Ton de Leeuw

Netherlands Music Archive

A series of books commissioned by the Board of Editors, CNM, Hilversum, in consultation with Richard King, Oberlin Conservatory of Music, Ohio, USA and composer Jenny McLeod, New Zealand in association with Centrum Nederlandse Muziek, Hilversum, The Netherlands

---

Volume 1
Ton de Leeuw
edited by Jurrien Sligter

Additional volumes in preparation:

Six Women Composers from the Netherlands
edited by Helen Metzelaar

Unico Wilhelm van Wassenaer
edited by Kees Vlaardingerbroek and Rudolf Rasch

This book is part of a series. The publisher will accept continuation orders which may be cancelled at any time and which provide for automatic billing and shipping of each title in the series upon publication. Please write for details.

Ton de Leeuw

edited by
Jurrien Sligter

translated by
John Lydon

h⬤ **harwood academic publishers**
ap
Australia • China • France • Germany • India • Japan • Luxembourg
Malaysia • Netherlands • Russia • Singapore • Switzerland • Thailand
United Kingdom • United States

3 Boulevard Royal
L-2449 Luxembourg

Originally published in Dutch in 1992 by CNM, Hilversum / Walburg Pers, Zutphen

This English language edition was made possible by financial support from the Prins Bernard Fonds, The Netherlands.

British Library Cataloguing in Publication Data

Leeuw, Ton de
Ton de Leeuw. – (Netherlands Music Archive, ISSN 1023-7127; Vol. 1)
I. Title   II. Lydon, John   III. Sligter, Jurrien   IV. Series
780.92

ISBN 3-7186-5695-7 (hardback)
ISBN 3-7186-5696-5 (paperback)

CONTENTS

Contents

PREFACE

Ton de Leeuw (b. 1926, Rotterdam, The Netherlands) must be considered one of the most important composers of the generation that emerged shortly after the Second World War. In a period in which Karl-Heinz Stockhausen and Pierre Boulez were still exploring the limits of serialism, De Leeuw made the first of his trips to India and was struck by the realization that most European composers have but a superficial knowledge of the great non-European musical cultures. This was the beginning of an international orientation that over the course of the years was to take him to innumerable countries in Asia, the Americas and Europe.

From the very beginning De Leeuw was critical of serialist dogmatism, but neither could he agree with John Cage's loose interpretations of oriental thought. He developed a highly personal view on the possibilities for musical acculturation between East and West, outlining this in numerous articles for UNESCO and organizing workshops in which European and Asian composers could meet.

Thus, De Leeuw was not only progressive in his composition, but also in his ideas on music and its function in society. Herein lies the importance of an English language edition of this book: the music and thought of De Leeuw have international significance. Many of the problems regarding the relationship between eastern and western musical cultures which occupied him are as crucial today as they were at the time of his writings, and the solutions he proposed merit broad attention.

The reader of this book will encounter an important selection of the many articles authored by De Leeuw over the years, most of which appeared originally in English and French journals. The articles are arranged in chronological order, beginning with his Indian travel diaries. Although each was conceived as an independent essay, a reading of the entire selection offers insight into the growth of De Leeuw's ideas on the contrast between East and West. In his most recent article, *Back to the source* (1986, rev. 1990), De Leeuw reviews the development of these ideas. Here we find his thoughts reaching their most highly crystallized form.

In the second part of the book, contributions by the American musicologist William Malm and the formerly Vietnamese musician Trân Van Khê deal with the international perspective in which De Leeuw's ideas must be seen.

De Leeuw's strong interest in music therapy, based on the eastern belief in the ethical and healing effects of music, is given attention in an article by Dutch psychiatrist Richard Hees. He relates the contrast between East and West to the mutually complementary roles of the various brain functions; music is an effective therapeutic tool because of its considerable capacity for integrating the various functions of the human brain.

Aspects of De Leeuw's music are analyzed in articles by Rokus de Groot and Jurrien Sligter, with works of different periods being reviewed. Because the composer holds material questions to be so strongly interrelated with spiritual values, aesthetic and philosophical matters play an important role in the musical analyses. Many of the compositions mentioned may be found in the discography and the interested reader may obtain copies from the Dutch music publisher Donemus. A bibliography and list of compositions round off the book.

Each text may be read independently of the others, but together they add to the separate thoughts and information contained in each, offering a broad view of the composer Ton de Leeuw and, more generally speaking, of the problems of composition since the end of the Second World War.

Jurrien Sligter

HOMAGE TO TON DE LEEUW
Olivier Messiaen

La musique de Ton de Leeuw est essentiellement diatonique. Il utilise des modes, des lignes mélodiques, des contrepoints, des accords, mais tout cela reste diatonique. Presque pas de dissonances. La couleur est blanche, ou délicatement bleutée, parfois une lumière d'or s'ajoute. Le traitement des 12 voix dans son œuvre sur le "Cantique des Cantiques" reste aussi diatonique, aussi bien dans le pianissimo que dans la force. Son œuvre sur un fragment de "l'Apocalypse", offre un nouvel élément de timbre, avec les staccato du cor et de la clarinette. Dans les Psaumes pour la Messe des morts, interviennent le plain-chant, et des effets dramatiques où les coups de tam-tam s'opposent aux ostinatos de marimba, aux appels de la voix de femme. Il y a même des accords en grappes utilisant des modes. Mais l'esprit est toujours diatonique, d'un diatonisme statique, très proche de ces musiques orientales qui pénètrent l'auditeur en le mettant dans un état semi-onirique, un état de rêve éveillé.

Olivier Messiaen

Ton de Leeuw's music is essentially diatonic. He uses modes, melodic lines, counterpoints, chords, but it all remains diatonic. Hardly any discords. The colour is white, or just a shade bluish, sometimes a golden light is added. Treatment of the 12 voices in his work about the "Cantique des Cantiques" [*Song of Songs*] also remains diatonic, both in his pianissimo and forte. His work on part of "l'Apocalypse" [*The Book of Revelation*] provides a new timbral element with staccato of the horn and the clarinet. Plainsong is introduced in his "Psaumes pour la Messe des morts" [*Psalms for the Requiem Mass*], as well as dramatic effects where the beating of the tam-tam comes up against the ostinatos of the marimba, against the calls of the female voice. There are even bunches of chords with the use of modes. But the spirit always remains diatonic in a static way that is very close to the type of oriental music which penetrates the listener and gets him into a semi-oneiric state, the state of a waking dream.

Olivier Messiaen

OLIVIER MESSIAEN
230, RUE MARCADET
75018 PARIS
TÉL. 627-99-34

22 avril 1981 - à Ton de Leeuw -

Cher Ami,

Merci de votre bonne lettre.

J'aurais été ravi de vous retrouver à la Haye en février, pour le concert de mon œuvre pour piano solo, cor solo, et orchestre : "Des canyons aux étoiles..." — mais j'avais secrètement beaucoup de scrupules & de remords à la pensée qu'on allait déranger le plus grand compositeur hollandais uniquement pour faire des traductions dans une conférence publique. Le sort a décidé autrement ; nous avons joué à cache-cache entre Paris et la Haye, et c'était mieux ainsi !

Merci pour ce magnifique programme Messiaen que vous organisez au Conservatoire d'Amsterdam. C'est très bien choisi : et cela donne une idée très complète de presque toutes mes œuvres. Je suis surtout émerveillé du nombre énorme des exécutants : je suppose que ce sont pour la plupart des élèves ou des anciens élèves du Conservatoire Sweelinck : l'interprétation va être extraordinairement variée !

Merci pour toutes mes œuvres d'orgue, de piano, et de chant — merci pour mon "Quatuor", pour les "Oiseaux exotiques", et pour "Et exspecto resurrectionem mortuorum" qui est une de mes œuvres préférées. Un merci tout spécial pour Almut Rössler qui joue partout ma musique d'orgue et toujours magnifiquement : si vous la voyez, dites-lui, je vous prie, toute ma reconnaissance et mes bonnes affections.

Merci aussi pour les salles. Je pense que la salle Bach d'Amsterdam sera parfaite pour le piano & chant, et que l'Église Saint Bavon de Haarlem donnera tout l'éclat nécessaire au "Livre d'orgue" & aux cuivres et tam-tams d' "Et exspecto".

Croyez toujours, cher Ami, à mes sentiments très admiratifs et bien affectueux.

Olivier Messiaen

Olivier Messiaen
230, rue Marcadet
75018 Paris
Tel: 627-99-34

                    22 April 1981, to Ton de Leeuw

My dear friend,

Thank you so much for your nice letter.

I would have been delighted to have met you again at The Hague in February for the concert of my work for solo piano, solo horn and orchestra: "Des Canyons aux étoiles . . . ."– but secretly I hesitated a lot and was quite reluctant at the thought that I was going to trouble Holland's greatest composer just to do some translations during a public lecture. Fate decided otherwise: we played hide-and-seek between Paris and The Hague, and it was better that way!

Many thanks for the magnificent Messiaen programme that you are organising at the Amsterdam Academy of Music. The choice is excellent and it gives a very comprehensive idea of practically all my works. I am particularly amazed at the enormous number of performers; I suppose that most of them are pupils or former pupils of the Sweelinck Academy of Music: the interpretation is bound to be remarkably varied!

Thanks for all my works for organ, piano and chorus – thanks for my "Quatuor", for "Oiseaux exotiques" and for "Et expecto Resurrectionem mortuorum" which is one of my favourite works. And very special thanks for Almut Rössler who plays my organ music everywhere and always beautifully: if you see him, please convey to him my infinite gratitude and fond affection.

Also many thanks for the auditoria. I think that the Bach Hall in Amsterdam will be perfect for the piano and the singing, and that the Saint Bavo Church in Haarlem will provide all necessary splendour for the "Livre d'Orgue" and the brass and tam-tam of "Et expecto".

With admiring and affectionate greetings I am,

Yours as ever,

Olivier Messiaen

Ton de Leeuw, 1990

INTRODUCTION
Rokus de Groot and Jurrien Sligter

"When I was quite young I once accidentally tuned in on a radio broadcast from an Arabian station. I was thunderstruck: I became deeply aware that there were other people living on this earth, living in thoroughly different conditions, having other thoughts and feelings. Since then, the way that all of this is translated into music, and why, has held my unceasing attention. This breakthrough of consciousness had all kinds of consequences. For instance, from that moment on I could no longer project my musical development merely against the background of a few centuries of European music. I quickly broadened my horizons: the twentieth century, the Renaissance, the Middle Ages, all music outside of European borders."[1]

No quotation is more typical of Ton de Leeuw's thought or better suited to head an introduction to his work. In the fifties, he set out on a quest aimed at broadening the sources of his musical experience. The anecdote makes clear that this expansion of musical interest is paired with a growing awareness of the role of music in man's experience of life. Ton de Leeuw's involvement with UNESCO has brought him around the world, inspiring him to advocate, among other things, an 'ecology of music'.[2] The central issues of this are his criticism of the superficiality of western musical life, and his concern with the threat posed to the authentic musical cultures of the East by indiscriminate orientation towards western examples. Because of this, a collection of articles written by, and about Ton de Leeuw deals with more than just the composer: the role of music in society after the Second World War, the changes in musical life brought about by the invention of the radio and tape recorder and other technological means of storing and manipulating sound, the significance of eastern thought to the western composer, all are issues whose growing implications far exceed the person of Ton de Leeuw. The unifying theme of this collection of articles is the acculturation between East and West. Thus, the book is much more than a homage to an important composer: post-war musical reality is reflected in Ton de Leeuw's thought and work.

THE 'EAST' IN TWENTIETH CENTURY MUSIC

The 'East' and 'eastern' music are western concepts that have served in breaking down – particularly in the twentieth century – western conventions. The need for new, vital sources of inspiration led Bartók, for example, to study the folk music of the Balkans and Turkey. With the invention of recording equipment, the music of each continent has become available to anyone wishing to hear it: the East has received the most attention.

In seeking alternatives to western conventions we often forget that eastern music also has its own conventionality. Too often we think of the East as a panacea for all our artistic, and even social problems. This misconception could lead to a modern form of 'exoticism'. Even among serious artists, the word 'East' is used as a generic term in reference to such disparate cultures as the Indian, Japanese, or Indonesian, with their Hindustani, Buddhistic, and Islamic backgrounds.

Various composers point out general tendencies in characterizing the notion 'East'. Olivier Messiaen's preface to *Quatuor pour la fin du temps (1941)*, pointing out the lack of a directed temporal flow, is related to this: the concept 'now' replaces 'before' and 'after'. This temporal conception is often manifested in music with cyclicity, a quality that starkly contrasts with the development orientated music of the classical-romantic tradition in the West.

Debussy was intrigued by the lack of development and the emphasis on varied repetitive patterns in Indonesian gamelan music, first hearing it at the World Fair in Paris of 1889. The famous passage in which he states that he would rather listen to an Egyptian shepherd playing flute than Beethoven's *Pastoral (Sixth) Symphony* suggests that not only was Debussy seeking 'naturalness' in music, but also indicates his interest in a different conception of time. In a commentary on his composition *November Steps* for biwa, shakuhachi and orchestra (1967), the Japanese composer Takemitsu proposes that western music is ordered by a horizontal thought process while music for shakuhachi, the Japanese bamboo flute, is conceived vertically, like a tree growing to the heavens. Ton de Leeuw has often quoted the renowned ethnomusicologist Jaap Kunst's reference to the music of Java: 'It does not evolve, it is.'

We will attempt to list a number of the characteristics of De Leeuw's aesthetic, one which is typified by an East-West polarisation.

EAST	WEST
'being'	'becoming'
static	dynamic
non-developmental	developmental
chain structures	genetic structural principles
intuition of universal correlation	avoidance of centre
listening to nature	subjection of nature
modesty	self-centred
inner peace	inner tension
non-subjective	subjective
emotional expression is not a goal in itself	main goal is expression
functional relationship to the universe	autonomic music
no thematic development, no 'subject'	thematic development, 'subject'
room for the listener	overwhelming the listener
modest means	expansion of musical means
emphasis on melodic/rhythmic aspect	emphasis on harmonic aspect
concern for the quality of sound	emphasis on structural relationships

Has an autonomic development in western music led increasingly to an overlapping with the music of the East? Qualities that are associated with eastern music have found a place in the music of Stravinsky and Varèse (chain structures, heterophony, anti-Romanticism), and in the music of Webern and Debussy (modesty, sober means, listening to nature, concern for sound in itself), although these composers were either unacquainted with, or had a very sketchy understanding of eastern music – an example being Debussy's experience with gamelan music. Or is it possible that eastern thought, long more or less known in the West, could only begin to play a dominant role in the twentieth century because of the crises facing western consciousness? Whatever the answer, the music of the East became more accessible, on a larger scale than ever before, after the Second World War. As early as 1957, a concert of Indian music, with the improvisational element standing central, was organized in Darmstadt.

It would seem that, after the 'spring cleaning' of serialism, non-western music is needed to fill the vacuums in our composition. The 'return to the source'[3] is not merely a way of breaking down western conventions, but is in fact also an endeavour to get a grip on a splintered universe.

Immediately following the Second World War, Olivier Messiaen and John Cage were particularly instrumental in giving the concept of the 'East' meaning in western music. Cage went furthest in this direction: by applying *I-Ching* in the compositional process, the individual contribution of the composer was reduced to a minimum, and the involvement of chance elements in performance led to the negation of music as a 'work', an 'opus'. But Cage seems more to have projected his own understanding of general eastern philosophical principles on music, than to have interpreted and incorporated eastern musical principles.

Ton de Leeuw firmly considers Messiaen the most important post Second World War composer. Although Messiaen's knowledge of non-western music has remained limited, the above mentioned list of qualities of eastern music seems equally applicable in describing his work. The reference of Messiaen's music to nature and cosmos, belief and mysticism, emphasizes ethical aspects of music that are so decisively important in eastern culture.

Since the seventies, Stockhausen has been leaning more conspicuously towards eastern philosophy than most composers. This former leader of serialism has turned away from abstract manipulation of musical material, a development that is manifested in statements like: "Sounds can do anything. They can kill. The whole Indian mantric tradition knows that with sounds you can concentrate on any part of the body and calm it down, excite it, even hurt it to the extreme."[4] The similarities between Stockhausen's ideas and those of Ton de Leeuw seem striking: where Ton de Leeuw speaks of 'trans-subjectivity' we hear of 'transpersonal music' from Stockhausen. De Leeuw's belief that tradition is a living process rather than a static entity also has parallels with Stockhausen's thought. "I have learnt – especially in Japan – that tradition does not simply exist, but must be created anew everyday."[5] But the cult of self, so typical of Stockhausen, is foreign to De Leeuw who objects to much of the former composer's work for its Wagnerian tendency of overwhelming the listener.

We could conclude that De Leeuw's deep interest in non-western music and eastern philosophy could be seen as being part of western tradition: the search for new points of orientation following the disintegration of tonality and the acceptance of musical plurality were in general a concern of innumerable composers. However, aside from Ton de Leeuw, there is hardly another composer who has so deeply and consistently pondered the significance of the East to western composition. He has studied non-western music and philosophy from the earliest days of his career: his thoughts on the East developed parallel to his musical evolution.

THE EVOLUTION OF CONCEPTS ON THE EAST-WEST RELATIONSHIP IN THE THOUGHT OF TON DE LEEUW

The interest in non-western music is not an isolated element of Ton de Leeuw's thought, but forms rather one part of his extensive musical curiosity. The composer considers his first contact with non-western music, at the beginning of his secondary education, to have had decisive influence on his intellectual and musical development. In 1949, at the age of 23, he travelled to Paris to take part in a course in musical analysis conducted by Messiaen. One may assume that De Leeuw's choice of mentors was influenced by Messiaen's distinguishing characteristics as a composer: his openness to the sounds of the world – whether those of another society, the past, or of birds – and his efforts to integrate musical ideas and concepts of other cultures.

On returning from Paris, De Leeuw approached Jaap Kunst, ethnomusicologist at the Royal Institute of the Tropics, seeking more detailed information than he had found from Messiaen. He studied with this teacher from 1950 until 1954. The *Three African Etudes* for piano (1954) evolved from transcriptions that he made for Kunst. The first high point of his career came with *Mouvements rétrogrades* (1957), an orchestral piece that is still frequently performed. In his introduction to the work, De Leeuw speaks of the eastern concept of time and points out how it contrasts with that of the West. Supporting this passage, he quotes Jaap Kunst; 'Western music is full of action and tension. On the other hand, we may characterize Javanese music perhaps best by calling it "time transferred into music".'

Mouvements rétrogrades does not directly borrow stylistic characteristics of Javanese music but there is a similarity on an abstract level: cyclicity in the form of a double rhythmic retrograde repeated ten times (see example 1). One could say that the concept of the East basically serves as a charter for musical renovation and as a means of breaking away from nineteenth century and neo-classical aesthetic. In this regard, the function of eastern influence is not fundamentally other than that of serialism as used by many young composers. But already from the fifties onward, there was no trace in De Leeuw's music of exclusive concentration on musical material, and in this he is exceptional. In his early articles, we find the aspect 'ethos' as the binding factor between non-western and antique Greek music and music therapeutic applications.

1 *'Mouvements rétrogrades', beginning of the first movement. Compare bars 1-5a with bars 5b-9 and bar 10 with bar 11.* [6]*' Donemus Amsterdam 1957*

De Leeuw made his first journey to India in 1961 to study classical Indian music on the scene. In his travelogue, *People and music in India* (1963), he optimistically proposes that contemporary western music is closer to that of the Indian culture than the classical-romantic: "The Indian, apart from the few who have studied in Oxford, has neither feeling for nor need of harmony". The thought that a partially autonomic process of development was taking place in the West, with remarkable parallels to eastern music, seems at this time to have served primarily in supporting the search for an individual path, as a reaction to serialist dogmatism. One of De Leeuw's compositions of this period that specifically reflects his Indian experience is *Symphonies of winds* (1963). It begins with an 'alāp'-like introduction (a slow introduction setting the turning and mood of an improvisation or composition), a way of opening a composition that was to return many times in the future. This work is at the same time a homage to a western composer that De Leeuw fervently admired: Stravinsky. In De Leeuw's composition, there is a quotation from Stravinsky's *Symphonies of wind instruments* (1920). Other pieces reflecting more or less strongly the Indian culture are the orchestral works *Ombres* and *Nritta*, both dating from 1961. In the first of these, there are structures that are patterned after yoga breathing, while the rhythmic patterns of the second were inspired by the tablā.

The non-western musical orientation, however, remained diversified. Traditional Japanese art was a stimulant for the solo piano piece *Men go their ways* (1964). In an introduction to this work, that was strongly inspired by Cage, De Leeuw outlines a stance for the composer, performer and listener derived from the haiku tradition, of openness, concentration on the moment, and the shunning of any self-willed act casting the musical occurrences in a context of purposefulness. In this work he experimented with automatic writing, but for the sake of discipline he also applied arithmetical automatisms. In this period of general interest in aleatoric principles, the East served once again as a guiding light in resolving the current problems of western composition at that time. De Leeuw raised objections to the lack of formal and intellectual discipline in the work of the many composers following Cage's line, a discipline that increasingly drew him in the direction of Japanese art. He composed various works with guided improvisation, *Spatial music* I / IV (1966-1971) for settings varying from orchestra to percussion ensemble, and *The magic of music* (1970) for a cappella choir. Here, non-western oral tradition stood as model. This served to counteract the arbitrariness that was characteristic of many western improvisations at that time. Instead of simply ploughing through the work, the musician is provided with a repertoire of musical patterns and selects ways of performance, ornamentation and the sequence of the various patterns, in accordance with the requirements of a specific composition or performance.

In a lecture held in 1971 at the International Music Congress in Moscow, De Leeuw went much further than suggesting the possibilities for integration between East and West. He proposed that western composers' apparent recent sensitivity to aspects of eastern music indicated the possibility of 'mental mutation'. This concept, the mutation of the mind, implies the understanding that the world's music, in all its diversity, is no longer foreign to us, 'exotic', but is a part of ourselves.

In an article relating to his trip to Japan in 1968, De Leeuw underlined the necessity of mental mutation in integrating the unparalleled profusion of information from other cultures. In this article, he wrote, notably, that he considered the traditions of India, Iran, and Indonesia to be closed systems, having hardly common ground with contemporary music: he clearly favoured Japan. The high point in this period of Japanese orientation is without doubt the superb work for soprano and orchestral groups: *Haiku II* (1968).

Lamento Pacis (1969), for choir and instruments, equally reflects De Leeuw's Japanese experiences. This work contains De Leeuw's most concrete musical references to non-western music. The second movement, dedicated to Zeami (1363-1443) – one of the founders of Nō – is very clearly inspired by Nō Theatre. The character of the flute music is related to that of the Nō-kan; the recitation of male voices is modelled on that of Nō. The strings are patterned on the shō (mouth organ) of the Gagaku orchestra (see example 2). The work also refers to several masters of the western tradition: Ockeghem and Gesualdo.

De Leeuw's publications since the mid sixties have been marked by a more explicit social commitment and criticism. From that time, his long cherished thoughts on the possibility of integrating eastern and western musical concepts evolved to a more comprehensive longing for peace and unity in the face of worldwide division.

In a presentation held during the Musicultura Conference in 1974, De Leeuw advanced a new element in answering the question of what could be considered a common bond between people of diverse cultures. Next to a summary of Jungian concepts of the archetype and the collective unconscious, he proposed human physiology as a common factor, in the sense that the central nervous system facilitates particular forms of human expression. In this he referred to the work of Jean Piaget. The renewed interest of French structur-

2   *From 'Lamento Pacis', the second movement. The model for the strings is the shō (mouth organ) of the Gagaku orchestra.*

Ps 1: [→ range ±1/2 octave. Ps 2: Each player has two prescribed notes (vl 1: e♭ and d; vl: a and g♯, etc.). Free choice.

alism for research into universal qualities suggests a theoretical basis for the understanding of thoroughly divergent cultures.

From this time modality began to play a more prominent role in his composition. Several works appeared with more or less explicit reference to modality: *Mo-do* (1974) for harpsichord and *Modal music* (1978-79) for accordion. It was also at this time that he wrote *Gending, a western homage to the musicians of the gamelan* (1975). De Leeuw lists three levels in which *Gending is* the result of a process of acculturation: material, structural and mental. The material level is a result of the use of eastern instruments, while the structural level is a consequence of an intentional borrowing of Javanese structural principles. He considers the mental level the most important. It is derived from a cyclic conception of time, a slow musical respiration, a tendency to not dramatize.[8] The central Javanese gamelan is not the only reference to a specific tradition in De Leeuw's works of this period. De Leeuw also mentions the North Indian *dhrupad* style in connection with *Mountains* (1977) for bass clarinet and tape. And in *Modal music* there is also a reference to classical Hindustani music. This is one of his first works to make large-scale use of the diatonic scale. There are even sharps and flats indicated at the beginning of the musical staves (see examples 3a and 3b).

3a   *The mode of 'Modal music'.*

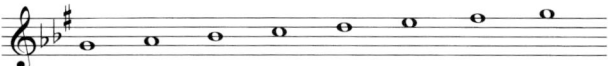

3b *'Modal music', the beginning. The bass part plays major triads (M)*
produced by the knobs on the left hand side of the instrument.

Thus, yet another aspect of eastern music was emphasized in De
Leeuw's composition of the seventies: modality, with its implied
technical and aesthetic qualities serving as a point of reference. It was
De Leeuw's solution to a feeling of general malaise in contemporary
western music. His renewed orientation reached a first high point in
the trilogy on biblical texts: *Car nos vignes sont en fleur* (1981), *And they
shall reign forever* (1981) and *Invocations* (1983). He also introduced the
concept of 'extended modality'; this principle may also be found in
recent compositions like the orchestral piece *Résonances* (1985) and the
Concert for two guitars and orchestra (1987-88). It is basically a pitch-
time model that manifests itself through numerous diversified selective tactics.

The concept 'East' is a broad notion and we have seen that it served various functions in the music of Ton de Leeuw. In the various shifts of meaning it underwent in De Leeuw's thought we can see reflected the succession of points of interest in western composition. Thus, we find the concept of the 'East' serving in the fifties as a means of gaining distance from the nineteenth century and neo-classical aesthetic; it has maintained this function up to today. The Webern revival in the fifties led to emphasis on aspects of non-western music such as austerity and inner peace. Since the sixties, there has been more attention for multiple significance and textures, and the physical aspects of making music, with references to, among other things, haiku and Nō. In this period of vehement social criticism, De Leeuw's thoughts on the place of music in society and the musician's part in bringing it about were equally drawn from models of non-western cultures. He characterized western music life as superficial, a form of 'poster art'. He contrasted this with the Indian musician, whose performance is highly influenced by his religious and social background. Finally, orientation on the East yielded in the seventies the building blocks for developing a new language in which modality is central, not only with regard to the musical material, but also as a philosophical concept.

ANTI-ROMANTICISM

The reader of De Leeuw's articles repeatedly comes across criticism of the 'subjective' and the romantic aesthetic orientated on feeling. His ideas relating to this are summarized above in the list of characteristics of the antipode 'West'. He praises Stravinsky as the first great 'anti-romantic'; he admires Messiaen not only for his oeuvre but also for his metaphysical aesthetic.

Nevertheless, De Leeuw's appraisal of romantic aesthetic seems at least to be tinted by his need to delineate his own position as a composer. He is more highly critical of the German Beethoven-Wagner tradition than of the Rossini-Verdi branch, or of a composer like Chopin. Regarding subjective expressivity of sentiment, one could propose that even if this were the main goal of a given composer, creating a piece of music still necessitates a certain personal distance, analysis, even 'calculation'. Limiting this argument to Wagner, for example, he was undeniably also concerned with symbols that are deeply rooted in tradition and the unconscious. In Schopenhauer's teaching, that wielded considerable influence on Wagner, music is not essentially a manifestation of the Ego, it gives form to the Universal Will. In De Leeuw's description of romantic aesthetic of feeling – self worshipping, rhetorical, tending to overpower the listener, expanding musical means, unstable – one can see that he equates it with the deification of the subject. These are the same qualities that he mentions in connection with another composer of his generation, Stockhausen, and there lies the source of his distance from the latter. Stockhausen does indeed seem to comport himself as the artist-magician, with a tendency towards self-glorification. In an explanatory note for movement 26 of *Aus den sieben Tagen*, for example, he writes that the musicians should link up with him as though flowing with a stream, and *Hymnen* closes with sound material modulated through Stockhausen's own breathing. In the last decades there has been an increasingly more spectacular formulation of a private mythology, culminating in a project for music theatre of enormous dimensions, *Licht*, whose performance fills the evenings of an entire week. One could propose that with Stockhausen, the emphasis lies on externally directed activity, on expansiveness and on that which one receives from the outside, from afar. In *Sirius*, Stockhausen seeks the centre, the 'central sun of our universe' far away, outside of us. Ton de Leeuw, in contrast, emphasizes the discovery of that within us.

Still, it would appear that De Leeuw's characterisation of nineteenth century western music is not absolutely just, not even on a music-technical level: one also finds in Romantic music textures having exactly those qualities that De Leeuw prizes as counterbalance. Notably, these characteristics appear in the context – already existing in the nineteenth century – of exoticism, folklore and archaism as well as in connection with natural images. In the Romantic era, one means of conveying the image of nature in music was through tone fields, for example in *Waldweben*, in Wagner's *Siegfried*, and the prelude to *Das Rheingold*, where a primeval state of rest, absence of pursuit and desire, is portrayed by a prolonged E flat major triad.[9]

On a philosophical level, there is also a relationship between De Leeuw's work and the challenged tradition, especially with regard to the concept of music as an art of ideas. As different as De Leeuw's philosophy may be, as far removed from the German-Romantic aesthetic as it is, that such an overt philosophy is brought into relation with music, and especially that so much importance is attached to music as a philosophical medium, is quite in keeping with romantic tradition. This blend of composer and thinker is precisely the reason that a book about De Leeuw offers a fascinating image of composition in a broad, international context.

1

PEOPLE AND MUSIC IN INDIA[1]
Ton de Leeuw

Karachi, January 3, 1961

Wake up in the morning in a sun-drenched city. A blinding white light floods through the shutters on the windows. Not quite 24 hours ago I stood chilled and trembling in a European airport. Now I look out on a tropical garden where men are working with slow movements. In my cool hotel room, and without having yet seen anything, I suddenly realize how the sun must be responsible for the art in these parts.

New Delhi, January 7

Invited by the Dagar brothers[2], last night at 8:30. A taxi carried me over the broad boulevards of this English built city. Mr. Kotari, secretary of the Sangeet Natak Akademi[3], met me at a gateway, behind which loomed a half obscure and unexpected world. I followed him through a maze of low white buildings, passageways and galleries, and suddenly stood in front of the older of the two brothers. He invited me inside. A small, bare room with stone walls.

The conversation is slow in getting started. It is clear that Ustad Nasir Moinuddin Dagar has little contact with whites. He seems almost embarrassed that I show interest in his music. He is the leader of the two brothers. A broad, calm visage, with a seriousness and dignity that make him seem older than he actually is. His younger brother, to whom I have been introduced by now, is enchantingly modest, is reserved and sometimes almost timid. The difference of character will also be expressed in their singing. Meanwhile a number of people have arrived – discreetly – all of whom greet me in the traditional Indian fashion, hands folded in front of the breast. Only then did I understand that the Dagar brothers had invited their accompanying musicians and several others, to treat me to a recital of Dhrupad song.

They are specialists. The two brothers sing almost exclusively in Dhrupad style, the drummer plays exclusively his pakhavaj.[4] All of this has been passed down from father to son, and the Dagar brothers pass it on as leaders of the Barathya Kala Kendra-Institute.[5]

After an introductory conversation over coffee – where I was buzzing with questions about the secrets of Indian music, things that the books hadn't made clear – Kotari told me that the recital would begin. We had to remove our shoes and I was invited to sit on a carpet in the middle of the room, placed immediately in front of the players. It was a place of honour. Next to the exquisitely beautiful wife of the elder brother, a princess escaped from the Thousand and one Nights, with all the accompanying attributes: magnificent eastern garb, two sparkling eyes behind a transparent veil and superb jewellery on her ankles and wrists.

So, kneeling in a circle, everyone's attention concentrated, the music could begin. First the performers tuned and warmed up. The tampuras[3], two in all, began their drone, the everpresent tonic, the singers' take-off point. They start gradually, from several isolated tones, expanding these to larger melodic patterns. The music does not begin suddenly, like it does with us, but gradually emerges from silence. It is as though the musicians use this opening phase to prepare for and to concentrate on what is going to come. The gathering listens attentively, some with eyes closed, emerged in the fascinating aural universe, others watching the gestures of the main singer. For he is not merely singing: his hands and facial expressions reflect the music. Each melodic contour is eloquently portrayed in exquisite gestures, making the sound tangible so to speak. Those listening are connoisseurs. They shake their heads with each special melodic turn, I think as a sign of admiration and emotion. And I must say, after one or two hours listening, I also became much more sensitive to the unusual melodic turns that the singers sometimes produced.

This is India at its best. The refinement and simplicity of these greatest of the Indian Dhrupad singers is unparalleled. The elder of the two was so kind as to give me many examples of the various manners of singing, of various ornaments, and of the nine rasas[7], through which, much became clear to me. One thing especially became quite clear. This style, old, strict, and noble, despite its highly developed technique, always puts the emphasis on conveying human emotion, but in a way that is so different, so much more direct and complete than in our music. For it is not merely music, or music and poetry, – it is an attitude to life expressed in this music. One must experience it in order to understand. No wonder these musicians, guardians of an age-old style, are not only great artists, but also great individuals.

They escorted me outside, guiding me back through the maze to the foremost courtyard and, after inviting me again to attend the singing of the morning rāgas[8] one day in the coming week, they gave the traditional farewell salute.

Wednesday January 11
Last night at 6:30 Yamini Krishnamurti performed Bharata Natyam and Kuchipudi dance[9] in the Fine Arts-Theatre. The difference between the more ritualistic first dance style and the 'romantic' second is lost on me. Magnificent dancers, also the Carnatic music[10], very pure and unadulterated style. The elder of the Dagarbrothers told me that he was not able to appreciate all of this South Indian music 'for a lack of knowledge'! The greatest surprise of this evening: at last a dance form where movement and music are *perfectly* synchronized. Dance is the visual portrayal of the rhythm. Or the other way around. In any case one whole.

Thursday January 12
Once again, but now in the morning, a visit to the Dagar brothers. The city-behind-the-gate looks rather less romantic in the daylight. I have difficulty to find my way through the cluttered passageways to my destination without a guide. The master awaits my arrival. He is alone, sitting on a bench (probably put there in my honour), and I may sit next to him.

The same ceremony takes place, although the bond created by his music on the first wonderful evening has been broken. The conversation stalls; we are both happy when his wife comes in, with a colossal platter of exotic delicacies. But even this subject is quickly exhausted. Mrs. Dagar stays with us without taking part in the conversation. The minutes pass slowly. I yearn for the arrival of the accompanying musicians: the Dagar brothers were going to sing morning rāgas for me? I tell about Europe, but feel that my words do not sound convincing. The music must start soon! But no one comes inside, it remains strangely empty around us. Finally footsteps approach. In the doorway a man appears with a briefcase. An unintelligible dialogue in Hindu. Ustad Nasir Moinuddin Dagar stands up, excuses himself and disappears outside with the other man.

I stay behind, alone with the princess from the Thousand and one Nights. She is dressed more simply now, but nevertheless equally beautiful. She speaks better English than her husband. With renewed courage I resume the conversation, introduce new topics. We talk, talk, talk... until I suddenly realize that it's no longer possible: the morning has passed. Leaving all eastern courtesy aside, I ask her directly what is going on. And then she explains, as though it is the most natural thing in the world, that her husband cannot sing today because he has a mild throat infection. The man with the briefcase was the doctor. Once again I realize that I am in a different world. A world where in such a case it is actually too simple to make a telephone call and agree on another appointment. . .

Friday January 13
The opening of the new Kathākali-centre[11] in Delhi. A hall full of people, just like at home. Steeped in snobbery. Important gentlemen address the public. They speak of culture, just like at home. Finally the curtain opens. Beautiful masks in these dance dramas. Wild, archaic. The main characters are archetypes. Here also: the whole person takes part. No acrobatics. But it lasts too long. It does not belong in this hall, full of well-dressed Hindus and foreign diplomats. New Delhi is much like European capital cities in this respect. Only everything is rather more provincial.

Monday January 16
Republic Day approaches. The entire country prepares itself to celebrate independence. Days in advance people speak of the fabulous procession organized by the authorities each year. This year Queen Elizabeth will be present.

The hotels are full. It is a good time for businessmen, but also for beggars and snake charmers. These latter sit crouched in front of the hotels and busy squares. The sound of their shrill, loud oboes carries far through the warm, dusty streets. Even the cobras react to it. Everything is large and spread out in this city. An enormous camp of tents, the Talkatory camps, has been erected between four boulevards. The tents are intended for the representatives of India's rich community of peoples. Little dark people from the south, good humoured sturdy farmers from Penjab, Mongolian tinted tribes from Assam and near the foot of the Himalaya mountains, and many more. They are rather unaccustomed to the large city, they do not understand each other, and the presence of many police officers is apparently meant to prevent conflicts. But later they will dance, on Republic Day.

Then they are the children of a single people, held together by Nehru, and by ideals and concepts, the secrets of which I do not know.

With the help of acquaintances, I penetrate into the Holy of Holies, the headquarters of the police, where an important looking officer grants me a permit to visit the camp freely. Armed with a camera, I head there the next day, roaming among the tents. I watch and listen to this colourful folk, look at the beautiful costumes. People who live thousands of kilometres apart are dancing here on the same ground. They are impervious to the heat and fatigue. Dance and music spur each other on, in many cases the accompanying musicians are also dancing. The drums sound from every corner of the camp. Everywhere, inexhaustible, brown, shining bodies, the women rolling their hips, often while carrying large brass bowls on their heads, singers who are aware of nothing except that they are singing. The intoxication of an endless, seething celebration. I realize all this only when I've left the camp behind and the noontime silence of the boulevard engulfs me.

Sunday January 22
Visited a mosque with S. in a Moslem enclave. S. is different from most of the other whites here, who – even after years – maintain the aloofness of 'the foreigner'. I sense that he has more contact with the country. But in his own way. Muttering, he walks through the beggars; but he would gladly give each a coin. He teaches me that I mustn't do this, 'because then there's no end to it'.

A small orchestra forms spontaneously. The wildly gesticulating solo singer addresses Allah. Scruffy girls, crouched in front of the mosque, in torn and dirty jackets. I film them, so that I can later show them as sights in our enclave of prosperity. The mosque is rather small, and not even pretty. But the white chalk walls are breathtakingly pure, set against the clear-blue light. The colours make me dizzy. In the shadow of these mosques and temples, set against the relentlessly clear light, Indian truths take on shape. But the sexton is standing in front of me, grinning amicably, with his 'Guest Book'. It earns him five rupees and I am rewarded with all the blessings of Allah.

Sunday January 29
Yesterday I held the most pleasing lecture up to now since my arrival here. I slowly begin to comprehend where the Indian's difficulties lie with regard to western music. There is an abysmal difference. Yet we

must bridge the gap if we want to establish a more meaningful contact than mere political or economical. Setting of the lecture: a classroom of Bharatya Kala Kendra[12] filled with teachers and students of the school. There is no longer any sign of distrust, because I've slowly grown to know them all, attending the lessons in singing, in various instruments and in Kathak dance.[13] This all takes place in small stone rooms facing the gallery. They work hard, something I've found in all art education here. Now they are staring at me with their large black eyes, and they try their best to understand something of the strange western music. According to plan, we will start with several European folk songs. They listen intently but without much reaction. Until a Greek folk song is played. Suddenly something changes. They are enrapt, they recognize something. The tongues loosen. May we hear it again? Once again the same melody is played, which indeed does sound peculiar with its lowered fourth tone.

Chromaticism seems to have a great attraction on the Indians. An old man, who speaks not a word of English, shakes his head ecstatically: he did not know this chromatic progression. The wonders achieved by such a simple alteration of a tone! But chromaticism is not so devalued in Indian music as it is in ours. The piano is really all too convenient.

Monday January 30
New Delhi lies behind me. While the reddish brown patches slide away beneath us, I try to assess what I have learned from my visit to this city. We are on our way to Bombay, thought of as the most westernized part of India. I am to hold various lectures there as well, and I would like to visit all the major institutions of music and dance. Music and dance are one. They are immensely exciting here, particularly for their unity. Much, almost all of the Indian art is fascinating. But, in contrast to the much more dynamic European art, music and dance are the only two forms of artistic expression in India that are still living today.

Friday February 3
Yesterday, with the help of a student of the Prof. Dheodar School, I got my first glimpse of Manipuri dance.[14] It's different and extremely attractive. Also education in Kathak dance.[15] The dance teacher was at the same time drummer. They teach here Kathak, Manipuri and folk dance. The latter seems to be very popular because of its greater

simplicity. All beginners' lessons are in groups. Only advanced students have individual lessons.

Bombay looks very much like a western city. The long avenue along the bay reminds one of Nice. But everything is warmer, larger and dirtier. There are many Parsis[16] living here. Drifting above the Towers of Silence, vultures trace slow circles in the sunlight.

Attended a concert in the evening at the house of Mr. D., an American. Mixed public, half western, which surprised me because I've not often met whites at this type of concert. But the evening was disappointing. Neither the westerners nor the Hindus seem to have come for the music. A childish form of snobbery. Men trying to look busy and – it can't be denied – beautiful women, who spare no pain in trying to be interesting. A poor imitation of our – in themselves so annoying – artists clubs. Pity. Because the citar player[17], Abdul Halim Jaffar Khan, performs beautifully. His playing seems to be influenced especially by vocal elements, while his more famous colleague Ravi Shankar relies more on the sarod technique.[18]

Later, on the balcony under the evening stars, I had the chance to exchange several words with the player. One of the melodic formulas used by him kept going through my mind as I walked home:

1.2

There are no more taxis. The streets take on the nocturnal greyness of all big cities. There is a rickshaw in the square, the coolie sleeping inside, curled up like a dog in a basket. I try to shake him awake, but growling, he pushes me away.

Bombay, Monday February 7
Like in New Delhi, I am warmly welcomed by the radio here. Several recordings made, introductions to Dutch and western music, that are gratefully received by the department of western music. This department is small and, as far as I know, similar ones are only to be found in Bombay and in New Delhi. They suffer an impoverished existence

for lack of interest. The official programming statistics for Radio Delhi are: Indian music 48% (of which roughly one third is classical), western music 2%, news 20%, spoken word 5%, drama 4%, publicity 1%, and other broadcasts (school, etc.) 20%.

Two per cent western music is not much. But I fear that we do not even come close to broadcasting two per cent of Asian music in the West. In any case, my lectures (each is sixty minutes) will fill the western program for several weeks. And they are also going to be rebroadcast. The same minimal interest is apparent in Bombay, the most western city, although in another way: the only (western) orchestra here has been dissolved for lack of interest.

I also meet here an Indian composer who had studied in New York. On his return he was a stranger in his own country. He poured his heart out to me but I couldn't follow him. There would be more understanding if things were approached differently. One cannot expect a musical culture that for centuries has been used to the most refined melodic-rhythmic chamber music, to suddenly convert to our heavy western ensembles.

The Indian, apart from the few who have studied in Oxford, has neither feeling for nor need of harmony. I encounter everywhere, notably, a much larger interest in electronic music, or in contemporary western music in which nuance and rhythm play a considerable role.

Many western embassies make the great public relations mistake of transporting artists from their own countries to India to perform classical-romantic music – more than any other European style – which is miles removed from Asiatic aesthetical conceptions.[19] The same tactical blunders are made in 1960 as in 1600. I am proud that the cultural section of our embassy is much more advanced.

Of the many acquaintances I've made in Bombay, meeting with the [South] Indian dancer Satyvati comes to mind. She demonstrated many things, among which were the nine rasas[20] in the Kathakali[21] style. She allowed me to film important dances from Bharata Natyam[22] and Kathakali, and she told me much about them. The training is incredibly disciplined. Training in eye movement and expression alone takes a year. The full course lasts at least seven years. Despite the great visual power of the dance, previous knowledge remains a necessity because of the many symbolical gestures. The religious background and acquaintance with the contents of the Old-Indian epic stories is nearly indispensable.

Although it is difficult to compare, it is probable that Indian dance, because of these elements, is more gripping than European dance forms. On the technical side, in any case, there is an enormous advantage: the perfect synchronization of rhythm in music and dance. Even in folk dance ankle bands are usually used, thus providing rhythmic accompaniment. This necessitates but at the same time guarantees synchronization of foot movements.

Heard an interesting concert on February 5, from All India Radio, in a hall in Bombay. The vocal parts were by far the best. The instrumentalists often indulged in a virtuosity that soon became musically annoying. Heard Ghazel songs for the first time: Persian love songs in a light classical style. The singers held a magnificently controlled nonchalance.

Wednesday February 8
Madras. In other words, a thousand miles southwards. And it's still India. But there are differences in the people, the climate, the landscape and the music. The few whites here generally lodge in a European concern, but I have landed in a Hindu hotel. Only my stomach protests. I may chose between two cooking styles: 'Madras' or 'Bombay', but India's achievements apparently lie elsewhere.

I remember the first authentic Indian meal. A dining den filled with people eating. It seems to be part of the ceremonial that some things that we are more timid about in the west are made audible here. A waiter brings me a banana leaf with a dozen or so scoops of porridge-like substances plopped on it. What now? I steal a glance at my pleasantly eating fellow diners and notice that knives and forks are not in use. Then and there I decide not to await them, but to dig in. But where should I begin? Which lump is salty, sweet or sour? On the right and left encouraging nods. Even tender expressions. Look at this Englishman! (All whites here are English, and the C major scale is an English scale!).

Encouraged by the picturesque scene, I withstand the proof by fire. At the end of the meal I rinse my fingers like a real Hindu at the appropriate little faucet in the corner of the dining room.

Friday February 10
The Radio Madras building is at the end of the endless ocean front boulevard. A concert has been organized in honour of a Russian

composer who I had already encountered in Delhi. First the radio orchestra, then tape recordings, and finally folk music. Rather without meaning. All light music, that at its worst is surprisingly like our Ketèlbey. Still waiting for the first concert of pure Carnatic music[23].

Saturday February 11

Finally heard the first concert of Carnatic music in the house of the veena player Vydya Shankar. Introduced by the French dancer Madame H. who lives here. She could not attend so that – as always – I am the only white in a group of roughly twenty music lovers. I am burning with curiosity. Finally we go upstairs. A low, stone room serves as music hall. We crouch on the ground along the walls. A bit in front of me sits an old man who apparently is revered for having been a great singer. The vocalist this evening is M. Ramanathan, with the violinist[24] T. Krishan.

The singer, homely, shaved half bald, has a deep voice, venturing at times – in acrobatic probes – to the lowest register. He hasn't the slightest notion of facial expression and looks incredibly ugly in his determined efforts to perform the music. But he is a great artist, richly imaginative, with a clear sense of humour.

In my honour, he uses at one point a mode that resembles our (ascending) melodic minor. But what a different approach. Rhythm is more important and vigorous in Northern India, and the style of singing more complex. A great number of worked out ornaments, less portamento. Someone once told me that the southern music is more cerebral, less emotional, than the northern. It's not true. There are superb, breathtaking moments in the manner of variation, in the alteration between song and violin (also with entirely individual and beautiful variations). Roughly speaking, the structure is like the Northern Indian. The same magical feeling for time: 'estimating the distance' by calling the (rhythmical) variations back to order at the right moment.

The old singer betrays no emotion. While others react enthusiastically, he generally stares sceptically straight ahead. It seems that artists here maintain distance from each other, and that it is usually painful to talk about colleagues.

I suddenly think of western music life: the sectarianism, the inhibition of the conservatives, the provincialism of the avant-garde. The world is small. However the communication between the singer and the public and the singer's ease in interrupting himself, making a (musical) joke, appreciated by all, is remarkable. An ideal form of improvisation within set lines. To thoroughly appreciate the music one must know the rules of the game.

In which Hindu writing did I read the deep wisdom: 'to fully appreciate art there are two prerequisites: knowledge of the rules, and the ability to intuitively sense the aesthetic.' In European terms: technical knowledge and an open heart. What a rare combination! Usually it is either one or the other.

Bangalore, Friday February 17
There they sit. The entire surface of the railway platform is sown with people, crouched or laying on the ground, conversing in groups, munching, suckling, flowing, sleeping. The early morning sun – it's only 7 o'clock – is still mild. I have just taken leave of the high, beautiful trees of Bangalore, the only things that interested me in this place. The train to Mysore is to leave at 7:20.

I pace back and forth, between and over the people planted on the ground. Occasionally a voice rattles through a loudspeaker. I can't even hear which language is being spoken. I'm comforted that no one reacts to it. It is 7:30, still no train. Strange how quickly the sun rises here. The light is sharper. In the distance the trees of Bangalore take on blurred contours in the rising warm air.

The loudspeaker rattles again. This walking back and forth is beginning to annoy me. At 8 o'clock I find a small pole to sit on. There I stay, on the pole, in the middle of this vast landscape, amidst a multitude that both literally and figuratively lives in another world and where probably no one can understand me. It doesn't matter. I must forget my haste, even if I am to be met in Mysore.

In this heat, in this vastness, much of what seems so important in Amsterdam is insignificant. Shortly before 8:30 a newspaper boy appears on the platform. Incredibly, he also has an English newspaper. I buy one, although the news does not interest me. I pace back and forth for a half hour with the newspaper under my arm. The scene at my feet hasn't changed. I wonder if they are waiting for the train. The sun is getting warm, fortunately there is still a place in the shadow.

I unfold the newspaper but don't read. My eyes glide abstractedly along the columns; then I realize I'm not alone; a thin, dark young man behind me is staring over my shoulder. He starts a conversation in broken English. Finally, someone who can tell me when the train is leaving! Apologetically, he says that there has been a slight delay (it is quarter past nine) but that it won't be much longer. I ask him if all these people are also travelling. Yes indeed, he answers. Most of them are en route, having arrived last night, they are waiting for the connecting train. The fact that they passed the entire night on the railway platform doesn't seem to bother anyone.

Madras, Tuesday February 21
Back in Madras, the undisputed artistic centre of the south. I have visited several of the many institutions for music and dance; among others, the Central College of Carnatic Music, and Kalakshetra. Musiri Subramaniam, the director of the Central College, receives me in his room. After the usual preliminaries, he introduces me to several teachers and a Japanese student who is here on a grant to study veena and mrdangam.[25] I roam through the building, dropping in on various lessons, and come finally to the director's class. A large room, looking out on all sides on a surrounding garden. He gives singing lessons, classical. Sitting in a circle on the ground are roughly fifteen girls, several of whom play tampura.[26]

First they sing a song together. Then the teacher begins again, separating each phrase which is then repeated by the students who use their own variations. When this is finished, the entire song is sung together again. Musiri Subramaniam has an intensely musical delivery. His interpretation of a composition by Tyagaraja[27] makes an especially big impression on me. Mr. D. recently said to me: 'Tyagaraja narrates when he makes music. He is in constant dialogue with Rama.'

This music education – based on an age-old oral tradition – is extremely efficient. The song is in a particular rhythmic pattern that the students count using slow hand gestures. The teacher enters with his phrase, each time at the same part of the pattern. His phrase may last for one or more rounds (complete patterns).

The student repeating the phase must enter at exactly the same point, one or more rounds later. The hand gestures are an important aid to the memory and their use from early youth on strongly help to develop a feeling for time-estimation of distances. It is an ideal solfège aiding in the development of three things simultaneously: a feeling for pitch, rhythm and musical fantasy (the variations that the students must improvise). It would be worth looking into how this age-old, successful system could be modified for use in European schools.

Kalakshetra, the renowned centre of Bharata Natyam dance, a highly respected South Indian dance style. Some think of it as the greatest training ground for dance, while others find it too academic. But I already know that reputations in Madras don't stand for much, and in the taxi decide not to allow myself to be influenced by anyone's impression. Rukmini Devi, the director, receives me amicably. She is an authoritative woman – so far the reports were correct, but then again she must be in her position. One of those rare women in India to have a respectable record that is both officially and generally appreciated.

Kalakshetra is actually a small village. Spread out over a vast terrain are a number of larger and smaller buildings that serve as classrooms, but also provide lodging for the teachers and students living on campus. Both form a closed community. And each person works, motivated by his own sense of responsibility. Disciplinary action is unheard of. All the students and teachers gather each morning in a central hall where the day is opened in group prayer. The services are conducted according to various rituals, depending on the religious convictions of the students, who come from far and wide. On the day I was present the service was respectively Hindu, Buddhist, Christian and Tibetan. Afterwards the multitude disperses to various class-rooms, some being open reed huts, some built in the shadow of large trees, probably for a lack of sufficient teaching space.

I meet the singer Ramanathan again, who is giving lessons in one of the huts. He looks like a beggar snatched from the streets who has been brought to Kalakshetra for his great musical talent. On my arrival, Rukmini Devi informs me that there had been another visiting Dutchman. Later I meet him on the grounds. I recognize his face but cannot quite recall his name. On being introduced I learn that our 'Dutchman' is none other than the American conductor, Lorin Maazel. Strange coincidence after Hilversum. With his international fame in the West, he is also a thoroughly anonymous great artist. A strange experience, to find oneself in a music world where even the names Bach, Beethoven, Wagner or Stravinsky are often ignored. It's humbling. But we also know nothing of the century old Indian music culture. On both sides there exists not only non-understanding, but most of all ignorance. There's still a lot to be done.

Wednesday February 22

At quarter to seven in the morning someone knocks on my door. I climb from under my mosquito net, tip something over, and open the door to Mr. Rangaramanujam. He sits carefully on the edge of a chair and apologizes by saying that he always starts his day at four in the morning, and that he has waited before coming to visit me. My lesson is to start, that is why he has come. In his typical exaggeratedly clear English, spoken by many Indians, he explains to me the basic ideas of this celestial music. He is the author of a standard work: a six volume edition of the compositions of Tyagaraja and his contemporaries.

Mr. Rangaramanujam's great dream is to visit the West before the end of his life, to bring the message of Indian music. He timidly asks if he would be required to wear European clothing and if he could remain vegetarian there. I comfort him on these points and offer to help, but in my heart, I cannot envision this large and rather clumsy man in the West. He would be like a helpless bird, and no one would heed his message in our hectic music world.

Thursday February 23

In the evening I walk home in the company of the Dutch journalist, Mrs. Van B. This is my last night in Madras. A vast multitude swarms through the dark streets. Dimly lit booths, restaurants, cinemas with hideous advertisements, shuffling people, people sleeping on the sidewalk; the bustle of an international city without motor traffic. A steer breaks loose. Men bolt through the streets. We withdraw to safety. It is quieter outside the centre of town. Here the broad streets are mostly unlit. The coolness of the night slowly comes over us.

Suddenly there is music, somewhere to the side. Vigorous percussion, bells and drums, and rising above it the shrill cry of the nagasvaram[28]. We head towards the sound but it is suddenly silent again in the dark side street.

A temple facade is silhouetted against the night stars; ghostly gods gaze down on us. Everything seems immersed in timeless peace. We stand there irresolutely until a man appears from the darkness, perhaps a kind of priest, with a painted forehead and shaved totally bald. He wants to be our guide but won't bring us into the temple. He disappears again, and then returns almost immediately with a key in his hand. We follow him through another small street and soon stand in front of a large dark house. We go inside. The man wants to show us wood carvings, he is obliging, too obliging. My companion begins to feel anxious. As the door closes behind us I also feel uneasy about this man's intentions. I make it clear to him that we are not interested in further sight-seeing. Shortly after we are standing on the street again and I feel relieved that I wasn't required to resort to heroics.

Again I feel the strange charm of the night life. In a few weeks I'll return home. Are the people there really different? Or is it only the change in decor that makes us feel, think and act differently?

POSTSCRIPT

Five hundred kilometres to the south of New Delhi, in the middle of the endless desolation of this land, lie the temples of Khajuraho. A thousand years ago, before our Gothic cathedrals, a complex of more or less twenty temples, overgrown with thousands of statues, sprang from the ground in a grand creative fury. I passed my last Sunday in India here, far from the inhabited world. This eruption of human creativity seems unreal. It's difficult to place it in the context of the silence and profound peace that one finds here now. The temples stand alone in the sun, like forgotten fortresses. Ages of obscurity immerse them in an impenetrable haze, despite all the tourism.

There, on that day, I suddenly remembered an experience. Several weeks previously I had visited the house of a European, who on my arrival was playing a recording of Bartók's *Music for strings, percussion and celesta*. It was the first occasion in quite a while that I had been confronted with music from 'my own turf'. And I suddenly sensed – thousands of miles away – the vitality of this little piece of ground: Europe. How there, not only in the past but today also, generation upon generation of new artists arise, painters, poets, sculptures, composers. How, despite the discouraging circumstances of the past, the will to create could not be subverted. One generation has scarcely gotten started and the next is already knocking on the door. There we find a continual dynamic development, here – Khajuraho – the symbol of standstill.

Can these two worlds live together?

Because I am a composer, I can answer this question with a full-hearted yes. For even though much of India's greatness lies in the past, it is nevertheless a land that is bursting with possibilities. This is forcefully expressed in the two art forms that still live today:

music and dance. The way in which these are practised, but even more importantly, the equilibrium and harmony to which they aspire, could be immeasurably valuable to western man. If, at least, he can still listen to something other than himself.

2

TRAVEL MEMORIES FROM JAPAN
Ton de Leeuw

A priest is making his way to the grave of a former protege. He meets a woman with whom he discusses the deceased. Then he recites prayers. The spirit of the deceased appears and speaks with the priest about his earlier life and the causes of his death. That is everything. The austerity of the story is only exceeded by the terrifying bareness of the scene.

Archaically clad figures shuffle with wooden movements across the stage, surrounded by a small group of musicians and helpers. The unreal sluggishness of movements makes a distance of several meters seem endless. The small stage required by the Nō theatre – for that is what we are speaking about – expands to a new reality liberated from space and time. Nō is perhaps the most concentrated, the most desperate attempt to transcend the boundaries of human life. An almost horrifying silence hangs about the figures. Their monotone speech-songs, the sluggish drum patterns, the Nō flute piercing through everything, all is bathed in this silence that seems to take you by the throat. Hours are no longer relevant. The priest converses with the woman, he recites his prayers. . . What does he say? Where is he? Who still understands anything of this fifteenth-century Japanese? It does not matter: there is so much that remains.

I suddenly realize that I am outside the theatre, carried along by a happily chattering crowd. It is raining in Kyoto. I take a taxi and in a short while I am standing in front of a hotel where a friend of mine is staying. He hasn't arrived yet, I am much too early. But the serving girl, draped in a kimono, lets me in without hesitation. All of old Japan seems to be a part of her. She serves me tea, and while I am drinking, she kneels across from me on the ground. Language problems inhibit the conversation. I release her from her charming attempts by signing that I would like to rest. She hurries away to find a blanket. Slightly later I stretch out on the reed mats. She covers me with the blanket and then goes silently away. I fall asleep with the rich feeling of having experienced today something of this age-old civilisation.

This is one side of Japan. The other is equally bewildering. The next day I return from Kyoto to Tokyo – a distance roughly equivalent to that between Amsterdam and Paris – with the Tokkaido train. In the restaurant car I am fascinated by the speedometer: 150-180-230 kilometres per hour. The fastest train in the world glides almost silently through the Japanese landscape. Within three hours the traveller is transported from the old temple city Kyoto to the largest and perhaps most dynamic city in the world. Tokyo is a gigantic, perfectly organized ant nest. The streets are overcrowded, swarming with people, the traffic races by, and under and above ground trains shoot by one another. In many cafes, restaurants and theatres, numbers of portable telephones stand ready, the visitor not even needing to stand in order to make a telephone call. Time is valuable.

The same people who created the timeless *Nō* theatre have fanatically surrendered to the twentieth century with more vitality and dynamism than most Europeans were able to do. Their break with the past is more radical than it is in the West. The Japanese want to forget *Nō*. The girls in Tokyo are more talkative, and soft music – always and everywhere, even in elevator shafts – does the rest to insure that silence is banished day and night.

In 1868 Japan was rescued from its isolation by the so called Meiji restoration. This meant the end of a feudally governed society. For a century, Japan feverishly imported everything that the West had to offer, ripe or green, without discernment. Music and its education were very soon transformed to western models and for a long time traditional music found itself, practically speaking, repressed. For many Japanese, western classical composers became a symbol of liberation. The piano became an exciting instrument: because the *koto* was too clearly descended from feudal tradition, people wanted to forget about it.

The Japanese legendary capacity for assimilation resulted in a good deal of the musical culture of Tokyo becoming thoroughly westernized. Western culture has acquired its own, broad public. It is this group of the population that comes to listen when the Concertgebouw Orchestra plays in Japan.

There are six symphony orchestras, many music organizations, and fully stocked music and phonograph shops. Like everywhere else in Asia, most shopkeepers look puzzled if I ask for Japanese classical music. It must be my fault.

But recently there has been a miraculous change taking place. For one thing, many Japanese are becoming increasingly aware of their own culture; people are beginning to reappreciate the old values. The era of frustrations is coming to a close. Furthermore – and this is an even more recent development – several western artists have discovered Japanese classical music and are looking on it with growing admiration. It's not a question of seeking an exotic tint, as we did fifty years ago, but rather the wonderful discovery that a number of classical Japanese concepts seem to be closely related to the music that started to ripen in the West after 1950. The technique of the *Gagaku* ensemble – the oldest living orchestral music in the world – is more closely related to our age than to the nineteenth century. *Nō* theatre – one of the oldest living theatrical forms – is both musically and theatrically rich in contemporary characteristics and can be seen as the prototype of today's music theatre.

At a UNESCO conference in Tokyo – dealing with the relationship between Japanese and western art – I pointed out five distinguishing qualities, of a concrete, stylistic-technical nature, that are characteristic of certain forms of classical Japanese music, and that – in retrospect and without any intention on my part – are also fundamental to my own recent compositions. Perhaps this is incidental but it is astounding that there is suddenly a bridge between medieval Japan and the contemporary West. This is not manifested in mere superficialities. We must dig further in order to find the deeper lying common particulars. Several Japanese avant garde composers have also made this discovery. Slowly but surely, the Japanese are freeing themselves from the folkloristic stage, that seldom rises above picturesque quirks and a quest for local colouring. Its day lies behind us. In search of the sources of music, Japanese and western composers offer each other their hands.

All of this became especially clear to me after a conversation with Toru Takemitsu. Roaming through the flashily lighted streets of Tokyo, along bars, restaurants, night clubs, gambling halls, amidst all this noise I began to form an impression of this Japanese composer, who in my opinion is the most important in his country. He is of my generation. That makes talking about him easier. To him, the West is no longer an imported product, but rather a part of himself. On

Ton de Leeuw in his house in Utrecht, 1956.

Ton de Leeuw in his study in Utrecht, 1956.

the other hand, he could quite naturally gain awareness of the great traditions of Japanese music. At the end of the evening, he took me to hear a *biwa* player, apparently one of the greatest masters of the instrument. The *biwa is* one of the purest and most enchanting instruments that I know, and is also exquisite to look at. Our hostess, a woman in her sixties, is one of those rare traditional musicians who takes an open stance to new music. She played one of Takemitsu's compositions for us and it was remarkable the ease with which a living musical language came into being without in any way doing violence to the so individual character of the instrument. East-West dualism, Old-New dualism were relinquished in this music.

One of my aims was to study playing techniques of Japanese instruments. During my short visit, I had the privilege of being introduced into many traditional milieus where musicians of the old school resolutely continued in the practice of their profession. The world of Japanese music is an enclave set in a westernized society. But in contrast to other Asiatic music cultures, I don't sense any of the suppression that is so painfully evident elsewhere. The practitioners of this art continue to live in their old Japanese homes, still wear Japanese dress and keep Japanese customs. But they also have television sets and tape recorders in their homes. *Kabuki* theatre makes use of the most modern technical devices in producing their ancient pieces.

Yoritsune Matsudaira, one of the most prominent of the older composers in Japan, arranged a *Gagaku* performance. This orchestral music – as has been said, the oldest continuing musical tradition in the world – was imported quite early from China and has since then played an important role, for example in the Imperial court. A fascinating aural world to modern ears, despite the seemingly archaic strictness of style and playing techniques.

The players are clad in equally archaic costumes. The instruments – winds, plucked instruments and percussion – are very direct, and they are matched according to their qualities: sharp timbres are set against each other, sharp attacks, nothing is polished in this music. The *Sho* is a wonder. Seventeen pipes, coming together in an air chamber that the player blows into. I almost wanted to write: a predecessor of the organ. And it is too, if we take the term for what it is without trying to interpret it qualitatively. There are analogous forms of the instrument in China and Southeast Asia, but it is the Japanese version that has attained perfect beauty of sound. It produces

Above:
Working visit to Munich in 1952, from left to right Ton de Leeuw,
Henk Stam, Walter Maas and Jos Wouters.

Above right:
On the roof of the Concertgebouw in Amsterdam, during the Dutch-
Belgian Composers Festival 1954. From left to right are Jo Elsendoorn,
Ton de Leeuw, David van de Woestijne and Karel Goeyvaerts.

Bottom right:
Preparations for the radiophonic oratorio 'Job', for which De Leeuw won
the Prix Italia in 1956. In the studio of the Nederlandse Radio Unie in
Hilversum with technicians Piet Bottema and Arie Brandon.

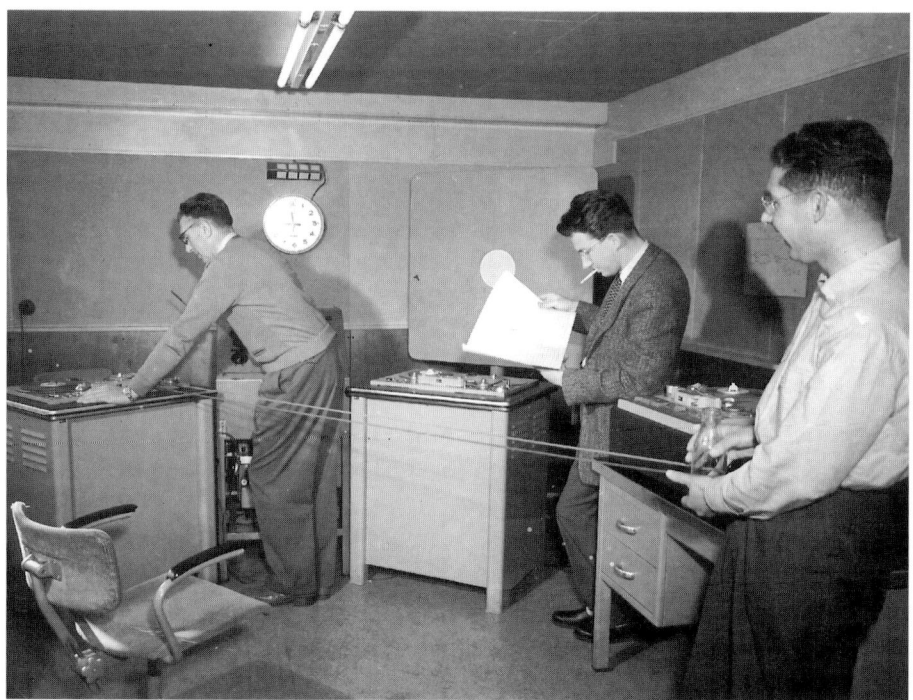

chords that envelop the sound on the entire ensemble, almost 'freeze' it, to use the description of the American ethnomusicologist William Malm.

After listening for an hour to this living witness to twelve centuries, I was very amazed when the *Sho* player produced an up-to-date camera from one of the folds of his ancient costume and humbly asked me to pose for him. The visitor encounters this type of comical contrast almost daily. In revenge, I took a photograph of him the next day.

One of the most notable characteristics of the *Gagaku* ensemble is its intentionally modest means. The clear intention – in other Japanese art forms as well – is to achieve as much as possible with limited means. This also applies to the way that instruments are used. I learned much about this while attending a *taiko* lesson. The *taiko* is a drum, laid on its side, that is beaten with sticks on the upper side. It seems very simple but the instrument is extremely complicated. The teacher showed me a number of drums which were exquisitely lacquered, especially the older ones – about two centuries old. The many sounds of this instrument would make a western composer's mouth water! But in Japan, only several basic sounds are used – conscious limitation – which are exploited, however, in producing refined nuances, so complex that one could only perceive them after making a detailed study. Sobriety and refinement: only several of the qualities to be learned from the ancient Japanese. The knocking about of much western music, particularly that of the sixties, seems very crude in comparison.

The intriguing situation in Japan was a point of discussion at a UNESCO conference attended by specialists in the field of literature, architecture, theatre and music. It may be interesting to outline the main streams of thought. There were two main categories of conflicting views. Firstly, the Japanese view contrasted to that of the westerners, in as much as these latter tended to embrace orthodoxy. The Japanese were more level-headed about their tradition than the western specialists in attendance, who were much more impassioned due to their life-long study of the subject.

A thoroughly different contrast of standpoints became clear when views of the scientifically orientated participants were set against those of the more creatively orientated participants. The first group was basically pessimistic, probably because they concentrated on the aspect of loss of older values. The creative group – writers, architects, composers – generally held a more positive view because they were concerned with the present, with all its new possibilities. In other words: whatever the result of the collision, the sparks that fly off are a stimulant to the work of the creative artist. Or as a Japanese writer expressed: "Let's not dig too deeply in the past, nor speculate about an abstract future, but rather do that which today asks of us. We live here and now."

Here and now.

There was one participant who wanted to return home immediately after the conference. He could no longer take Tokyo, the city that violated his thought. There was also Bill Malm, the ethnomusicologist mentioned above, who thinks of Japan as a second home. Each free hour he took me to new places, temples, or another performance. Proud and enamoured, as though it were his own country, he showed me places where foreigners never come: *Gidayu* (a special type of story where Japanese speaking techniques excel) performed by women; an old tavern where *saké*, the national drink, is still served in wooden cups, a custom that most Japanese have forgotten; a neighbourhood bar for communist workers where Russian songs are sung to accordion accompaniment. . . It did me good to meet a specialist who hadn't buried his soul in the past. People who thrive on their own era and contemporary phenomena are unusual.

In any case, it became clear to me that it was time for we Europeans to broaden our views. As long as we limit these to the most recent centuries of western culture we will continue to live in a state of cultural colonialism. Each western musician of standing should be reasonably acquainted with Asiatic musical cultures. This would not only result in inner growth, but more importantly in a change of consciousness, an intellectual adaptation to the present day. Regardless of how stiffly ideological and political differences are maintained, the true tendency of our time is one of broadening and doing away with borders. The artist should lead the way. Slowly but surely, interest is growing, especially in avant-garde circles. But dilettantism, that can even be heard among the leaders of this group when speaking of eastern music, is immensely irritating. We have become more critical; but I wonder if we have finally passed the stage of our former exoticism.

High above Kyoto, on the Heiji Mountain, lies a Zen monastery. The monks still follow their Buddhistic regimen, as they have done for ages. There is an exquisite view of the Lake Biwa, surrounded by hilltops, so characteristic of Japanese prints. Peace, quiet. Behind these are the plains, thickly populated centres of industry, harbours, traffic. A good deal of the hundred-million Japanese live in these parts, working in factories like we do, surrounded by the same appliances, experience the same social environment, are involved in the same world political problems.

All of this is only eighteen flying hours away. Japan has become a neighbour.

MUSIC IN THE EAST AND THE WEST
A SOCIAL PROBLEM
Ton de Leeuw

Over the past few years, various articles have appeared in this review concerning one of the great cultural problems of this century: the East-West relationship. The points of few differ markedly, of course, some, like the following, being too sure of themselves: 'The music of Asia and India is to be admired because it has reached a stage of perfection, and it is this perfection that interests me. But otherwise the music is dead.' (Pierre Boulez, *The World of Music*, no.2/1967, p.3) Others betray a somewhat disillusioned misunderstanding of western values: 'Apart from the virtuosi who only play, there are composers who only write, a public that only listens, conductors who only conduct, and when under these conditions an artistic impression is created, it is only through a highly organized adjustment between the isolated spheres.' (Edith Gerson-Kiwi, *The World of Music*, no.4/1968, p.9)

I shall take a different point of departure. The decline of most traditional musics is in fact largely due to extra-musical causes. It is not a lack of inner vitality, but rather the inadaptability of musicians and musical life to today's sociological changes that is the essence of the problem in the Orient. Moreover, this problem is not confined to the East; western music is equally threatened by extramusical forces that are to some degree analogous. Thus, instead of contrasting East and West, it would be more relevant to identify common threats and from these seek ways of resolving the problem, which ultimately centres on the relationship between music and modern society. To begin, we should briefly consider the main external causes of this problem in the East (excluding Japan which occupies a place apart in Asia).

The relationship between music and society is much closer and mutually influential than is generally realized. Sociological conditions in the East have been radically altered, and without the gradual transition that took place in the West (adaptation here also has been problematical due to the extraordinary rate of change).

In some cases, political circumstances stemming from a strongly emphasized pursuit of independence have had repercussions on the cultural sphere. There is a tendency to cultivate isolation, closing all doors to foreign influence except those of an economical or technological nature. On the other hand, the material needs are enormous, if not to say thoroughly overwhelming. So many things need be done, be done again, overcome, resolved, that monetary allotments to cultural development are limited to a strict minimum.

These phenomena have a paralysing effect and generate an underlying malaise, a provincialism that hovers over all the great capitals of the East. In these surroundings, the eastern intellectual finds himself in a grave dilemma: how to reconcile his past with western thought and the future of his country. To take a concrete example: what are the prospects open to a young Indian composer who, having studied for six years in the United States, returns to his native country? He would like to contribute to his national culture but because his craft and profession are not part of the local social framework, he works in a vacuum. Would he be betraying his country in returning to the United States to live the life of a western composer?

A paradox of the twentieth century is that there is most often no real bridge between the East and the West even though communication has increased dramatically. Despite the exchange of students, the activities of cultural-scientific institutes, aircraft crowded with diplomats, merchants and industrialists, most of this operates outside the immediate sphere of cultural life. So it is that a westerner who had lived for more than ten years in Bombay, confided to me that he had never seen a performance of Indian dance. He is no exception. Tens of thousands of westerners honourably exercise their professions, living in enclaves surrounded by oriental domestics, without ever acquiring an interest beyond that of a tourist. Worse yet, many western governments do not permit themselves the luxury of a cultural attaché. Consequently, cultural exchanges and contacts on an official level are minimal, and even these few are often ridiculous. Culture is a closed door.

The Easterner is not always more enlightened either. What he sees of the westerner in his daily life is taken as representative of the West as a whole. Too many orientals have told me that they find the West only powerful in its material resources. They almost completely ignore true western civilization. The 'westernized' oriental, unfortunately, has in many cases been stripped of his sense of judgment. There is nothing worse than those eastern Oxford alumnists who cherish the divine Bach, the heroic Beethoven, the nostalgic Chopin. They are the new bourgeoisie of the Orient, the social elite that have progressed in all fields but, as far as culture is concerned, have preserved the intellectual servitude of the colonial period. From here, it is only a small step to disinheriting one's own past. Traditional music is too often associated with memories of the past that many prefer to forget.

One case that made a great impression on me was that of a master of traditional music who earns four to five times less than his colleague who teaches western music in the same school. Training in western music has become the rage. In the same spirit, conservatories based on western models are springing up around the globe. An ignorance of western music has led to widespread training of eastern young musicians based on the fundaments of tonal harmony, which has been on the way out – in the West itself – since the beginning of this century. Another form of this superficial imitation is the founding of unmentionable ensembles so as to have real 'orchestras', the horrid background noise of the radio, cinema, cabaret, etc.

There are also other consequences, even more distressing for they operate internally. Eastern musical instruction was traditionally oral. Notation – if it existed – hardly provided any indication of nuance, rhythm, ornamentation and timbre, all these being subtle matters that could only be learned through the master's living example.

Since the appearance of schools on the western model the specific features of eastern musical training has tended to disappear although, admittedly, there have been advantages such as the increased number of students and greater technical possibilities. The same former intimate contact between the teacher and his pupil was reflected in the relationship between the musician and his audience, but the introduction of large concert halls to the East has altered the situation. The close and profoundly human communication between the artist and the audience – I think one of the most precious treasures of eastern musical life – is fading away. And finally there is the introduction of cheap, western manufactured instruments to the eastern market, steadily defacing the true musical qualities of the older instrumental practices. Good intentions have always been diluted by economic interests.

This sketch of the threats beleaguering eastern music has underlined the significance of sociological and material aspects. The fatal influence of these external factors is inevitably comparable to the threats posed by chemical products to the flora and fauna, if not the human beings themselves, of a given area. It is absurd to propose that the creatures mutilated by these products were merely too weak for survival. The same holds true for music, not only in Asia but equally in the West. Here also, many problems are caused by material factors. We should remember that the musical life of any country here would come to a complete standstill if funding ceased to flow. Without official subventions, no musical institute, no orchestra, opera, conservatory or festival could exist. Remember also that the great majority of westerners consume exclusively the products of 'commercial' music; that most western composers cannot financially survive through their craft alone; that our orchestras are gradually dying out.

Enough said. . . We live in a period of transition between the patrons of the arts in former days and the future society we dream of. Nowadays, one can only hope for the barest minimum of material guarantees. But even this would be tremendous! This is the deeper meaning of what Trân Van Khê wrote about his own country: 'A solution to the problem of the preservation of traditional music in Vietnam will only be found when traditional musicians throughout the country, like those in North Vietnam, can earn a living giving concerts and transmitting their skills to students without being obliged to take up a second profession.' *(The World of Music, no.2/1969, p.51)*

But we are not condemned to complete inactivity while waiting. It seems to me that there are two tasks we must undertake: the preservation of the great musical traditions and the preparation of the future. I think that the truest solution to the problem of preserving the past is that proposed by Daniélou (see *The World of Music*, no. 2/ 1968). This plan entails the training at the highest – and genuinely eastern – level of a small number of gifted musicians. These professionals would be selected to keep alive and pass on the great musical traditions. It would be a comparatively inexpensive solution and would circumvent the levelling process of westernized teaching. I should like to add that this plan – to be implemented by an international organization – ought to be complemented by measures of a social order. The government concerned should guarantee the young musicians of this programme the possibility of honourably earning their living by practising their professions. But with this thought we enter the realm of wishful thinking.

Regarding the preparation of the musical future, I have on several occasions submitted a plan that also aims at a concentration of forces. It basically calls for setting up study centres in the crucial areas of musical life in order to examine, on the scene, the following aspects:

– all genres of musical hybridization, their positive and negative aspects, their functions and influences;
– the part played by industrial and technical progress in socio-musical structures and the present day relationships between music and society;
– the possibilities of a new teaching of music based on the essential data available today.

The team – consisting of musicologists – should be carefully selected. Even now, note well, western composers too often think of eastern music as an exotic raw material from which one could, at very most, extract some picturesque detail for repolishing. The team would stress that the western composer take deep interest in every music that is valid as a human language by putting his creative ability at the service of the investigations. The musicologist, for his part, should concentrate chiefly on acculturation. His musical training should be broader than is usually the case today, and he should be equipped with a deep knowledge of twentieth century musical concepts. Finally, the sociologist would be entrusted with the research of a broad field: the optimal conditions for establishing rapport between musicians and their public. Should one aim for mass consumption of music (large concert halls) or to split up today's anonymous public into small groups, each with its own points of reference and interest? It also goes without saying that it would be essential for the young musicians of a given country to collaborate closely. These centres, experimental and even pragmatic, could lay the foundation for the future actions of governments and international organizations. Instead of passively awaiting the effects of hybridization, as massive as it is inevitable, we could try to forestall events.

This plan aims at direct action and could be put into effect without too much expense. We would only need four or five such centres with a staff of about twenty in each. Placed under the auspices of an international organization, these centres could be incorporated in existing institutes, provided they were assured sufficient autonomy. In any event, these proposals could secure an advance on our long term recommendations and wishes. They would help further the discussions on numerous matters, for instance on musical education, but all this has already been brought up at congresses organized under the auspices of UNESCO. The summaries of these meetings are proof of the awareness of our age and it would be difficult to add any fresh points of view. If the decade of 1960-1970 has been one of general discussions, the decade 1970-1980 should be one of action. UNESCO'S attention to these problems over the past ten years justifies every hope for the future.

4

INTERACTION OF CULTURES IN CONTEMPORARY MUSIC

Ton de Leeuw

The influences of cultural interaction in the music of this century have been widely disparate. Many times, they have been rather superficial or even negative, for example, the colourless mixtures of commercial music furnishing background noise in non-western countries. These make use of whatever is purported to be the local characteristics but, set in a western idiom, they fail to achieve any authenticity or have any character of their own. Many changes have been brought on by extra-musical circumstances, like the industrialization and urbanization of countries of the non-aligned world and the impact of technology imported from the West. Despite their disastrous proportions, these phenomena hardly constitute conscious cultural confrontation. Only in the comparatively esoteric field of 'serious' contemporary music may symptoms of a new attitude and of modern man's intellectual adaptation to the changing world be discerned.

The present article deals primarily with this evolution and its consequences for musical composition. Since all this is intimately bound up with the notion of tradition, I shall put forward a few preliminary remarks:

- Tradition could be defined as the sum of values handed down from the past and as our interpretation of these values. Through this interpretative aspect, the notion of tradition is filtered through our contemporary consciousness. Thus, this notion is as dynamic as it is essentially subjective.
- But the sum of values we have inherited from our predecessors has been greatly enlarged in the twentieth century. At the same time, our attitude towards them has been modified. First of all, tradition is not as much the local phenomenon that it had been and it is less impenetrable. Interaction among cultures is taking place on an international scale. We are also nowadays conditioned

by something more than mere local or regional values. We are subjected to common experiences, like the technological, industrial and urbanized environment of modern society. Modern education is another of these experiences: we share the common heritage of the major currents of thought influencing mankind, from Buddhism to Marxism. Conditioning factors are therefore more uniform in the world today than ever before.

These developments do have some positive aspects: as our field of action widens, opportunities of fruitful interaction between widely varying spiritual and musical sources increases. Already, local customs now exist as part of a global tradition, to be experienced by the whole of mankind. The modern situation has a parallel in the thought of Carl Jung for whom all men and all races are bound together by the collective unconscious. Since the beginning of this century, creative artists have sensed the truth of this idea. They discovered that the African mask is not only an exotic – 'foreign' – artifact but is also something that they recognize deep down in their own being. Does this imply synthesis between different cultures or is it the intuitive discovery of a common, archetypal source?

In any case, dramatic foundations have been laid for a positive change in human thought. Ironically, this also will bring about the dissolution of specifically local cultures. Even though this would be lamentable from a historical and scientific point of view, it may well be highly beneficial from a creative standpoint. The generic values of a given artistic evolution, those objects of scientific research, are rooted in the past and cannot be re-lived. They can at best only be reconstructed. In the final analysis, 'relative' values, those collected by and filtered through our contemporary consciousness, are the most authentic and will prove most fruitful.

But, the negative consequences abound:

1.   The limited field of action of most local traditions also constituted their strength. The art in question operated within the framework of a fairly well defined society. One consequence of a relative continuity of their evolution was the unity they achieved between the conception and its means of expression. These vanishing aspects cannot always be replaced by new ones. Today, we even see the creation of works of art that consciously

draw from the most widely divergent materials and resources from every corner of the world.

2.   Secondly, music, at least in the West, has become largely a matter of individual research without any obvious reference to social context. As restricted as ever, the musical public has in addition become anonymous and amorphous, especially since the arrival of large concert halls in the West. But in the East, as well, the trend towards enormous concert halls has begun to distort the habits of the musical public. Intimate and profoundly human communication between an artist and his public is beginning to disappear. The interaction between music and society is much closer than is generally realized and, with radical, sudden changes rife with sociological conditions, we are afflicted with innumerable problems of adaptation and a rupture between the requirements of modern society and musical life.[1]

3.   Then there is the psychological problem arising from the fact that today the very overabundance of information generates serious perceptive difficulties. Modern man tends to shield himself by limiting his choices, arbitrarily accepting or rejecting as he sees fit. He feels threatened and overwhelmed by the flood of new things, whether they be the music of Japan or contemporary western music, and he ultimately rejects them. It is too much for him; he prefers to relax in the familiar world of the classics, the romantics. He has been neither mentally nor musically prepared. What is lacking is not so much the stimuli in themselves but an adequate system of education that would enable us to digest them. In short, the worldwide interaction of which I was speaking is beset by serious problems.

EASTERN INFLUENCES IN THE WEST

At first sight, it would seem that the negative consequences of this evolution outweigh the positive. Even if we confine ourselves to authentic activities in the field of contemporary music, the situation gives little grounds for optimism. Without even stepping out of doors – and this is important – the contemporary artist has much greater access to foreign cultures than ever before. Modern western art has been vastly enriched while remaining firmly anchored in western ways of thinking and doing. Because of this, nearly all the recent major developments of present-day music still transpire within the narrow confines of a typically western process of evolution. All too often, the western composer thinks of eastern music as something exotic from which he will at most extract a few picturesque details. Every time a few idiophones are scored, or any other instruments even remotely resembling Javanese types, the composition is beleaguered by meaningless comparisons to gamelan music. A chorus of superficial likening to oriental mysticism follows whenever a western composer mentions the role played by intuition in his work. Admittedly, our ignorance of non-western music is practically complete. In this regard, we have made no progress at all since the turn of the century with its trivial oriental cults. We tore down the barriers separating us from the past instead of surmounting them. Granted, western musicians have discovered eastern music, but it is still a precious object far beyond their reach.

To make matters worse, many musicians who are interested in integrating eastern concepts in their music approach the task from the wrong standpoint. They envisage the synthesis of styles but in fact they do no more than to treat the various musical sources as if they were merely making a setting of them. This is a grave error, for, as I have already stated, the merging of cultures is brought about in the mind, internally and not externally. True synthesis has nothing to do with a more or less successful assemblage of heterogeneous materials. The decisive turning point comes when we no longer think of the various musics of the world as being 'outside of us'. The point cannot be logically argued; it is a subjective truth, but none the less profound for that. The two crucial factors in effectively fusing divergent sources are our ability to change and the extent of our creative powers. Both are instrumental in, for instance, Bartók's superiority to the innumerable stitchers of folkmusic patchworks throughout the world.

EXAMPLES FROM THE FIRST HALF OF THE CENTURY

Much has been written about the revelation of oriental art experienced by Debussy at the Universal Exhibition of 1889. Four years later he wrote:

> 'Let us rediscover tragedy without forgetting what can be gained in total effect from pantomime and dance, while developing the use of lighting to its very highest degree – to the proportions of a crowd. To this end, we can find useful information in the entertainments given by Javanese princes, where the inescapable seduction of that language without words, that is called pantomime, attained almost the ultimate heights, because it worked with acts rather than formulae. The poverty of our theatre consists in our having confined it to intelligible elements alone.'

And in 1913:

> 'The music of the Javanese conforms to a counterpoint compared to which that of Palestrina is child's play. And if we listen, without European prejudice, to the charm of their "percussion", we are forced to conclude that ours is nothing more than the barbarous noise of a country fair.'

Although their sentiment is exaggerated, these remarks show the great degree of Debussy's receptiveness to other musical conceptions. Perhaps it was this alone that drove him further than any of his contemporaries dared go. And yet, what concrete evidence can we find of first hand familiarity with eastern music in Debussy's musical language. At that time, knowledge of non-western music was at a minimum. More probably, Debussy listened not only 'without European prejudice', but also without any knowledge of the subject whatsoever. It may well have been this very ingenuousness that led him to experience a freedom from form in eastern music – a liberty he was to cherish for the rest of his life. But the case of Debussy shows us how subtly phenomena react on the mind. His affinity with nature was quite different from that of the great romantic composers. The romantic artist tended to project himself into nature, whereas Debussy was above all else capable of listening. Profound silence is made audible in his music *(Nuages)*. He detested subjective outbursts. His attitude, as far as we can judge by his music, was more receptive than anthropocentric.

From a structural point of view, this implies the absence of classical development of themes *(La Mer)*. The traditionalist concludes that Debussy 'does nothing' with his subjects. On the other hand, at his finger tips is a very subtle and elaborate art of variation *(Pelléas et Mélisande)*. There is only the barest shadow of the causal relationships characteristic of the classical masterpieces in Debussy's music. Various elements take shape, mingle together and disappear in a free and anti-hierarchical manner. Functional harmony is abolished and metrical context is relaxed. Though seemingly innocuous, Debussy's innovations are extremely radical and foreshadow concepts 'pioneered' in the Fifties of this century. Western music took a decisive turn with Debussy. His was an internal evolution, for note carefully that at least some of its resultant aspects – derived without direct external influence – are closer to certain non-western concepts than they are to those of European classical music. I shall return to this point at the end of this article.

In Stravinsky's music, the case is both more clear and more complicated. The elementary explosion of *The Rite of Spring* is revealed not only in the work's violent expression but also in certain structural features of the musical language. This is true of its rhythm – which is highly complex – and, even more essentially, of its melodic substance which is surprisingly similar to certain primitive melodic forms.

Stravinsky uses a limited number of notes, often revolving round a central nucleus (Ex. 1a), a falling cadence beginning with a strong beat (Ex. 1b), lengthy repetitions of melodic units (Ex. 1c) and a predominance of 'archetypal' intervals: the major second and minor third (Ex. 1d).

1a

1b

Primitive melodic forms are pre-modal, in the sense that the musical consciousness in which they originate knows neither the octave nor any divisions within it. Melodic structure evolves, so to speak, around a note that is more or less fixed, the only constituent part being the interval (which is more or less defined). In some cases, particular intervals are favoured and 'nuclei' of intervals may be formed. One such especially common nucleus is the combination of a major second and a minor third, found frequently in the *Rite*. Only at a much later stage is the use of melodic intervals subordinated to other imperatives, like the division of the octave and, more generally speaking, the demands of a modal system.

We know that in the nineteenth century western composers began to turn away from classical tonality by integrating certain modal and other elements into their music which, from all other points of view, remained basically tonal. Also, those among them who, like Debussy, rediscovered at least some essential aspects of modality were rare.

In my opinion, Stravinsky – setting out on this path – exceeded its limits in approaching the 'pre-modal' melodic foundation. If this is true, then the melodic substance of the *Rite* constitutes a very special, almost archetypal, element in a highly complicated, contemporary context. Stravinsky blends two highly divergent structural elements in this composition. This is not surprising if we remember that *The Rite of Spring* was composed at a time that the disintegration of the classical tonal system had reached its peak. From that time on, mixing absolutely heterogeneous elements became normal practice in twentieth-century music.

We should bear well in mind the gulf separating Stravinsky's 'pre-modal' melodic concept in *The Rite* from the richly tonal, chromatically saturated melodies of his predecessors. And, given the period in which *The Rite* was composed, Stravinsky could not have been acquainted with examples of what is called 'primitive' music. He was familiar, at most, with the folk songs of his native country, which, in comparison to those of western Europe, are much more elaborate and rather modal. While there are no direct quotations of eastern European folk music in *The Rite,* the piece frequently approximates its melodies (Ex. 1e).

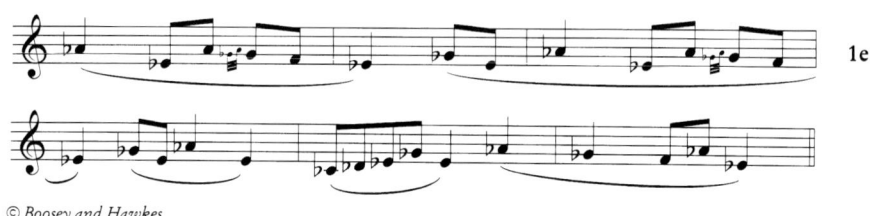

1e

© *Boosey and Hawkes.*

Another important work in our discussion of Stravinsky is *The Wedding.* It in no way resembles our western ceremony and seems more akin to those arcane, but potent rituals that man uses to mark the main stations he passes in life. Just as it is difficult to distinguish between a lament and a nuptial hymn among certain peoples, the musical language of *The Wedding* has this same liturgical, non-subjective flavour, and this in spite of the creative liberty that the composer never ceased to proclaim throughout his life. In *Chroniques de ma vie* (1935) Stravinsky says of *The Wedding*:

> My idea was that this spectacle should be a divertimento, and that is precisely what I wanted to call it. I had no desire to reproduce the ritual of peasant weddings, and I paid little heed to ethnographical considerations. My idea was to compose a sort of scenic ceremony, using however I pleased those ritualistic elements so abundantly prevalent in the age-old village customs of celebrating Russian marriages. I took my inspiration from those customs, but reserved to myself the right of using them with absolute freedom.

Is the Stravinsky of *The Wedding* a Russian or is he drawing from the deep wells of the human subconscious? And what are we to think of his successive metamorphoses, from the Latin world of neo-classicism to the serialism he reached at the end of his life? We never cease to be astonished by the extraordinary vitality of this musician and his flexibility of mind. Stravinsky's field of vision is vast and the sources he draws from are widely dispersed. But in spite of all that, despite its many divergencies, his work shows an astonishing internal continuity. Stravinsky is one of the best examples of that positive sense of mental flexibility that I spoke of previously.

Bartók, unlike Stravinsky, had an active interest in the sources of folk music. He made a study of it, with the result that the composer and ethnomusicologist were united in one and the same person. In this regard, 1913 was a significant year, for it marked the publication of Bartók's first scientific publication *(Rumanian Folk Songs of the Bihar Department).*

With his eminently creative mind, he was able to avoid the pitfall of deliberate, forced synthesis. This folk music aspect of Bartók's composition is not like a superficial layer grafted to a basically tonal idiom. His style was intrinsically enriched by elements he borrowed from it, integrating them in his language. Bartók's 'mutation of mind' is deserving of the highest praise. He, the modern, the rational composer, traced the very sources of folk dance and song of the Balkans. Let us take a closer look at one of the many effects that this had on his composition: the Bulgarian rhythm. Below is an excerpt of one of the *Bulgarian Dances* published in *Microcosm* for Piano (Ex 2a).

2a

© *Boosey and Hawkes.*

According to Y. Arbatsky *(Beating the Tupan,* Newberry Library, Chicago, Illinois, 1953), 'aksak' rhythm is to be found in certain regions of the Balkans. The rhythmic formulae are based on two values, a short and a long (*a* and *b*). The proportion represented is one to one and a half, and not two to three, which is same as saying that we must not count in quavers (*c* and *d*) but in two unequal crotchets; ternary interpretations of these two values would therefore be: *e, f, g,* etc. In his *Dances,* Bartók uses this rhythm and the basic values making up the bar are divided in various ways – the common practice in the Balkan folk music.

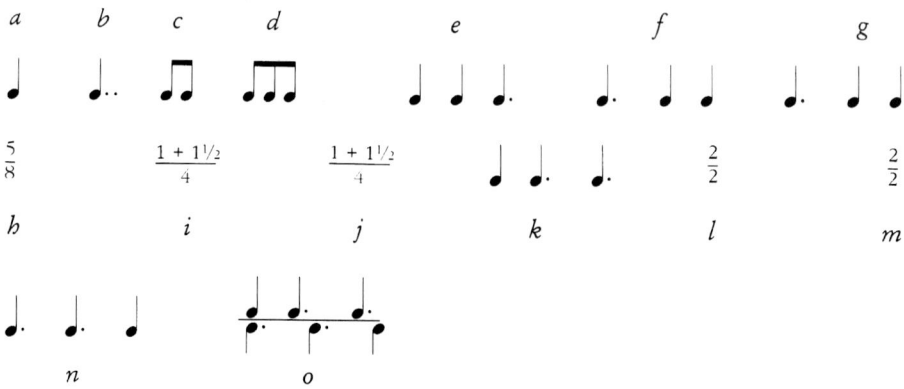

In the example above, the composer erroneously designates *(h),* which actually should be *(i)* – a binary bar with unequal values. The difference is essential. Based on quavers, the performance could only with great difficulty recreate the slightly 'limping' (aksak) binary rhythm suggested by *(j).*

The same notational problem arises in *Music for String Instruments, Percussion and Celesta.* The theme of the fourth Movement is written in the aksak rhythm in ternary metre as follows: *(k),* Bartók's *(l)* signature, however, suggests a syncopated binary rhythm (with a metrical accent on the F sharp of the first bar). If we are correct in assuming what was intended was an aksak rhythm, then Bartók seems not to have realized that a *(m)* signature is quite inadequate and misleading. In passing, it should be noted that the accompaniment also has a slightly different ternary aksak rhythm: *(n).* There are thus two ternary metres superimposed one on another: *(o)* (see example 2b).

Allegro molto

2b

In exploring cases of musical synthesis made in the West, we mention the amazing turn about made by Manuel de Falla. After a period of composing expressive folklore and impressionistic Andalusian scenes, he hit upon a far more concentrated form of expression in *El Retablo de Maese Pedro*. This is a pot-pourri of sixteenth and seventeenth-century court dances, medieval liturgical chant and neo-classical trends of the period. It was to reach to the very depths of the Castilian soul – alone among all his work, except perhaps for his *Harpsichord Concerto*.

A year later, in 1923, Darius Milhaud wrote his ballet *La Création du monde*, adding the foreign element of jazz to his already heterogeneous ingredients. The result was a mixture of free polyphony, syncopated rhythm, melodic 'blue notes' and a very special type of orchestration. Incidentally, the aesthetic values of the Twenties were conducive to the growth of interest in jazz among a number of composers. The freshness and audacity of the New Orleans polyphony, its direct and spontaneous expression and the improvisation – all this was an unexpected source of support in their struggle to find a new musical art form. Later on, when 'Cool Jazz' came in, the evolution of 'classical' music and jazz once again crossed paths. Despite this, it would very difficult to find other works where the fusion of jazz and classical elements was so substantially evident as in *La Création du Monde*. The two worlds are apparently incompatible, which is all the more curious when we consider that Jazz itself was born of the happy marriage of African and western sources. Perhaps the cause of this setback is the element of improvisation that determines the structure of jazz and is its true essence. This element, remember, has long been ignored in western classical music.

If this hypothesis is correct, and if jazz is not dead as the pessimists claim, a more substantial fusion between the two may perhaps be expected in the near future, for it is only in the last fifteen years that western musicians have begun to explore elements of improvisation in their music. *La Création du Monde* holds yet another precious indication of fusion – neo-classicism. The neo-classical idiom, we should remember, is essentially pluriform. In the best examples, it far exceeds superficial 'patch-work'. This use of various classical materials and structural principles was initially motivated by a search for a new type of equilibrium that turned to the old masters for guidance.

THE POST-WAR PERIOD

From the point of view of heterogeneousness, the music of Olivier Messiaen is certainly one of the most astonishing phenomena we will encounter. The diversity of sources and musical material blended in his work is beyond imagination. His is a very universe of elements, embracing bird calls, Hindu rhythms, almost medieval theological concepts, mathematical permutations, etc. Each is subjected to far-reaching transformation. The bird calls are strongly conventionalized, the Hindu rhythms – long forgotten in India – are handled in a purely western fashion. Messiaen defies purism. One moment he is fashioning a curious mishmash of Japanese Gagaku *(Sept Haikai)* and then he invents the famous 'modes with limited transpositions' in which a fascinating array of modal concepts are laid out with great precision. Messiaen believes that this eastern quality of his music is rooted in another of its many facets. He considers his rhythms, derived from an ancient Indian treatise, rather than the modes, as lending that certain oriental aspect to his music. He claims to have discovered their structures, laws and symbols. Figuring in many of his works, these rhythms reinforce, to his mind, qualities he has always striven to attain in his music. To him, these rhythms constitute something of a pre-existing affinity, so to speak. Even if the mysticism of his approach is to a degree responsible for the qualities of his music, we cannot ignore the purely cerebral aspect of Messiaen's approach. Long forgotten in India, these rhythmic forms were merely an object of scholarly research, rhythms on paper, until Messiaen came upon them. And his manner of treating them is purely western. So far as I can judge, Messiaen's rhythmic language has nothing whatsoever to do with the music of India.

Where his 'modes with limited transposition' are concerned, the composer distinguishes between the mathematical impossibility of transposition in his own modes and what he calls the reflexive 'defence system' of the Indian modes (embracing all conventions of modal improvisation).[3] Despite the many differences, the characteristic consistency of Messiaen's modes is reminiscent of certain aspects of eastern modal music. Moreover, their symmetrical structure precludes a vertical, harmonic approach to the music, quite naturally lending itself to horizontal arrangement. Heterophonic textures and rhythmic-melodic writing predominates (Ex. 3).

3   *Olivier Messiaen, 'Les eaux de la grâce', taken from 'Les corps glorieux' (Leduc, Paris)*

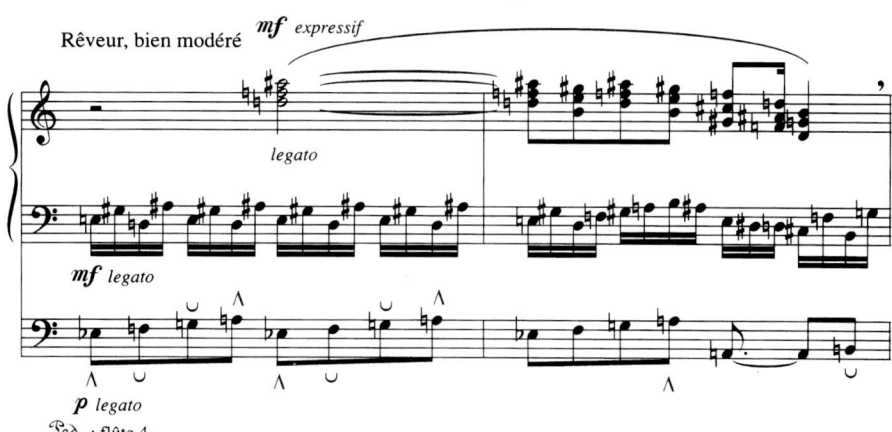

The heterogeneous language of Messiaen's writing never strikes one as being eclectic. Even lesser successful pieces come across as being absolutely authentic: mutation of mind and creative power.

With Messiaen, we have made our way to the contemporary post-war period. Significant facts: in the period between 1950 and 1960, a number of rationalist trends blossomed, among which were the introduction of the computer into music and serial, mathematical and electronic research. Emphasis was placed on musical evolution as an autonomous sonorous phenomenon. After 1960 came neo-romanticism and neo-expressionism. All this fits well in the evolution of traditional western thought. The same period was marked by an appallingly superficial assessment of so-called 'orientalism' in music. Composers like Britten, Boulez and Stockhausen are often quoted. But neither the eclecticism of *Curlew River,* nor the Cartesian intellect of the composer of *Le Marteau sans Maître,* nor even the German mysticism of Stockhausen's recent work is imbued with that quality of mutation of mind which is the subject of the present article.

The work of John Cage is much more interesting in this respect. In it there is no dualism between expressionism and formalism. He tries to tackle music in a new way, void of preconditioning. He aspires to 'allowing the sounds to be themselves' and eschews concepts like control and musical form: 'The rational intellect will never be able to assess nature.' In an effort to avoid the intermediary of human intellect, he resorts to radical chance techniques. One of these methods involves the use of the Chinese 'I Ching'. Why, then, does he compose music? 'I am not interested in the why, I deal with sounds.' Still, Cage is more a philosopher than a composer of music. 'Each and every thing in all time and space is related to every other thing in time and space.'

Several remarks on this:

- This idea is similar to ancient Taoist philosophy where the artist's task, it was thought, is to identify with nature so that he will be able to create the right forms spontaneously, rising above the intermediary of consciousness. Zen Buddhism, in many ways the successor of Taoism, has always emphasized spontaneous, irrational, direct action in art, without fear of the illogical or eccentric.
- Cage is not a 'fashionable' imitator of the East. He has integrated Sino-Japanese thinking into his own western conception, which, although somewhat strange and certainly exceptional, is quite consistent and authentic.
- But there is a fundamental difference: even the most radical Zen art has always maintained a high degree of structural consistency and technical superiority (the best known Japanese haikus provide sufficient examples).

Cage's spiritual radicalism, on the other hand, has quickly led to a complete dissolution of the musical language, not to mention the disastrous effect it has had on many of his disciples. To attain the 'purposeful purposelessness' John Cage seeks, it is necessary to get away from the basic dualism governing western art.

Rather than give a musical example, I refer the interested reader to two of Cage's books, from which I have quoted the passages above: *Silence* (Wesleyan University Press) and *A Year from Monday* (Calder and Boyars, London).

American avant-garde composers were, from the very start, less rooted in the great western tradition than were their European colleagues. The Japanese, on the other hand, were confronted by a different problem. Since the Meiji Restoration in 1868, the two civilizations – Japanese and western – have existed side by side, a condition that has made Japan the absolute testing ground for the future. Here again, we can see that adaptation of the mind cannot be forced. Despite their natural intellectual flexibility, most Japanese composers have gone astray either in a type of exteriorized traditionalism or in some form of surrogate western music. Only particular works of Takemitsu and Ishiyanagi, to give an example, have effectively fused the various elements. Written in a thoroughly contemporary language, they nevertheless exude ancient musical expression from the historical depths of the Japanese soul.

Many of the concepts of ancient Japanese art, incidentally, seem astonishingly up to date, even today. Nō Theatre, for example, is well-known to have had great impact on many western writers. Ancient Japanese music also has many fascinating qualities:

1.   Nō and Kabuki music characteristically superimpose various independent units that have no apparent rhythmic or melodic relationship. In Kabuki music, we find the sounds of the flute and the taiko being combined with independent motives of the shamisen. Divergent musical functions and groups, such as Naga-uta, Gidayu and Geza, are also combined. Some western composers are famous for creating textures in which independent groups are bound together only by a common space-time dimension.

2. Gagaku – the court orchestral music – is remarkable for its highly concentrated musical expression and the reduction of musical strands to a minimum. Making allowances for the obvious differences, this quality of limiting elements to the barest essentials has a parallel in Webern's concepts. The harmonies of the Sho – a type of mouth organ – function in the polyphonic ensemble more like the vertical amalgams of recent music than classical harmony. Moreover, the essentially linear structure of Gagaku could be likened to certain developments in modern western music.

3. The highly elaborate forms of *Sprechgesang* in Gidayu, a sort of musical narrative, is also very instructive. We in the West have made little progress in this technique since it was introduced by Schoenberg.

4. Then there is the exceptional flexibility and consummate subtlety of the sounds of the biwa, the shakuhachi, the shamisen and the ko-tsuzumi. Speaking of the instruments of Japan, Toru Takemitsu remarked: 'Japanese instruments, the biwa and the shakuhachi for example, produce sounds that are quite vivid and near to man. The moment I hear one of them I see a whole world open before me: this is my idea of music. Holding such an instrument in my hands, playing on it, I am closer to music's essence than when I compose something for it. The sound of European instruments, on the other hand, is very abstract (removed from nature), but I am better able to shape something new with it, that is, to compose with these abstract sounds. The two categories of sound belong to different worlds.'

What Takemitsu calls abstract (removed from nature) may perhaps not only be an intrinsic quality of western instruments, but more importantly, a consequence of the classical use that has been made of them for several centuries. Western musical tradition has always demanded 'pure' sounds. The jazz musician's inflections and expressive distortions, for example, are an object of scorn among orthodox musicians, who tend to think: 'They just can't play their instruments'. Contemporary composers, on the other hand, are beginning to rediscover the beauty and force of so-called impure sounds. There is a tendency to abandon the classical ideal and the contem-

porary composer now listens with admiration to the jazz musician
as well as the players of many types of non-western music. The
instrumental and vocal art of the Far East has attained an even greater
degree of refinement than jazz. What we call 'ornaments' are often
in fact nuances and subtleties that are thoroughly integrated in the
musical language. In this regard, it should be pointed out that new
music in the West, especially since 1950, also tends to differentiate
musical language down to the smallest detail. It seems to me, however,
that there is a basic difference between the eastern and western traditions. In serial composition, differentiation is a consequence of
formal planning and is more closely akin to rationalism than musical
sensitivity.

As a composer, I have always been much impressed by the
great instrumental and vocal traditions of the East, as the intricately
detailed notation of some of my compositions would indicate. Obviously, detailed notation does give rise to problems of execution. In
Music for Violin (1967), for instance, I call for thirteen different types
of pizzicato, while most western violinists have as of yet barely
discovered the 'Bartók-pizzicato'. The use of micro-intervals is faced
with similar problems. Here, the East has everything to teach us.
Especially in listening to Iranian music, I became aware that our
western approach to micro-tones is utterly arbitrary and appallingly
lacking in precision.

Micro-intervals in Iranian music, far from being mere approxi-
mations of 'normal' intervals, have their own, individual characteristics, just like any other intervals. This led me to consider the theory
that certain frequential proportions lend themselves more readily than
others to establishing musical individuality (obviously, everything
depends on the degree to which these intervals are consciously handled
within a given musical system). In any case, seeing that micro-intervals
also are endowed with this quality of 'individuality', the performer
could learn to recognize the individual character of each by ear, before
trying to reproduce it. The vagueness of many modern scores – 'a little
higher' or 'a little lower' – is totally unnecessary. These intervals
already exist as characteristic musical entities. This being so, I have
cautiously introduced certain 'standard' intervals in my work, even
though I am aware that the western ear is not yet accustomed to them.
By way of example, here are two excerpts from *Music for Violin* and
my instructions in the score for reproducing the micro-intervals
(Ex. 4).

4   'Music for Violin'

I propose the following notation of micro-tones: a - sign added to the accidental raises or lowers the tone by a comma (a Pythagorean comma is 24 cents; a tempered semitone – 100 cents – is comprised of roughly four commas).

1 = semitone minus two commas (± 50 cents)
2 = semitone minus 1 comma (± 75 cents)
3 = semitone (100 cents)
4 = semitone plus 1 comma (± 125 cents)
5 = semitone plus 2 commas (± 150 cents)
6 = wholetone minus 1 comma (± 175 cents)
7 = wholetone (200 cents) etc.

The following micro-intervals are used in this piece:
± 50 cents   (quartertone)
± 75 cents   (the small semitone, 25:24 is 70 cents)
± 125 cents   (a very large semitone that is approximated in the
                 Arabian Higaz and the Javanese Pélog scales)
± 150 cents   (Arabian 3/4 tone). This amounts to a division of the
                 minor third in two equal parts. ± 175 cents (the minor
                 wholetone, 10:9 is 182 cents).
± 250 cents   (the average interval of the Javanese Sléndro scales is
                 roughly 240 cents. This is also the division of the perfect
                 fourth in two equal parts).

In the examples dealt with above, I have made no attempt to exhaustively outline their many qualities and characteristics. It seemed more fruitful to briefly demonstrate the different ways that cultural interaction is manifested in each case.

These, then, are some of the elements contributing to contemporary western music, a western musical form that is more highly differentiated than any before it. As we have seen, only a few of the examples above achieved true fusion of the elements in our contemporary crucible, but, alongside these isolated, individual efforts, general advances have also been made. Since the beginning of our century, the following general trends have come into play:

– The renunciation of the classical era's genetic concepts in favour of more basic and universal musical forms (free, non-causal succession of parts, like those of *The Rite of Spring*).
– A preponderance of linear structures and heterophonic textures replacing nineteenth-century vertical harmonic treatment.
– Autonomous rhythm, liberated from a metrical context. Increasingly differentiated rhythmic structures.
– The increased importance of other musical parameters, for instance timbre. Here again, we are not speaking of the rational exploitation of timbre, as it is approached in serial music, but rather a heightened sensitivity to it such as we find, for instance, in the work of Debussy, Varèse and Webern. More recent examples are provided by the efforts of some composers to revitalize instrumental sounds with a more direct contact between the player and his instrument (Berio, Kagel, Globokar).

This quite naturally brings us to:

– The growing importance of improvisation in recent music – a phenomenon long neglected in the West.
– An underlying current in western music – the tendency to shift emphasis from the work as such to the language it uses.

This subject merits in depth exploration in a more extensive article. Let it suffice to note here that the evolution of musical concepts in the West is becoming increasingly further removed from the classical tradition. Western musicians today are exploring phenomenon that bear similarity to certain features of oriental art.

July 1957, in Mase (Valais, Switzerland), during one of those early mornings of work on 'Mouvements rétrogrades'.

WESTERN INFLUENCES IN THE EAST

I have dealt up to now with western composers, for the simple reason that the situation in the rest of the world is far more complicated. As I said at the beginning of this article, the West has had enormous influence throughout the world, but its impact has been basically negative and superficial. One important phenomenon should, however, be noted: in many non-western countries, typical composers, that is to say composers whose work in some sense builds on the western tradition, can be found next to the performers of traditional, authentic, local music.

Most of these composers have been trained in one of the many conservatories based on western models that are to be found throughout the world. These artists, offspring of a relatively traditional western musical education, find themselves in a rather difficult position. They have been alienated from their own musical traditions by their education, but, because this has been rather orthodox in most cases, they also have little contact with the main currents of contemporary music. Finding themselves in a 'musical no man's land', they usually attempt to follow in Bartók's footsteps, setting their particular folk music in a traditionally western idiom. The many shortcomings of this approach have already been outlined above. While these composers may, of course, attain a degree of artistic quality, their work by no means amounts to a fusion of cultures as the term is understood within the context of this article. We must not, however, rashly rule out the possibility of meaningfully blending these divergent elements. Attempts to nourish modern composition with the resources of folk music have been widespread in twentieth-century music. In the long run, a trend of such dimensions will probably not fail to have a profound influence on the attitudes of musicians.

Remaining to be dealt with is the question of western influence on the mainstream musical traditions of non-western countries. Apart from the many negative developments – and it was agreed not to speak of these here – is there anything that would be of interest to mention in this article? I cannot answer this with any certainty. Firstly, non-western musical traditions vary widely from one another. The influence of any given western source may thus lead to vastly different consequences, depending on where it is exerted and the nature of the local musical tradition. Moreover, most local musical traditions are passed down by word of mouth so that it is quite difficult to know precisely the musical behaviour of earlier generations. Seeking comparison with the past in order to assess the extent of deviations in musical habits is in most cases a speculative exercise.

Finally, because these musical traditions are mostly oral and the weight of tradition in itself plays such an enormous role, eventual changes would be felt more slowly than they would in western music.

Nevertheless, despite these many limiting factors, it is fairly safe to predict that some long-term internal transformations will appear and that will be very subtle in their initial stages. And let us admit straightaway: they are not necessarily negative. Everything depends on the attitudes of the traditional musicians concerned. Are they aware of what is going on? Or do they seclude themselves in an impregnable past, shunning the influences of modern life? If this latter is the case, there is a risk that their music will sooner or later become no more than a museum piece. Only by accepting the facts of modern life can traditional music fight for survival, as paradoxical as this may appear. Let us offer several examples:

1. Many western instruments have, for economical reasons, found their way into the music of non-western countries. In several, though admittedly very exceptional cases, the interplay between eastern and western types has enriched the music of the countries concerned. The appearance of the violin in twentieth-century Iran had widely divergent results. A fourth string was added to the Kamantché – the Iranian counterpart to our western violin – and its silk strings were replaced with metal ones. These innovations were made at the cost of the intimate and delicate character of the Kamantché. On the other hand, Iranian musicians had developed a new instrument of their own. Moreover, one could reasonably claim that the violin has been integrated into the Iranian musical tradition. The integration of the violin in a local tradition is even more strongly the case with Karnatic music: tuned and played differently, the violin has proven admirably suitable in rendering the traditional art of the great musicians of Southern India. As no other bowed string instrument is to be found in Karnatic music, the introduction of the violin has amounted to a great enrichment.

2.   Evaluating the various uses made of electro-acoustical devices is rather more difficult. In some cases, performers have abandoned the intimacy of the small musical gathering in favour of large halls. But because their musical language is not always suited to the larger dimensions of modern concert halls, many musicians amplify their sound with microphones. This seemingly insignificant fact has had far reaching consequences for the microphone is capable of picking up barely audible sounds, the details of which pass unnoticed to the naked ear. If this development were to be approached from a creative standpoint it could be used to enhance the musical language; with regard to the ornamentation for instance. People sing and play differently in front of a microphone. This phenomenon is well-known to western musicians, although they do not always make good use of it. And how does the act of recording affect musicians' behaviour? To be able to hear yourself playing and critically study your performance after the fact is not without benefit to the advancement of music. With these same instruments, traditional musicians, long strictly conditioned by their own environment, can now hear music from any part of the world. This constitutes an extraordinary turn of events which in the long run must have an influence on musicians' attitudes and therefore on the musical habits of the future.

3.   Finally, I would draw attention to the changes in musical education brought about by applying western methods to traditional musical training. Previously, oral tradition was the rule. Notation, if there was any at all, scarcely gave any indication of the shading, rhythmic ornamentation, or various modes of expression, all of which could only be learned from the living master's example. These special features began to disappear as soon as music schools based on western models were established. The image of the old-time master surrounded by a few faithful pupils has now been replaced by that of the music school where teachers have access to books, recording apparatus, transcriptions, and so on. Here as well, there is a constant struggle between the positive and negative consequences. One must not overlook the advantages of this new type of teaching greater numbers of pupils, greater technical resources, and the possibility of widespread dissemination of information. In other words, what the

teaching loses in depth it regains in breadth. Perhaps there is a simple solution to the detrimental aspects of this development. The benefits of oral training could be preserved for a limited number of the most gifted pupils. These, the professionals, would be responsible for maintaining and passing on the great music traditions (a solution suggested by Alain Daniélou). On the other side, the growing number of pupils in schools of music would benefit from a broader education. We should not forget that musical sciences are becoming increasingly diversified. If only to ensure the place of music in the world of the future, we shall need teachers, musicologists, sociologists, technicians and other specialists. Growing activity in all these fields cannot fail to affect the evolution of musical conceptions in the future.

These few examples demonstrate that traditional musicians are not sheltered from the great changes taking place in the world. But these changes are not necessarily or exclusively destructive. What is needed is detailed research into all aspects of the cultural transition that is now taking place. Although it will not alter the course of history, if musicians and musicologists were fully aware of the situation, they would find themselves able to take greater advantage of it and probably help us to avoid many useless errors.

QUESTIONS, IDEAS AND EXPECTATIONS: PREMISES AND AIMS OF AN EAST-WEST ENCOUNTER

Ton de Leeuw

The theme of *Musicultura 1974* is the confrontation between the musical cultures of the Far East and the West. The underlying idea is that this confrontation is taking place on a worldwide scale. Consequently, this project, which will be spread out over several years, will bring together composers, performers and scholars of very different backgrounds, each having their own methods of addressing the subject. But, all are involved with the issue in one way or another. This is the experimental aspect of the project. Besides having a common interest, we must also find a common base, and, if possible, a common terminology.

This is the main reason that I am speaking in general terms today and not in the specialised language of the composer. In fact, I think that one of our most important aims should be to contribute to the increasing awareness of all who are involved with music and culture in one way or another. In order to clarify this point, let me begin by formulating a number of ideas, and more importantly, broaching a number of questions that I hope will stimulate and channel our discussions. The issues discussed generally in this introduction will undoubtedly re-emerge over the coming weeks in more precisely defined terms.

1

Times are changing. The oil income of the eight leading Arab countries increased four-fold between 1973 and 1974. What is to be done with all this money? At this very moment, five mammoth tankers are being built in Kuwait as the first vessels of a veritable Arabian armada which is to be completed over the next five years. Impressive hotels and banks are springing up in Arabian capital cities. Astronomical sums are being earmarked as credit for less fortunate Arab neighbours. The Arabs have bought an entire island off the coast of South Carolina. They own property on New York's 5th Avenue, as well as in Las Vegas, Georgia, Kentucky and California. Even if every Arab were to own several cars and a villa in Switzerland, there would still be oceans of money left over. So much, in fact, that western financial experts are becoming concerned. In 1974 alone, these resources were estimated to be in the region of 74 billion dollars. Such astronomical reserves could be used to dramatically enlarge the budgets of Arabian Ministries of Culture. It is quite feasible that Arab cultural officials will soon have greater funds at their disposal than their colleagues in the West could ever dream of.

Let's daydream for a moment. If you were one of these fabulously wealthy ministers of cultural affairs, what would you do for music in your country? Such a fortunate minister could set up conditions essentially improving musical life within a single generation by founding good training facilities for musicians, securing them material guarantees for a reasonable standard of living and by organizing the most efficient, optimal distribution of the musical product within the society. Our daydream conjures visions of a renaissance of Arab musical culture reminiscent of the golden age of Ziryab and Al Farabi.

Unfortunately, matters are not so simple. Our minister has much more on his mind than mere material matters. He must take account of the lengthy political and cultural developments of less prosperous times where hardly a moment's thought could be spared on cultural activities. They have remained at the mercy of random forces and, because of the generally prevailing ignorance and lack of interest, out of our hands. Although we musicians cannot gain control of the 72 billion, we undoubtedly could increase our knowledge and commitment. If we fail in this, what right have we to complain when the minister turns a deaf ear. He is preoccupied with a number of crucial problems, some of which I will enumerate here:

−   Lack of trust: is all of this necessary? After all, music is a luxury, and luxuries are imported from the West.
−   Lack of self-esteem: Why stimulate Arabian music? It is a thing of the past, now we must modernise.

The myth of progress: progress is a superficial phenomenon. Musicians may employ new technical devices but what is lacking is an internal impetus. Given these issues, our minister is confronted with a basic problem: what criteria should be taken into account in forming our cultural policy? If he is unable to solve this problem, everything is left to the whims of the supplier and music will become a consumer good, to be fabricated in a way that it is quickly and easily digestible by the public at large: don't aim too high. This is good enough for the background sounds of the radio, television, film, restaurants, commercial airliners, lifts. The labour will be delegated along the lines of mass production. One person makes up a tune, another adds the harmonies and a third arranges it for orchestra. In short, the minister is faced with a new and perilous development, namely a music industry dominated by nineteenth-century liberalism.

I shall return to this point later. For the time being, we could say that the widespread, prevailing assumption, that music is an insignificant factor in human development is at the source of this laissez-faire attitude. Everything the old thinkers and musicians stated about music, the lofty modal ethics of the ancient Greeks, Arabs and Hindus, concepts from the Far East and those of our own medieval philosophers – all this has become increasingly impoverished and void of meaning. Music has been reduced to a luxury article. The resultant superficiality must be one of the gravest threats that demands our concern today. In the final analysis, all dialogue between East and West will probably fall back to these key questions: what is the actual significance of music to the development of the human personality; and, what should its role be in today's society? These problems form a common peril to musicians and musicologists of all countries, irrespective of local differences. Local solutions are no longer tenable. We must learn to think on a larger scale. This being so, we can now pose the following question: to what extent can one meaningfully reflect on the function of music – man and society – without taking account of the enormous backcloth of eastern and western cultures?

I think my thoughts on this question should be clear to you already. The need for an answer is the justification of conferences such as this and illustrates their necessity. We are the ones who must take a stand on this difficult issue. We cannot and should not expect a minister of culture to solve this crucial problem for us.

2

When my children were still young, they believed that our neighbours would have different children's television programmes than those we had at home. After all, the neighbours had a different television set in a different room, and they were other people. They were deeply shocked to learn that everyone is offered the same programming; a first flash of insight into the efficiency of organisation and technology. This common property becomes a communal nuisance if you realise that people must endure *Bonanza, Mission Impossible* and *Peyton Place* not only in Amsterdam, but in New York, Bangkok and Tokyo as well. The internationalism of what television has to offer is in fact no more than the tiniest communal bond that can still unite men. Technological signalling across national boundaries has not enriched or broadened human expression, but rather has lead to appalling impoverishment of the mind in the form of superficial consumerism. The situation is paralleled in music. Light music, which has always had legitimacy in serving a necessary need, has deteriorated to commercially determined, mass produced merchandise. We are subjected to the same aural decor in Amsterdam, New York, Tokyo and Bangkok. Regional dialects, evolved over many centuries, are now being replaced by a sort of touristic patois.

Radio is the main villain in this development. As an example of this, let me relate an experience I had at the last ABU Festival of Folk Music. As part of the festival, radio stations of many countries exchange tapes of their own local music. Only a pitiable few of the roughly twenty tapes I listened to at the beginning of this year were of any value. Not only that, but time and again the technical quality of the recordings was also bad; many were either too short or prematurely cut off. The commentaries spoken into these tapes were typical of the problem. More often than not, they were styled in a clichéd international jargon, so often adopted in reference to folk music: 'the joyous, peaceable folk, singing and dancing after their daily toil'. One South East Asian country came up with the following gem: 'The items of our contribution may not actually be authentic examples of our folk music but they have nonetheless been arranged and re-orchestrated to be played by our local musicians'. One neighbouring country clarified the anomaly: 'Like most young countries, the younger generation of our land is very trendy and easily influenced by anything new. Today, after years of the sounds of world's corners invading us, the traditional customs of our country can take their place alongside the orchestrated works of the world's musical giants'.

Utter nonsense! The inferiority of these selections devaluates the in itself well-intended international exchange, making it very dubious indeed. As we have seen in the case of television broadcasting, technological broadening of our horizons has not enriched but rather impoverished humans. That internationalism is no more than the tiniest common bond between men also applies in music. When we realise that international confrontation and exchange must for a large part rely on mass media, then we as musicians are confronted by a new set of important questions, two of which I will mention here: how could a medium like radio function best within the framework of our set-up? What is lacking in musical education if in radio as well as many other facets of our musical life – especially the economic and technical periphery – we encounter an outrageous shortage of professionals sufficiently rooted in their own musical and cultural background?

Sadly, the direction that music is heading throughout the world is increasingly determined by these above mentioned peripheral interests.

3

Before we know it, a new technical wonder will be knocking on our doors: the transmission of television and radio programmes, throughout the world, by satellite. Then, we will find ourselves sharply divided, even more so than now, between those who are basically commercially oriented and those who are decidedly ideologically motivated. I will confine the discussion to this first type of person for, in the West and much of Asia and Africa, they are the ones we are going to have to deal with.

What will happen? The same concerns that are now churning out the mass produced Peyton Place genre have a finger in the economical pie of the coming satellite era. We will be inundated with commercial productions on an even larger scale and a considerable number of the world's youth will be raised under the influence of these standardized heroes of large scale television productions. There are two obvious causes of this distressing turn of events: it is both more economical and time saving for the world's broadcasting companies

Above left:
*Performance of the 'Four Preludes' at a concert in the Collège
Néerlandais in Paris, February 1950.*

Bottom left:
*Ton de Leeuw with his wife Arlette at the Gaudeamus 'composers'
house' in Bilthoven, where he lived in 1951-52.*

Above:
*In 1950 with composer Bep Geuer, who held a weekly artists salon in
her atelier in Montparnasse, visited at the time by the Groupe des Six.
Ton de Leeuw was a frequent guest during his Parisian years.*

to subscribe to pre-fabricated programmes than it is to set up their own productions; these rented programmes guarantee high viewer ratings because they are easily digestible.

This parallel with the television industry has brought us to the core of the problem in world music. Western economic factors with global influence, and an apparent lack of cultural policy are the two major determining influences of what happens in the world of culture. The situation is comparable to the economic reality of nineteenth-century liberalism: freedom for all actually means freedom for the strong to amass wealth by exploiting the poor who are thus doomed to poverty.

What are the implications for music? In this case, the strong are the commercial interests who fabricate and distribute the musical product. The weak are all minorities, each with their own set of cultural needs, but lacking the means of maintaining, developing and disseminating them.

What are the consequences? We have already mentioned the proliferation of mass produced light music, to the detriment of the skilled traditional musician. Another less obvious symptom is the economic exploitation of concert life and the cultivation of worn, outlived forms, discouraging living, up-to-date, creative develop-ments in music. In the realm of East-West relations: a non-stop stream of by-products of the music industry: cheap instruments, transistors, and records, all of which threaten the already vulnerable, independent life of many non-western musical traditions. We have already learned that pervasive governmental disregard for the problems of ecology, urbanisation and food production leads to disastrous consequences. We have not yet reached this point in music.

Why not? Probably, and I repeat the point, because music's right to existence has been dealt a severe blow over the past few centuries. It is still considered a luxury item. Looking at things from this point of view, East-West antagonism, of which we hear so much, is less essential than another form of antagonism – thriving in both the East and the West – that raging between global economic forces and local authentic, artistic, socio-cultural developments. In point of fact, the western classical musician is threatened by the same problems as the Japanese koto player or the ud player from the Middle East. Cultural liberalism is a common danger.

Can we somehow oppose it? What realistic recommendations could we offer our governments and authorities to open the eyes of responsible politicians to these dangers? This is, again, one of the difficult questions offered today.

4

In addition to economical and political realities, there are a number of other matters with which we should concern ourselves. One of them has to do with the range of our musical experience.

Today's listener is confronted with unfamiliar musical idioms much sooner in life than he was in the past. There are two important factors involved: (a) our conditioning, that is, our perception and patterns of expectation moulded by our environment; and (b) the accessibility of other, non-indigenous idioms – more or less closed systems, aesthetics and backgrounds that developed in foreign parts among specific groups of people.

All the factors involved here seem to be very complicated and have not yet been sufficiently researched. This is also true of the individual's listening process: what processes are at play in the mind from the time a sound is generated, through the stage of sensorial stimulation, up to the musical perception? Until recently, our musical knowledge was primarily empirical. This worked as long as music and our approach to it was strictly regionally defined. But now that national and regional borders are less of an obstacle, the question of music's effect on the human mind – and vice versa – has become more pressing.

I brought up this question a moment ago in a different context. Now I will attempt to outline the issue from a cognitive-theoretical standpoint. A well-known and widespread hypothesis has long existed that all human knowledge originates from the senses. According to this theory, sensory perception comes first, and only after this does the complete process of coordination and interpretation take place in the mind. This view, according to which the process of cognition is divided in successive phases, is disputed today. One of the most important authorities in this field is the Swiss psychologist Jean Piaget. Piaget contends that sensorial perception basically functions as a signal and leads to a somewhat independent process in the human mind that utilizes what he calls the total action. A great number of human faculties are actively involved in this process, and from the very start there is a close correlation between the object conveying the information and the subjective processes interpreting it. Piaget writes: 'It is a violation of the perennial, fruitful, constructive character of cognition, intelligence or action, when it is reduced to the passive role of simple registration'.

If this is true, what are the musical implications? It means that there is no such thing as an autonomous musical object that we first perceive sensorially, then classify, interpret, and so forth. From the very beginning, there are mechanisms at work that have far reaching influence on the process of musical perception. Allow me to formulate this more radically: musical information is already being transformed at the very moment of perception; active integration is set in motion by different sorts of constructive mechanisms. The passive listener does not exist. One way or another, he moulds the musical object in a positive or negative sense. Perhaps, the unconscious listener does exist. He is the willing customer of the music industry, called by Adorno the 'unconsciousness industry' ('Unbewusstseins-industrie').

The most important question to emerge from all this, one we can no longer ignore, is: what kind of mechanism is active within us? Of course, I cannot answer this question because it is ultimately involved with the brain's internal structure and the bio-physical processes of the central nervous system. We must await the answer from future biologists. But there is also a philosophical approach. In illustration, I will relate a radical concept found among several neo-Hindu oriented circles: because of the logical/mathematical structure of our intelligence, we are incapable of acting in any but logical and mathematical terms. Human intelligence, thus, pierces matters like a drill, never seeing further than the grooves made by its own bore.

Here we touch on the key *philosophical* issues of the pros and cons of determinism. But our *cultural* problems are difficult enough, and in this connection the following question becomes important: to what degree does everyone who considers himself human react in the same way as a result of identical built-in mechanisms? This could be a decisive factor in the success or failure of 'mutual understanding', the key to successful international congresses. Perhaps archetypes are indeed a living example of communal human action. The hypothesis of the collective unconsciousness, through which we are supposed to have the ability to recognise different musical idioms at a certain level, by means of musical archetypes, and to experience them as something familiar, can now be seen in a different light. But there are also points of reference with a theory current among some French structuralists; i.e. our nervous system determines a number of possible creative forms of human expression, limited in number and mutually related.

Finally, it should be noted that the idea of universally communal elements of languages has been the subject of much recent linguistic research. Aside from these physiological matters – projections of built-in characteristics of the human mind – music is also comprised of socio-cultural elements. Do these perhaps determine the local characteristics of various musical cultures?

Or is it that the physiological aspect of music is the cause of its specificity? In the light of the above discussion, does it make any sense to look again for basic communal elements in the various musical cultures?

5

During a recent visit to Bulgaria I learned about a radio ensemble consisting of a choir and orchestra. As is usual in Eastern Europe, such ensembles specialize in performing arrangements of folk music. The members of this ensemble were recruited from all parts of Bulgaria. Thus, the best singers and players in the land are given employment in the capital city, where they subsequently remain. Broadly speaking, the process is as such: recordings are made of the local repertoire of each individual musician. Then he undergoes a period of training and adaptation. The musician is confronted with the musical idiom of other regions; he must learn to cooperate in a relatively large ensemble, and to read music so that he is able to perform the arrangements written by prominent Bulgarian composers. The repertoire is collated from the various local sources, of which Bulgaria is rich. In solo passages, the musician is free to do as he was accustomed at home, but these individual traits are inevitably ironed out in the ensemble playing. For example, a certain intonation that is characteristic of a given region is smoothed over because the arrangements are most often practised with piano accompaniment.

It would be interesting to delve more deeply into the many aspects of such a policy – the more so because the Bulgarian example made a more positive impression on me than that of many other East

European countries. What we have here is the cultivation of a broad national style at the expense of regional styles. The same is done on a larger scale, and in a different form, on a worldwide level. Curiously, western cultural liberalism and the cultural policies of many Marxist countries both tend to iron out the differences between local traditions. We know that to the present day regional styles have flourished within the context of smaller regional communities. In Asia this was the case for a longer period than in the West. The Arab musician, working in the closed, small society of which he felt himself to be a spokesman, or the Japanese drummer who for many generations dedicated himself to a particular performing style, equally reflect cultivated regionalism. Music in the West has also known such versatile and variegated traditions but symptoms of their decline appeared early on, especially in the realm of art music. Let us take a closer look at several of these symptoms.

Artistic regionalism is probably dependent on the close bond between the musician and the community. The musician is a spokesman and he has direct contact with his listeners. This contact ended with the arrival of the western type composer in music. The composer is no longer a performer, he has delegated this task as far as his public is concerned, and his musical activity takes place in the seclusion of his study. From the moment of this development, music began to live a life of its own. What the composer writes can just as well be performed elsewhere, by musicians and in communities unknown to him. Because he no longer performs, he loses contact with the instrument, so that his musical creativity develops along quite different lines. This 'de-physicalizing' of musical creativity has had a striking parallel in our century in the introduction of electro-acoustic apparatus. Recording techniques make it even possible to eliminate the performer in the sense that his physical presence is no longer necessary.

Today sound itself has a life of its own, dissociated from its source, no longer emanating from a singer, a player, or a specific place. As a result of this and other developments, Western art music faces a dilemma that has become acute today, namely: are we to have 'regional' or 'world' music? We have already looked into the negative and impoverishing aspects of internationalism. But, we should also be careful not to over-idealize musical regionalism. It also has drawbacks in the form of provincialism and isolation.

In an age of the large-scale destruction of regional traditions, the following questions would seem essential. Should we support and stimulate regional traditions, not as museum pieces, but because they may fulfil the most essential needs of man? In what way, then, should we take advantage of the opportunities for exchange that the world of today has to offer? How should we evaluate our own activities, in this regard? What are we actually doing? We do not promote regional activities, but we nevertheless study them with the passion of the zoologist documenting various species. On this point, Edith Gerson-Kiwi states: 'Traditionalism has become an ethno-philosophical concept'. Through increased scholarly interest, concert tours and recordings, regional traditions are acquiring a status of their own, one of a cultural product, internationally promoted for the benefit of a relatively small group of fans. Thus, with due respect to the positive aspects of this, is there not a danger of regional traditions being driven into the same social isolation as Western art music?

6

Regionalism, if deprived of the openness and expansive nature of our age, deteriorates into provincialism. It is typical of our smugness that we Western intellectuals choose to view the more or less backward societies, far removed from our world, in just this way. But we do not consider it cultural provincialism when:

–   it was not until the middle of the 20th century that we came to realize that music outside of our own tradition was also of value;
–   music history books, in the best of cases, begin with the ancient Greeks, and our students are taught that polyphony is a European invention;
–   non-Western music is largely ignored at most of our conservatories;
–   the acquaintance with Eastern knowledge is limited with most of our intellectuals to a reading of a popular book on Yoga or Zen Buddhism.

Thus, many myths must still be swept away if we are to see the values of the East and the West in their proper proportions. The myth of western dynamism, for example, which is closely linked to that other myth about the originality of creative artists. If we hold this for a basic truth, then the Eastern artist does not fit in. We must therefore learn that other conceptions of art are also feasible. If the artist is a spokesman

of his society, as he was in our past, then originality is not a virtue
but rather a deviation. We should ask ourselves whether our efforts
to be original and individual do not lead to isolation from society.
To what degree is the search for originality an expression of Western
ego-preoccupation and of the inability to live in the here and now?

Professor Han Fortmann quotes American economist Keynes
on this matter: 'This man, aim-obsessed, is always preoccupied with
securing a false and deceitful immortality for himself by transferring
the meaning of his actions to the future. He does not like his cat, but
only his cat's kittens, and actually not really these kittens, but only
the kittens of his kittens and he continues like this, until the end of
the cat kingdom.'

On the other hand, critical self-observation also means that we
become conscious of the positive values of the West. Western music
has created a unique type of composer. The possibility of fixing musical
ideas in a score has resulted in a different approach to the musical
experience. Composition has acquired the allure of audible architecture. Composition today has something of the fascinating beauty of
a game of chess, not necessarily lacking an element of human contact.
It would therefore be unfair to emphasize only the negative side, the
abstract character, the absence of direct creative expression. The same
applies to technical matters; here again the positive possibilities for
music are exceedingly great. Think of the perspectives opened by
recording technique, such as the recording of single performances,
coming into contact with a much broader repertoire, its use in music
education, the opportunities it provides the performer with evaluating
his own performance, etc. Technical aids have led to the historical
consciousness typical of our twentieth century which brings a
thoroughly new perspective to our thinking and actions. Critical self-
observation is not only a necessity for the West, but for all the world's
important cultural regions. It can keep us from becoming self-satisfied,
chauvinistic and contemptuous of other values. This is one of the
prerequisites of mutual understanding.

7

To close these considerations, I shall perform a simple act well-known
to us all. One press of the button and the record starts turning. What
we hear, music of the Australian aborigines, is nothing new to the
insiders among us. But the way I have set it up has so many conse-

quences that it is better if we remain quiet for a moment. [De Leeuw plays the recording; ed.]

Leaving aside our subjective reactions, what was our collective experience?

1. We have been culturally transplanted. This technical miracle makes it possible to detach the acoustic reality from the socio-cultural one, i.e. from the people who made this music at a very specific place and time. We receive this de-rooted message. We may react in many ways, but whatever we do, we should remain aware of the small miracle that is occurring here. Otherwise, we too are the victims of the 'sleepers-industry'.

2. This transplantation is not successful. The displaced musical organism cannot thrive in another community. Despite this, we still acknowledge a process of acculturation, even though it is difficult to measure. In fact, this music also contributes in broadening our horizons. An exchange is taking place, because we listen and interpret the music through the filter of our present day consciousness. In doing so, we transform the original musical message. But this too broadens our awareness and effects change. Consequently, we think and compose differently.

3. We now come upon a paradoxical situation. This musical expression of a world bound by tradition, with a strong tendency towards continuity and relatively fixed and permanent patterns, this symbol of immobility has precisely the opposite effect on us: it generates mobility and transformation. As is probably the case in most acculturative processes, a shift in values is effected in the recipient culture. We therefore ask:
    – Are there basic laws to acculturative processes?
    – Do selective systems merge well with alien influences?
    – What types of qualities should changes in value have so that foreign elements can be integrated in our own culture?

4. This recording is but one small drop in the overwhelming sea of information inundating us in today's world. In itself, this is not a problem, but our inability to adequately digest this stream of information is. Selective systems are operating in our minds as well. We apparently have the ability to keep things out of our view, as many teachers could tell you. In my youth, I hitch-hiked to Paris to hear *Pelléas et Mélisande*. Later I went to Berlin to see

a Kabuki performance. Since 1960, however, students have access to practically everything the musical world has to offer. And to our great surprise, we see that few young musicians have much interest in it. This concerns us because we are again confronted by a choice between two alternatives: between active or passive listening. What teaching methods can we come upon to stimulate the first of these two?

5.   The recording we just heard brings the aboriginal music from a closed to an open society an immediate transferral. Perhaps I could illustrate the weight of this point by bringing up the example of the Australian aboriginals who within a few short years were transformed from being tribesmen to the pilots of war planes, and who did quite well in their new functions. But something was irrevocably lost in the process: their unique manner of thinking and acting. This process is taking place on a worldwide scale. On a different level is the example of some Indian musicians who when presenting me with tapes of their own music implored that they should only be listened to in small groups. Can such exclusivity be reconciled with our present day democratic concepts?

6.   At the same time, this shows enormous respect for the music and belief in its worth. I think this is one of the most important things we can learn. Whatever role we relegate music, it is always more than just that. The fact remains that man has cultivated sound from the very beginning. The music we heard of the aborigines has two fundamental aspects: it is the bearer of a semantic reality (Lévi-Strauss) and it is music as a specific entity. Both aspects are inseparably intertwined with each other. Together, they are the treasure that we call the phenomenon of music.

6

BACK TO THE SOURCE[1]
Ton de Leeuw

This article deals with the backgrounds of the East-West relationship in my music. In our age of growing intercultural confrontation, the need for reflection on this topic seems self-evident. I further hope to clarify for the interested reader several matters and terms that are often brought up in discussions of my work, but are most often left undefined.

Our path has three stages. First, there is an autobiographically orientated review of the post-war years, followed by several basic concepts of eastern, and particularly Indian philosophy, and finally the concrete effect that all this has had on my work.

Asian and non-western musical forms in general have from my youth onwards played no less important a role in my development than have the great western examples. In retrospect, I think that certain characteristics of Asian music correspond to my personality: a penchant for introspection, a strong feeling of affinity with nature; the idea that nothing need be conquered, nothing need be invented, everything already exists; an inclination towards spirituality coupled with a deep distrust of its sectarian expressions; and, in connection with this, an instinctive aversion to all ideology, equating this with an assault on true inner freedom.

Much of this had already given a certain tint to compositions like the *Sonata* for two pianos (1950) and the *Sonata* for violin and piano (1951). Next to this, in experimenting with non-western musical elements *(Three African Etudes*, 1954) it became clear that any form of imitation was senseless and without substance. Meanwhile, my interest in non-western music had led me to study (1950-1954) with the ethnomusicologist Jaap Kunst.

Given this background, it is understandable that it was not easy to join ranks with the schools of thought emerging in contemporary music. In 1953 I visited Darmstadt where I met with the veneration of Anton Webern, led by the – at that time – still young Stockhausen. It made me deeply uneasy and to this day I wonder at my continued admiration for Webern in the face of this ideological smoke screen.

Still, I was deeply impressed somewhat later, in 1956, by the first performance of Stockhausen's *Gesang der Jünglinge*. The undeniable potency of this work temporarily attracted me to serialism – until about 1959, although its formal and technical precepts quickly struck me as being richly simplistic. Its underlying intellectual backgrounds were also foreign to me. The entire experience was most clearly expressed in *String Quartet I* (1957-1958), which technically speaking has an exceptionally consistent serial structure, but at the same time it is very austere and transparent, in flagrant opposition to the latent expressionism and expansive overabundance of so many serial compositions. There were already references in this string quartet to specific forms of Japanese music.

Another significant influence in those days was the arrival of John Cage – bursting with references to Zen Buddhism and Taoism – in Europe. I met him at the 1958 World Fair in Brussels. Our contact seemed natural and was very refreshing in the context of the rather fanatical serial climate of the time. But it was difficult to support his ideas wholeheartedly. Cage's advocacy of chance, which without the right frame of mind would lead to uncontrolled and noncommittal products, struck me as being incongruous with the high degree of structural discipline and concentration characteristic of Zen art.

I was equally excited by the work of the other great opponent of the serial bastion, Xenakis – its brilliant moments, his personal commitment, and his broader vision of the relationship between art and science. But even he remained a product of the restless, extroverted western thought that was behind the musical renewal of the European avant-garde in the fifties.

Musical revision, yes, but what more?

With my first visit to India, which accelerated my thought processes, I was able to make a timely escape from the neo-romanticism – music that does not even aspire to renewal – emerging at that time. That was around 1960. From that moment on I became an inspired, though not actively involved, witness to the equally rich and fragmentary evolution of western music.

This does not mean that I consciously sought alternatives. Many things became increasingly clear in outline, but my composition remained basically intuitive, instinctively guided in a particular direction. One factor that became significant as time went on was the feeling that all things are connected to one another. This had already become a guiding premise in the composition of *Mouvements rétrogrades* (1957). Unity manifests itself in at least two ways. First of all, contrasts must be relinquished. The opposition between static-dynamic, motion-rest, becoming-being (as I formulated it at that time) is illusionary, each group being in fact two aspects of the same thing. Next, to attain unity one must abandon the ego-consciousness (the contrast between 'me' and 'the rest'). The connection between both aspects was not yet clear to me. On the one hand I concentrated on the dialectic 'static-dynamic' and on the other on a non-subjective approach to composition. I was more or less aware that non-subjectivity must not lead to that Cartesian 'objectivity' put forward by Boulez, and that Cage's method of dispelling the creator's influence with chance manipulations ignored the real nature of the problem.

From today's perspective, it seems perhaps more accurate to leave the subjective-objective contrast aside, thinking rather in terms of 'trans-subjectivity'. This term refers to that part of our personality that is not based on egocentric variables (the 'me' in narcissism, vanity, ambition, *Weltschmerz*, power, violence), relating more to a sense of fundamental belonging, as part of a higher unity. At this level, the desire to manifest one's self as 'me' disappears. The composer becomes a mediator: directly responsible for his creative actions, while functioning as an instrument, influenced and guided by a deeper, trans-subjective experience of being. The ideal seems utopian in the individualistic west. Almost everything in our society, even in the art world, offers resistance. The me-cult is exaggerated. The incessant ego trips in art, the ridiculous glorification of the traditional soloist, the festival fads, the publicity factor, the economic conditioning, the absence of an ethical, artistic, and spiritual foundation have resulted in a deceptive world, a superficial culture that appears difficult to mend.

Yet, there are signs of change, coming it would seem – alas – from outside of the world of art. The re-evaluation of spirituality, taking many different forms, the growing openness to the achievements of other cultures, more attention to a natural lifestyle, to the environment, the relationship between man and nature, are possibly all signs of a slow transition in western society. It is probable that the West will become more conscious that the music of our culture is also subject to pollution and inflation caused by our inane overproduction, consumerist behavioral patterns, and the inundation of inferior background products. This realization will run parallel to the thought that the aural energy generated by music does not simply disappear in nothingness; that music is a form of nourishment, with a real influence on the human organism, and that the terms 'pretty' and 'ugly' need be paired, complemented with the at least equally relevant terms 'rich' and 'poor'. In short, a growing awareness of the need for musical ecology.

The sixties – years of hope, optimism, democratization, slogans, salon revolution, mythologization – yielded no actual change. Like so many times before in the history of European culture, artists and intellectuals sheltered behind half truths. The most profound values of this world were once again packed in rigid 'right' and 'left' equations. The tide of musical renewal of the fifties had ebbed away. A new magic word appeared: socialization. Music entered politics, took to the streets and stepped in line with society.

In my opinion, an even more important phenomenon – of historical significance – went almost unnoticed in those days. For the first time in history, thanks to audio technology and the greater ease of travelling, a new generation of musicians was confronted with, on a large scale and from their formative days onwards, the great sources of other musical traditions. The cultural horizon had been pried open. The spiritual heritage of almost the whole of mankind has become both geographically and artistically tangible and can take part in moulding the younger generation. But we are still waiting for the intellectual breakthrough. Most people, by far, behave as tourists. Travel is becoming more popular but almost all of us travel for their personal interests instead of for the sake of the world. What had seemed a new phenomenon has been revolving, just like before, in Eurocentric confines, only slightly diluted by American ingredients.

With regard to my work, I underwent more a period of expansion, of stabilization, then of renewal. The old Japanese aesthetic, to mention but one aspect, continued to tint my composition, from the opera *The Dream* (1963), through *Men go their ways* (1964) and *Haiku II* (1968), up until *Music for strings* (1970). The techniques of chance used in these works were absorbed – in contrast to Cage's doctrine – either in strict intellectual discipline or evolved along unconscious paths (automatic writing). I explored the relationship between space and music in a number of works, of which *Spatial music I* (1966) went to the furthest limits, setting it far outside the codes of traditional performance practice. Some of these elements, like the worked out ornamentation and the microtones, also play an important role in many Asian musical cultures.

My fascination with the world of forms in nature can be traced in *Symphonies of winds* (1966) and *Schelp* (Shell, 1964). My renewed interest in electronic music, since the introduction of frequency modulation in electronic studios, is thematic in *Syntaxis I* (1966). Finally, *Lamento Pacis* (1969), an appeal for peace, is in its three consecutive movements a homage to the richness of the past: Gesualdo, Zeami – the spiritual father of *No* Theatre, and Ockeghem. The second Movement, dedicated to Zeami, is closely related to (my conception of) *No* music. Much of my time was taken up in non-musical activities, both home and abroad. Regarding the East-West relationship, a growing interest in the gigantic processes of acculturation of our time regularly brought me to Asia, sometimes in affiliation with UNESCO, despite the crippling political climate of this organization. I have spoken at UNESCO conferences (in Manilla, Teheran, Tokyo, Moscow, and Sydney) on the increasing pollution of the music industry, and called for a broader, ecologically orientated view of music.

It is possible that all these activities have slowed the – in my opinion – sluggish evolution of my creative work. Be that as it may, it was only in the seventies that two new elements gradually surfaced. One of these was philosophy. Passages that I had read long before this – especially from Indian metaphysics – began to penetrate more deeply, taking on their own meaning. It was a digestive process, if you will, that once again showed me how small the margin of intellectual understanding is. Next to this, or perhaps in relation to it, the first traces of modality appeared in my work, at first on a modest scale, in the form of isolated modal elements like tone rows, rhythmic patterns and such like. Examples of this can be found in *Music for oboe* (1969), the *Sweelinck-variations* for organ (1973), *Mo-do* for harpsichord (1974), *Mountains* for bass clarinet and tape (1977) and *Modal music* for accordion (1979).

Gending (1975) for gamelan ensemble anticipates perhaps most forcefully the modal concept that since about 1980 I have termed 'extended modality'. It was a tentative answer to the challenge of generalizing principles of the great modal systems (Asian, Arabian and early Christian). Naturally, this contemporary version has little in common with the original local forms. In any case, I became increasingly aware that extended modality was the most effective step

I could take in surmounting the late-western tonality-atonality dilemma, while at the same time avoiding the undifferentiated character of the tempered chromatic system. Furthermore, it all seemed to mix remarkably well with my long-standing philosophical interests.

In this brief retrospective summary, the East-West relationship, disregarding other elements, has played prominently. My evolution, as outlined above, passed through four stages. It began with my affinity with Asian music, then ethnomusicological studies, personal contact with Asian music on the scene, and finally the growing significance of the philosophical backgrounds that had always interested me. Equally important was that the East was no more than a catalyst in my evolution, which was basically a western and contemporary process of development. Speaking more generally, the accent in my thought does not lie on East-West contrast, but rather has always centred on that which connects these worlds, both in their common resources and the threats to them, the gradual undermining of the cultures of the West and of modern Asia.

INDIAN THOUGHT. SEVERAL MAIN THEMES

Indian thought is internally orientated and existential: instead of seeking the absolute highest truth, the central issue is the human condition. Another basic premise is that thought (and also the senses, feeling, and will) is seen as a product of Prakriti (nature, material, in contrast to Purusha, spirit, soul).[2]

One could say that our thought is tied up with the temporal-spatial reality, dependent on cerebral structure, memory, perception of the senses, processing of information, and all kinds of conditioning. We think of rational thought as a phenomenon existing on a plane of binary structures. A formidable weapon in contemporary technical-scientific development, but it is doomed to operate within these terms and to generate a world view that is the reflection of its own limitations.

Although strongly conscious of these limitations, we also believe that man can surmount them. In other words, there is an alternative and more direct path to a higher reality. But one must learn to speak a new language, find other methods to reach this higher plane of experience. It is not solely the domain of visionaries and prophets, and is in principle available to all, so long as we make the proper efforts (one of these is yoga technique).

The language of the Upanishads grew from these thoughts, conceived in terms that are basically non-rational, intended for those who have tasted something of this higher level of existence. These writings, which according to orientalists came into existence between 800 and 500 B.C., are an intermediate culmination in the long evolution of Vedic thought, spanning the period 3000 to 1000 B.C. The ideas set out in the Upanishads are not 'vague' or 'pre-scientific', but reveal, in another type of language, a grand vision of human existence. They were later elaborated on, but also overrun by numerous scholastic and metaphysical speculations. In the past century, the West has added its share with an extensive series of publications ranging from trust-worthy to irritatingly vague.

We will sketch several basic ideas of the Upanishads. The universe in which we live can be thought of as a perpetual flux of becoming and perishing. Everything, including human existence, is transitory. We think of human existence as suffering because of this bond with mortality. The insight that the cosmic maelstrom and the plurality of phenomena actually emanate from a single ultimate reality can liberate us. Our temporal-spatial reality and the timeless ineffable reality are in fact one.

In the following paragraphs I will try to clarify this point.

1

The concept that life is suffering (even Buddha was to later make this one of the cornerstones of his learning) has led to the misunderstanding that the Indian view of life is negative and pessimistic. But we must not isolate this concept from its underlying ideal of liberation from suffering. This, as Mircea Eliade[3] has pointed out, is the main objective of existentially orientated philosophy: striving towards another level of existence that transcends the *condition humain*. One central tenet is that human suffering is not the result of 'sin' or 'guilt' or 'punishment', but is caused by our ignorance of its actual raison d'être. Thus, to rid ourselves of this ignorance and gain insight into the human condition is our most important task.

2

The path leading to insight into the true nature of our existence is not outside of us, but is found in man himself. The internally directed tendency of Indian thought has led to an unprecedented exploration of the conscious mind. 2500 years before Freud, it was already clear that human personality is formed by the interplay of conscious and subconscious forces. But at the same time, the Indians believed that we have another and higher consciousness at our disposal.

Let us consider this more closely. Consciousness, as we experience it in our daily lives, is based on our perception, thought, feeling, in a set of more or less conditioned patterns of reaction that are at the same time nourished by unconscious dynamic forces. Patanjali, the founder/compiler of classical yoga (second century B.C.?) speaks of Vâsâna, subconscious forces of a personal and impersonal (historical, cultural, racial) nature. The interplay of conscious and subconscious elements determines our character and behaviour. One is tempted to say that a balanced relationship between the two is the basis of a balanced, mature personality. But Indian thought considers this to be too narrow a foundation. Psychological substance, as manifested in a never ending stream of conscious states, is considered to be primarily an expression of Praktiri, an element of transient cosmic material.

There are two other aspects to be considered. The previously mentioned dualistic character of our thought has strongly contributed to the formation of our ego-consciousness. The ego is an entity that is isolated from the world outside itself and our fragmentary view of the plurality of what is around us is a direct expression of this. But it is not only thought: the whole of the human psyche is an extraordinarily complex interplay of reactionary patterns that are both conditioned and egocentric. Human actions are constantly geared towards and adjusted to the egocentric tendency of our consciousness, and are thus anchored within their own limitations. This eliminates the possibility of making actual choices, a recurrent theme whose many guises are still found in our own time. Vimala Thakar[4] speaks of the 'silence of the mind' that will aid us in evolving from 'reaction' to 'action', the path to true inner freedom. It could be put otherwise. Rather than conditioning one's self (the method of most ideologies), one can opt for a task as difficult as it is inevitable, namely deconditioning.

In short, it is not enough to explore the limits of the conscious and the subconscious; there are other levels of consciousness. Einstein once said that if a fourth dimension did exist, man would experience it in one way or another. In analogy to this, we could say that if higher consciousness does exist, man must have the capacity to penetrate it.

Acceptance and development of this capacity is, in my opinion, one of the most singularly important messages of ancient Indian thought.

3

Liberation. Liberation from the confinement inherent to human existence within the cosmos. This is the vast, recurrent theme, so immense that it sometimes is given as much, if not more attention than its ultimate goal. After all, godhead, Brahman, or whatever we call it, is beyond comprehension and cannot be expressed in terms of dualistic thought. Remember, we are speaking of a philosophy of life. The immediate experience of reality is worth more than juggling with abstract concepts. Meditation begins where thought ends. There are many different methods traced out, depending on the school of thought and local traditions. The most fruitful seem to be those that make no attempt to suppress the aspects of human nature that are considered negative. The path leading to higher levels of consciousness is not one of suppression, but rather entails the recognition of, and insight into the true nature of the human organism. And we must not take this task lightly. Its most radical implication is roughly equivalent to the eradication of what we commonly call personality. Surmounting this personality most often entails years of struggle using highly disciplined techniques.

4

This is far removed from the soft techniques of meditation found in contemporary western society, and equally so from the romantic artist's non-committal musings on Eternity and Mortality. The stake is a radical transmutation of human personality in order to reach a more immediate experience of reality.

What does this mean?

Let us return to the opening premise. As has been said, the universe - in perpetual movement like a cosmic maelstrom, in myriad perishable forms – is by nature One, as a manifestation of the ultimate reality beyond time and space, and above all discrepancy. Unity is manifested in multiplicity; the eternal as time-space; the transcendental as immanent.

The Isha Upanishad, one of the oldest upanishads, begins:

'Au Seigneur tout ceci qui est, pour qu'il l'habite, et chaque chose, univers se mouvant dans l'universel mouvement. De tout cela détache-toi et jouis-en; ne convoite aucun bien que s'appropient les hommes.'[5]

The fundamental concept is postulated in two sentences: Le Seigneur (the One, immovable Being) 'dwells in', manifests itself in the multifarious, moving universe. Each part of this universe represents the whole. The individual participates with (is identical to) the universal. 'De tout cela détache-toi et jouis-en': all that exists finds its reason for being in the universe. By accepting this unconditionally, and by not being bound by it, man can discover his actual freedom.

The experience of reality discussed above is a product of 'seeing', of feeling the fundamental unity of the universe, thus freeing ourselves from the divided, dualistic view of the world that has been constructed by our consciousness.

Hopefully, this summary will give some idea of this world view that was born, in an explosion of insight, about three thousand years ago. There is much, too much in fact, that I have left out, like the role of Taoism, or that of the fascinating Buddhism that was to develop several centuries later. Also unmentioned are the striking similarities between the visionary cosmology of ancient Asia and contemporary science. Leading figures of modern physics, like Niels Bohr and especially Werner Heisenberg, have explicitly referred to this, and the number of publications dealing with it continues to grow.

In this article, we are concerned with the significant contribution of the Asian heritage to my work. Let us start with a general proposition. The concepts of Indian metaphysics sketched above basically led me, after nearly thirty years of study, to a general purgation. Involvement with these ideas has transformed many of my thoughts about the world, people and art. But this Asian metaphysical framework can and may not result in the construction of intellectual and ideological certainties.

History teaches that it is unfruitful to lose ourselves in metaphysical speculation. Schools of thought, systems, sects, quickly affix the human spirit in stereotyped thought patterns or anthropomorphical visions of a reality that exists on a level far beyond human reach. It is precisely this multiple conditioning, the concept of man as a product of his past, of his intellectual and psychological mechanisms, that obscures our view of a freer and broader path. The ultimate revolution is therefore nothing other than remaining strictly individual. This is also the real meaning of the 'non-commitment' outlined in our century by thinkers like Krishnamurti and Vimala Thakar. It is also the background of the previously mentioned term trans-subjectivity, as the foundation of my creative activity.

MUSICAL RESULTS

These perspectives place both music and the act of composing in another light. Several aspects of this latter – trans-subjectivity, experience of unity, an 'ecological' approach to sound – have already been mentioned in this article. One of the major implications is that the renewal of musical material – long the motivating force of much new music – is no longer a primary concern. The emphasis lies rather on a new attitude towards making music: a higher awareness of values that one could perhaps call spirituality. In a world that seems to have lost all touch with this value, or is only concerned with it on Sunday mornings, it may seem strange to speak of spirituality, but the need for a spiritual view of the world is becoming stronger.

It has long since surpassed the role it held at the beginning of our century, that of occupational therapy for well-to-do women. It does not imply a flight from reality, or a return to the familiar mother church. It is the only possible solution in this final phase of our thoroughly materialistic culture in which music thrives only in economic and consumers circles. On rare occasions one has an inkling of how everything in the universe is interconnected. This existential experience is perhaps the essence of spirituality. Its effect is felt in creative pursuits, but also in the most mundane daily activities.

A composer's expressive powers remain dependent of course on his musical talents. But talent, genius, and aesthetics alone are no longer sufficient to free us from (too) individually orientated art, and to help us reach a more universal expression. 'Return to the source' also implies a new attitude, a path to the future.

Music can serve as a stimulant, an outlet, a social or political manifest, an intellectual game, a background, and many more things in innumerable variations and combinations. To me, (my) music is primarily a symbol. It is a symbol of unity, the resolution of discrepancies; a quest for equilibrium; unity is expressed in multiplicity; the audible reflection of the laws of nature (for instance in cyclic structures) and the supreme symbol of mortality.

But precisely in this image of mortality in music, in this brief moment, we may find the concentration of all human expression. We touch eternity with music and because of its fleeting nature. In this sense, making music is like spiritual training. The human spirit finds its greatness, not in clinging to constancy, but in its capacity for continual transformation.

Looking for a general description of the path taken by my music since about 1980, I coined the term 'extended modality' . Modality, in a broad sense, is a generic term referring to a number of characteristics that are the source of phenomena within particular musical traditions, like Raga (India), Maqaam (Arabic music), Patet (Java) and – probably – Nomos (ancient Greece). In our day – following the period of tonality and atonality – we look back to the sources, with a new and better insight than was previously possible. 'Extended modality' is in a certain sense a reappreciation, a generalization and an extension of earlier modal principles, put into twentieth-century perspective. It is also a reaction to the impasse reached in our music, and is foreign to the background that bred both late western tonality and atonality.

AN ATTEMPT AT CHARACTERIZATION

– In contrast to the inherent expansive compulsion of late tonality and atonality, modality is a phenomenon that occupies preferably a confined space, one whose components include both musical and non-musical aspects. The whole of these components determines the individual character of a particular modal idiom. Extended modality is centripetally orientated, in contrast to the centrifugal tendency (its expressive / expansive quality) of late western music.
– The non-musical qualities mentioned above are for the most part of an ethical and symbolical nature. In so far as they are related to 'my' extended modality, I have already dealt with them at length. One could tentatively propose that with the rise of individualism in Europe, modality was superseded by tonality and musical emphasis shifted from ethical to aesthetical values.
– As has been said, the musical elements of modality form a consistent whole. Considering the limited conception of modality held by most, it is important to stress that modality is not merely the result of a series of tones, but is determined by the mutual interplay of a large number of elements. The nature of these elements is rooted

in the centripetal basic premise, the ethical and cultural backgrounds, and the musical tradition in which it appears. This also applies – mutatis mutandis – to extended modality.

– In this regard, the qualifying term 'extended' also means that the musical structure is determined to some extent by fifteen centuries of western musical tradition. Thus, 'Return to the source' refers as much to Asia as it does to the beginning of our own culture. The relationship to earlier modal systems lies not so much in the structure as in the orientation. One could say that extended modality is as much an attitude as it is a technical approach.

THE MUSICAL ELEMENTS OF EXTENDED MODALITY IN MY WORK SINCE ABOUT 1980

As I have said, (extended) modality is a product of the interrelationship of a large number of elements. In earlier compositions, namely those works written from about 1970 onwards, several of these elements are usually demonstrably present, varying from work to work. These elements were for the first time grouped in a model in the opening movement of *Gending*, and, since 1980, the model concept has become increasingly significant. What is a model?

A model is a synthesis of many modal elements to form a greater whole, and it is responsible for the signature of a composition. Its material consists of a predetermined arrangement of a number of pitches, in most cases several hundred. The model is continually repeated in the course of the composition. But – and this in basic opposition to earlier thematic and serial techniques – these repetitions are not always thoroughly realized, or in other words, not all tones of the model need be sounded with each appearance.

The tones of the model are filtered in the repetitions by a 'time grid', so to speak, so that some remain while others are removed. The constellation of tones passing through the filter do not constitute variations or developments, but are other versions of the same constant foundation. This foundation may be explicitly stated in whole, in part, or not at all, but its presentation always lasts the same amount of time (see examples 1a-d).

The model is characterized not only by its sequence of tones, but also the choice of tones: which tones are present in the model, which are not, and what are their hierarchial relationships. Which

1 *'Résonances', excerpt of the model with three versions.*

Basic model (total of 144 tones)

intervals dominate, which specific melodic curves are formed, and which registers are used must be weighed very carefully because each detail of the model could have repercussions on the composition as a whole. To put it differently, in our age where statistical music reigns supreme, it is suddenly crucially important to choose whether an E or E flat is to be played!

Partially because of this, most models chosen by me are rather lengthy, making it possible to achieve greater variety of characteristics within them. The entire group of these characteristics determines to a certain degree the individual structure of each new work. To demonstrate this, let us examine *Transparence* for choir in eighteen parts and wind instruments (1986). In the basic model we find a highly unusual and extreme case of tonal hierarchy: the beginning is dominated by the tone C sharp which gradually dissolves in a constellation of tones revolving around the axis F sharp - A. The music unfolds from C sharp in the middle register towards the F sharp - A axis. This characteristic can be found in a modified form in most of the repetitions (see example 2).

2 *'Transparence', the model, with its realizations below.*

Basic model (total of 324 tones)

Rhythm takes on a new and fascinating role in model technique. Because time and pitch are simultaneously fixed, both elements are inextricably connected. If a rhythmic formula serves as the basic

premise – as is the case in the example below – the pitches will fall
into place according to their position in the model. If, on the contrary,
a tonal formula is the basic premise, then the rhythmic context will
be derived in the same manner. This special dialectic is often a feature
of my work. One example can be found in *Invocations* for mezzo
soprano, choir and instruments (1983). A Gregorian melody, *Libera
me*, appears in the middle of the piece, followed by its transformation
according to model technique (see example 3).

3 'Libera me', with its transformation in 'Invocations'.

When in the course of the composition the model is repeated, components can take shape in such a way that they form recognizable
macro-rhythmical structures over larger distances. Naturally, this can
occur in varying degrees of recognizability, ranging from vague outlines
to crystal clarity. The result is complicated networks of correspondence. Such patterns may serve as signals (indicating structural components), by drawing attention to all or part of the model when it is
repeated. This function, with which I became acquainted in Japanese,
Indian and Indonesian music, had already been part of my composition since *Mouvements rétrogrades*. Here is an example from *Résonances*,
where a composite pattern (melodic/harmonic/rhythmic and at times
orchestral) is repeatedly used to underline the end of the model (see
example 4).

4 *'Résonances', end of the model, on pages 9, 13, 17, 19, 51, 55 and 60 of the score.*

Similar to earlier modal idioms, extended modality is primarily melodically-rhythmically oriented. Sonorities serve to colour, accentuate, profile, or in some other way distinguish the passage, according to the situation. Parallels can often be found within a basically single-voiced, heterophonic texture (see also example 5).

Tonal fields are also used, at times resembling a prolonged group of bourdon tones. There are also many bourdons, both continuous and shorter. Sometimes they appear to generate vital energy, for instance at moments where certain tones of the model come to the forefront in solidified form, seemingly suspending motion within the continuous progression.

They may also serve, both generally speaking or with regard to a particular work, as symbols of the centripetal background of extended modality. This latter is the case in the beginning of *Car nos vignes sont en fleur* for twelve vocalists (1981) (which, incidentally, does not use an integrated model). The bourdon tones A-D-A give musical expression to the image of the perfectly balanced inner self of a person in a state of deep rest. The core of fundamental peace expands and contracts in various phases in a slow, respiratory motion. The modal character of this composition is in part brought about by a note in the score directing the singers to try to experience the states of consciousness aimed at in the music, and to adjust the progression of musical motion accordingly. The musical performance is not only an activity requiring technical and musical expertise, but is also an emotional/intellectual process of experiencing.

Phase 1 – Process of assimilation on the tone A. Inner concentration. Continue until ready for the following phase.
Phase 2 – The entire centre unfolds. Singing must be guided by a state of inner balance. Serve as a perfect soundboard for the centre.
Phase 3 – Small fluctuations from the centre. These are accompanied by small movements of in and exhaling. Do not disturb the acquired equilibrium.
Phase 4 – Return to phase 2. From here, prepare the first externally orientated activities of phase 5.

It may clarify the part played by the model in determining the work by comparing the compositions already cited in this article with the last movement of *Alba* for chamber orchestra (1982). The model's strict stepwise structure is reflected in the scale-like textures of the music.

Additions to the model have consequences for the form (melodic figuration, harmonic or instrumental colour, differentiation of the textures, etc.). Here is a simple example in which parallels have been added. In *Les chants de Kabir* for vocal sextet (1985), the part of the model corresponding to the passage with which we are concerned is characterized by see-saw motion. Through the rhythmic treatment of the upper voice, and the addition of a parallel fifth below it, a new tonal characteristic is created, an extension of the lower voices, that follows a more direct translation of the model (see example 5).

5 *'Les chants de Kabir', the model with its realization below.*

In *Résonances* we find a more complicated example, an enrich-ment of the musical texture, where a secondary model is grafted to the original, so that a new layer is created that co-exists for some time with the basic model.

Generally speaking, a model represents the ideal realization of various elements while allowing great flexibility as to their actual appearance.

Cyclical structures are formed by repetitions. These have always been a part of my music, perhaps in connection with my idea that music is not merely a temporal art, but – at very least – a temporal-spatial art, and with this last dimension, it touches on timelessness. Thus, I cannot wholeheartedly accept many of the speculations on the temporal aspect of music, in as far as they remain too unilaterally/ intellectually fixated on a linear approach. Music is just as much a temporal/spatial phenomenon as is the human organism, of which it is a projection.

One could compare the model to a time-harp, in which varying aural events are produced by successively plucking a different string in a continuous progression back in time.

In conclusion, two comments.

Musical material, as used by a particular composer at a given time, is not just a means. The use of diatonic or chromatic passages, the choice for or against tempered tunings, of instruments, and so forth, reflects backgrounds that far surpass a personal aesthetic. That is why

*Dutch composers in the Vondel Park in Amsterdam, May 24, 1957.
Standing from left to right are Jurriaan Andriessen, Ton de Leeuw,
Oscar van Hemel, Herman Strategier, Henk Badings, Karel Mengelberg
and Hans Kox; seated from left to right are Anthon van der Horst and
Rudolf Mengelberg.*

I attach the utmost significance to the purest possible refinement of material, form and sound, the basic concepts of the music. Prevailing musical practice does not always facilitate the realization of this goal, but it is worthwhile to reflect on this (age-old) thought.

This article so strongly emphasizes technical and philosophical aspects of composition that the reader may justly wonder where the music begins. The quality of music is not determined by theories. In our century, many artists have, to varying degrees, been led astray by stuffing their work full of theory, psychology, politics, and what have you. It should be clear that the creative fantasy never frees itself if we remain immersed in speculations. We must work from living experience. Only then can we reach a dimension in which music blossoms, guided by intuition, imagination, uncertainty, technical discipline, in short all the attributes that have always been a part of creative work.

Hopefully, these considerations will provide the reader with useful information and help the author become conscious of processes that ultimately take place on an intangible level.

CONTINUITY AND CHANGE IN JAPANESE MUSIC
William P. Malm

Japanese art forms have fascinated westerners, Ton de Leeuw being one of the most recent among them, for over a hundred years. Given the long period of this interest, it is only logical that attempts be made to generalize about the many forms of Japanese art in ways that might help to better appreciate them and understand their basic principles. The only problem with these generalizations is that they are sometimes taken to be comprehensive and accurate statements on the Japanese arts throughout their long histories. De Leeuw has shown too much intelligence and sensitivity to make such statements.

In the case of traditional music, however, the two most common assertions one hears others making are that: (1) traditional Japanese music has remained 'pure' and unchanged over the centuries, and (2) traditional musical arts are dying out in the face of modern mass communication and Western music.

The purpose of this article is to help us correct these aphorisms in the hope that we can then follow a truer, more De Leeuw-oriented path towards an understanding of the place of traditional Japanese music in the late 20th century.

Let us begin with the best known ancient Japanese music, Gagaku, music of the court and imperial shrines. Anyone who has attended a Japanese film set in the ancient culture, an elaborate traditional wedding, or an imperially oriented festivity, will know that Gagaku is still a living art form. The ensemble of flutes, oboes and mouth organs with the koto zithers, biwa lutes and percussion are heard performing in a tempo and texture that literally seem out of this world. Sometimes one witnesses stately, symmetrical dances, the performers garbed in costumes whose designs trace back over a thousand years. Many of the performers themselves come from families whose professional ancestries stretch back an equal length of time. Certainly, one's first impression of Gagaku is that it is an amazingly well-preserved, ancient tradition. But it is obviously a living tradition as well for it continues to be practised by professional musicians, some of whom have found permanent employment in the Imperial court. There is a special edifice on the Tokyo palatial grounds reserved for such music and dance.

But a visitor to this building may also note that there is a separate rehearsal chamber furnished with a bass drum, piano and other western materials. In the late 19th century, Gagaku musicians were required to learn playing western style reception and band music, in addition to performing their own music. In fact, during the Meiji period (1868-1912), Gagaku musicians spoke with pride of wearing western band uniforms and doubling on brass and Gagaku instruments. It was in this period that the various styles of Gagaku and its musical interpretations throughout Japan were consolidated into a single 'official' Gagaku tradition. Being the musical symbol of the newly established imperial culture, Gagaku music tended to be performed in a 'dignified', i.e. slower style. At the same time writings began to appear likening Gagaku to the Japanese imperial tradition; ancient and unchanged. From these observations, however, it should be clear that Gagaku today is different not only from that of ancient times, but also from the Gagaku of barely one hundred years ago.

In the early 20th century, Gagaku and many other traditional Japanese musics were still learned by the use of *shōga,* sung mnemonics that represent the instrumental parts. This learning method is very important for it reinforces the fundamental Asian concept of music as an oral or aural, rather than visual, art. The fact that Gagaku musicians had to become equally proficient with the print oriented western music generated an intellectual/aesthetic conflict that ultimately 'changed' things. Such changes in Gagaku were furthered by university and religious groups who used the ancient medium as a viable medium for their intellectual and religious needs. Moreover, they tended to resort to notation in learning its ways. Thus, today Gagaku can be heard in temples, shrines and concert halls performed by either professional or amateur ensembles. The Gagaku ensembles of Japanese universities are much like the collegium musicum of ancient European music.

These latter may be found in places as distant from Europe as Tokyo, Mexico City or Detroit. By parallel, note that Gagaku may be heard in such distant parts as Los Angeles, California and Dallas,

Texas, played entirely by non-Japanese. Gagaku in Japan, played by Japanese, fills its performers with a sense of their cultural/musical roots while American or European Gagaku ensembles provide their members with an exotic musical experience. All amateur performers tend to think of Gagaku as 'pure', ancient music, even though they may be playing on plastic ryuteki flutes.

Foreign Gagaku ensembles may serve a special function in the future for, under the anthropological principle of marginal survival, one seeks the oldest forms of things not at the centre of the culture but at the furthest point of their travels. Thus, the oldest form of Gagaku in the 21st century may turn up in Texas rather than Ise. This same principle has led many to think that in hearing Gagaku, one is experiencing the ancient music of continental Asia. This is partly true, for it is only in Korea and Japan one finds pieces of music and instruments that are known to have existed in at least the 9th century in China. Recent non-Japanese research into Gagaku implies, however, that the Chinese and Korean traditions, from which the Japanese version was to grow, used livelier tempos and strikingly different interpretations of all the lines. For example, the tone clusters of the Shō mouth organ, that have thrilled western composers for decades, seem to be unique Japanese readings of the limited original notational symbols and have no precedent in continental East Asia. Whether this is the result of an original approach or an error in reading is not significant to Gagaku's present day sociological/emotional function. Both of these last named factors have produced musical textures that have inspired contemporary composers to imitate Gagaku's present day 'ancient' style. Some composers have even gone so far as to write specifically for Gagaku ensembles.

So much for the concept of Gagaku as unchanged and dying. It has changed many times in its long history and will continue to do so for as long as it lives on. If you were to try to purchase a Gagaku instrument or accessory your efforts would be frustrated by back orders that imply a living, growing (and expensive) art form. Gagaku is not some stone fossil but is more like a living fish, though having reached a ripe age it tends to swim more slowly than its ancestors. Ton de Leeuw, on his 60th birthday, can reflect on the heavy currents and seas through which he has swum. He has cut some of the most significant paths through the sea of Japanese music, leaving a sonic wake that the entire musical world can enjoy.

A contrasting but equally venerable tradition in Japan is that of the folk festivals. Every agricultural society of the world has used ritual to reassure the growth of crops after a dormant period of seeming death. Those among us from northern climes (like Holland and Michigan) have an even stronger sense of the magic and importance that such an action must have held for mankind before the modern sciences of agriculture and meteorology gained powers of prediction and explanation. To use the catch words of the beginning of Japanese modernization at the close of the 19th century, 'enlightened and civilized' logic seems to have brought on astonishing progress unaided by the gods and rituals of ancient farmers. Of course, they have also resulted in pollution but computerized area models are now proclaimed as being the tools we need to overcome these problems. Things have changed. Every household has its colour television with a selection from the international market of programming. But on Japanese television one also sees folk song programmes and contests, slick folk dance presentation and films from the massive annual festivals that are held in every region of Japan. These latter are known for their financial benefit to the tourist industry and for fortifying regional pride. Regional folk music and dance groups are often as popular as the winning baseball team. They also draw more local people into direct participation. These large urban festivals originally functioned to drive away or prevent pestilence and disease. Now that science has taken on these problems, the festivals fulfil equally important but different economic and emotional needs.

National folk theatricals (geino) function in a similar manner. They, along with the folk song shows and contests, also provide opportunities for personal glory in a modern world where sameness has become a problem. Thanks to modernization, Japanese are provided with adequate but very similar clothing, transportation and housing, as is the lonely crowd of the rest of the urbanized world. But in Japan, one also finds the karaoke bar where one can shine for a brief moment by singing in an electronically accompanied urban folk genre called popular music. In this modern world of sameness, regional folk music has also become important in Japan. It identifies the singer not just as a member of a nation but as a member of a smaller segment of mankind that, in former days, consisted of individuals who knew one another and who worked together. With populations moving from the farm village to the factory complex, this need is met by the newer Japanese idiom, the company song.

Youth always turns to that which is new, and in Japan newness is often thought of in western terms. But look again. Note the present fad for the driving jangara shamisen playing and for the formation of new Japanese drum ensembles. Another modern fad is the appearance of Japanese folk song preservation societies. These are not founded for one style of music but for one specific piece! Members meet regularly to practice the singing of their one song. National contests are often held between different groups to determine who has the most perfect version. Thus, amidst the dramatic change in the function of folk events in Japan, we find a concern for quality control that implies continuity.

What about the old farm traditions? Examples of these are the January snow (yuki) or flower (hana) festivals (matsuri). These festivals are still maintained as supplications for agricultural continuity. The author observed such an event in the village of Toyonemura in Aiichi prefecture in the winter of 1984. In a special hall, erected for this one event near the village shrine, action began at 5 PM with a dance blessing the drum sticks. Then came a series of dances and songs, accompanied by drum and flute, that wove around a cauldron of hot water in the centre of the sacred square. Although the costumes and accessories changed, the general tune, rhythm and choreographic gestures remained the same. There were different generations of performers. When the young children appeared they were tutored by veterans who made certain that the youthful participants carried on the tradition correctly. As evening passed into early morning, the masks of gods and demons appeared. But the same tune was continued, the flute players often plunging their bamboo instruments into the boiling water to keep them playable. Saké, rice wine, and food warmed and reinvigorated some 200 local inhabitants and a few outsiders during that long night in a snowy valley under the cold, star filled sky. As the steaming flutes played on, dance followed dance, in groups of three, and often repeated three times in accordance to the magic numbers. By ten o'clock the following morning, the last dance had finished and the hall was closed for the year. Some of the old timers said that things had changed; the festival used to last three nights. But as the families wandered back to their homes carrying special good luck papers taken from the festival hall decorations, one felt that the essential power of the tradition still lived. The incessant tune and drum beat swirling in my head after hearing it for ten hours at the festival, I realized that its redundancy was vital. These repeating messages were a communication with the gods who rule over the crops of the future, and with ancestral generations who had farmed in the past. Maintaining such traditions and renovating old or inventing new ones all are important to the future of mankind. They are still part of the true picture of the arts in Japan today.

Ton de Leeuw may not have seen such a festival but its message to the modern world is of the kind that only a person of De Leeuw's sensitivity would understand. It is my privilege to send him a Japanese hommage from Ann Arbor, Michigan. What more international gift could be offered one of the world's best musicians, composers, and thinkers?

8

TRADITIONAL MUSIC AND CULTURAL CHANGE: A STUDY IN ACCULTURATION
Trân Van Khê

Almost all of the countries of Africa, Asia, Oceania and Latin America are non-industrial societies. In these lands, as in certain strata of western countries, music for the majority of the population – which consists of workers – is closely interwoven with everyday work and life: it is not merely an entertainment, a source of satisfaction or an art cultivated for its own sake. Music, for the professional musician or the cultivated amateur on the other hand, must have more artistic depth. It is the subject of theorization and it is made to conform to certain cosmogonic or philosophical ideas. It then becomes a principal source of entertainment or an essential adjunct of ceremonies.

Yet, for both the popular and the upper classes, music remains intertwined with social and religious functions.

Since the beginning of the nineteenth century, political and social upheavals have restructured political geography and modified social structures. In all non-industrial societies that are striving for industrialisation, the character and nature of traditional music and of musical life have undergone profound changes. A new phenomenon – seen as desirable by some and dangerous by others – is attracting attention: the acculturation of traditional music in Asia, Africa, Oceania, and Latin America.

Before discussing the pros and cons of this phenomenon, let us examine the role that music previously played in non-industrial societies and what it has become today.

SOCIAL AND RELIGIOUS FUNCTIONS OF MUSIC

In non-industrial society, man relies on his physical strength rather than machines to earn a living. He works in the fields, the mountains, on rivers or at sea, rather than in mines or factories. Both the nature of his work and his environment make him want to sing. Singing helps him forget the monotony and difficulty of his labour and aids him in coordinating his efforts with those of his co-workers, thus achieving greater productivity. It not only stimulates the zeal for work but is also a source of entertainment for those at rest. Then there are the songs meant to enable young people to get to know one another, appreciate and love one another, music that is often a preliminary to betrothal and marriage. Work songs serve manifold functions: the socio-economic by helping to increase production and diminish fatigue, entertainment for singers and listeners, and, in playing a part in the preliminaries leading to marriage, in a sense it helps perpetuate the species.

Work and, even more so, leisure are accompanied by song. In the spring and autumn, after the day's heavy toils of ploughing or harvesting, young men and women meet in the farm yards, by the rivers or in the foothills to sing and dance.

In many countries, boys and girls sing responsorially. A boy and girl stand opposite each other and, after the customary greetings, they exchange questions and answers. The words are often improvised, as is sometimes the music; the rite may or may not be accompanied by dances and games, like the tossing of a ball of silk back and forth. These responsorial songs – with alternations between the groups, the sexes, and even the place of origin of the participants – are all love songs, betrothal songs of a collective and competitive nature. Their function is similar to that of work songs.

Itinerant singers, often blind, travelling from village to village and singing in the market places, are also part of the musical life. They accompany their art on very simple, self-made instruments, singing love songs, satirical, humorous and sometimes erotic songs, and epics relating the achievements of popular heroes. They also recite poems. The crowd gathers round, all eyes and ears, roaring with laughter at each joke, blushing at each ribaldry, and weeping in sympathy with the tragic fates of the heroes and heroines. Popular singers often broach subjects that are taboo; they criticise the authorities, whether local or colonial, human weaknesses, avarice, cowardice, cupidity, luxury and adultery. Although it is a dangerous sport to poke fun at powerful people in everyday life, in song it is possible to portray them in ridiculous situations, to compare them to insects which are crushed underfoot. Who dares speak openly of sex in puritan societies? The itinerant singers do, not shying from any subject. Their satire is biting, subject matter free and sometimes even lewd. But in each story, the good are always rewarded, the honest are praised and traitors are punished. These itinerant singers are the 'safety valves' of peasant societies.

In real life, sickness follows health as rain follows sunshine. The ailing turn for help to the shamans and witch doctors who implore the gods' pardon or try to reconcile their patients with the guilty evil spirits. There are healing songs. Different from the religious songs, these consist of the recitation of prayers and psalms and the reading of sacred texts and liturgical chants, which vary from belief to belief. When neither medicine nor prayer effects a cure, the soul leaves the world of mortals to the sound of funeral music played by a few instrumentalists. Weeping and lamentation accompany the deceased to his final rest.

This type of music is anonymous and is transmitted orally, each performer having the right to stamp it with his own individual style. The players are mostly workers or semi-professional musicians.

Because this music is essentially functional, it differs from the artistic types which are performed by professional musicians or aristocrats, who try to improve the instruments, perfect vocal and instrumental techniques and extend the repertoire. Some are engaged in working out the theory of their music and laying down the rules of composition and performance. Art music may have its roots in the music of the common people but it differs in its artistic level and function. It is more sophisticated and more difficult to master. Those who spend years learning this art must be able to earn their living from it, unless they are wealthy enough to regard music as a pastime. Professional musicians, often of humble backgrounds, are forced to seek employment with the chiefs, aristocrats, or the music loving sovereigns. They are often attached to these priviledged households as domestic servants or menials. For example, according to Gaston Knosp, writing in A. Lavingnac's *Encyclopédie de la musique* (Vol. 5 [1914], p.3125), palace musicians at the former court of Hué (Vietnam) were:

> . . .usually thought of as servants rather than palace officials, [they were given] . . .jobs to perform that were quite unconnected with their qualifications. They had to carry out all sorts of tasks imposed on them by the majordomo; in this way they

went from one service to another in accordance with the requirements of the various branches of the administration, always occupying the lowest rank. It would be quite wrong to suppose that their profession ensured them a superior position among menials; they did not even object, for it had been this way for centuries. [When performing, they were expected to sit on the ground], . . . for they could not be allowed to be at the same level as the audience, composed mostly of mandarins sitting at ease in comfortable Chinese armchairs.

Scholars whose parents were musicians were not permitted to enter the tri-yearly competitive examinations. In 1592, Dao duy Tié was refused permission to take the examinations because his father, Dao ta Han, had been a musician at the court of Lê Anh Tên (1556-1573). Even though musicians received somewhat better treatment in China, Korea and Japan, there also they were not held in high esteem. In ancient Persia, as in India under the reign of Emperor Akbar, musicians and singers enjoyed the favour of the sovereigns, but in modern Persia, according to M. C. Huart (in Lavingnac, *Encyclopédie de la musique*, vol. 5, p.3067),

> . . . music performed at the mealtimes of wealthy Persians is provided by two or three musicians...seated on the floor, in a corner.

In Mauritania, according to A. Leriche, quoted by Michel Guignard in his *Musique, honneur et plaisir au Sahara,* the griots, or professional musicians, '. . . form a separate caste, the lowest of all, together with the blacksmiths'. Leriche quotes a Moorish proverb:

> Slaves are better than craftsmen and craftsmen better than griots.

Michel Guignard has attempted to explain the contradiction between the contempt in which the griots are held and the esteem with which the muezzin is regarded as follows:

> . . .to place the griot on any but a very, low rung of the social ladder would be to imply that entertainment and amusement

are equal in value to the courage and political strength represented by the warriors or the religious and scientific learning embodied by the marabouts.

Be that as it may, professional musicians, even in countries where music is highly regarded, are not treated with the respect they deserve. In present day Iran, masters of traditional music still do not dare to admit their profession: they refer to themselves as employees of the Ministry of Fine Arts or as conservatory or university professors. A young player of the Iranian transverse flute told me he was going to stop performing in public because he had recently passed his final examinations for architecture and it is unsuitable for an architect to play flute in public. But 'amateur' musicians, on the other hand, are held in high regard. Last year, a retired general and former finance minister were proud to give this writer a demonstration of traditional music as it was played in Iran fifty years ago. In China and Vietnam, music, chess, poetry and painting were the favourite pastimes of men of letters, and music was principal among them.

The six 'Arts', of the elementary school curricula, were listed in order of their importance: the rites, music, archery, horsemanship, literature and mathematics. Music, according to Yue Ki (Memorandum on Music) is

> . . . at the root of everything. [It] . . . produces profound impressions, changes habits and transforms customs. That is why the ancients encouraged its teaching.

Thus, music is considered suitable as a pastime and is thought beneficial in education, but it is not regarded as a worthy profession. Among the aristocratic classes and the professionals, music no longer serves its socio-economic function but it still maintains its value as ritual and entertainment.

MUSIC IN MODERN SOCIETY: THE ACCULTURATION PROCESS

After attempting the subjugation of the lands of Asia and Africa using the 'peaceful' method of conversion to Christianity, in the nineteenth century western powers attempted to overrun them by force of arms. Some countries lost their independence while others came under foreign economic control. The recently introduced capitalistic system of production and the beginnings of industrialization brought about an upheaval of social structures and the way of life in these countries. Monarchs and tribal chiefs were stripped of authority. The former men of letters, savants and marabouts gradually gave way to the new 'intellectuals' trained in the western fashion. These 'native civil servants' who 'drank milk in the morning and champagne in the evening' were an object of scorn, but they were also envied. The vast majority of the population in these colonized countries consisted of country-folk, deeply attached to the traditions of their ancestors: landless peasants working as share-croppers and tenant farmers at the mercy of landowners and money-lenders. Craftsmen, tradesmen and petty officials belonged to the 'middle' class, forming a new, moneyed and partly westernized bourgeoisie. With the introduction of capitalism, a new proletariat was created, working in mines, factories, mills and plantations. All these political and social upheavals brought about profound changes in the musical life of non-industrial societies.

Some genres fell into disuse or disappeared entirely:

– *Work Songs.* While science and technology liberate the worker from some forms of heavy labour, they are also responsible for the impending or actual disappearance of a number of work songs. Previously, peasants travelled on foot from one village to the next, as work in the fields required, singing as they went. Now, with public transportation networks of buses, the noise of the motors and the crowding of passengers, the modern conditions are no longer conducive to poetic or musical inspiration. Modern irrigational methods have supplanted hand-turned bamboo water wheels, and, with this transformation, so fade the irrigation and water-carrying songs. Now that mechanical ploughs and machines are used to cultivate and husk rice, the ploughing, threshing and pounding songs are no longer heard. Sampans, canoes and sailboats have surrendered the rivers to steamboats and the boatmen's songs have become a thing of the past. The arrival of western science and medicine has put an end to the old superstitions in many countries. The sick now consult a medical man instead of the shaman and incantations for healing, driving off demons and communicating with spirits are beginning to disappear. Transistor radios have encroached on even the remotest parts and the peasants and shepherds, who can now hear music in their homes, no longer flock to the marketplaces to hear itinerant singers, just as many city dwellers have abandoned the concert halls and theatres for the sake of the television at home.

Listening to the 'new' music broadcast on the radio, peasants have started to imitate the urban style of singing, especially that of well-known singers and musicians. Perhaps most detrimental of all to the popular traditions is that young peasants have given up making new songs in a traditional style as a result of this bombardment of 'new music' composed by young people trained in a western style. The older peasants have resigned themselves to the situation, saying: 'Youth must have its say'. The youth, through their contacts with city-dwellers listening to 'arranged and harmonized' versions of folk music, have adopted a new repertoire composed by young musicians who are often unaware of their own traditions and have merely picked up a few rudi ments of western style composition. They take the 'variety' type of song as a model. Creative talent and the artistic level of folk music is in general decline.

– *Musical genres.* After the fall of the monarchies, court music in China, Korea and Vietnam served no useful purpose and is now dying out. Today it is performed only on special occasions: on national holidays, at diplomatic receptions, or touristic amuse ments. Confucian temple music is no longer performed in China and Vietnam, and is only heard in Seoul and Tai Pei, where societies for the preservation of musical traditions have been struggling to save the ancient repertoires.

In practice, the rites in Confucian temples are no longer cel-ebrated as they were formerly. In Iran, the Ta'zié (a historical and religious spectacle comparable to the French medieval passion-plays), which commemorated the martyrdom of the Imams (the legitimate successors of the prophet Mahomet), is no longer seen in the big towns, except Shiraz, where it was performed at the international festivals of 1967 and 1970. While the custom lingers on in the countryside, the plays are no longer performed with the same spontaneity as of old. In present day Mauretania, the nature of the griot has greatly changed.

Michel Guignard, whom we quoted above, writes of the future of the griot and his music:

> Political and cultural life tends to move towards the capital and the centres of administration and of course the griots move with it. They are becoming less and less the minstrels and familiars of the nobility . . . Nowadays, anyone can go and see the griots or listen to them on the radio. They thus reach a wider audience, with tastes and needs different from those of the minority whom they formerly served . . . In any case, music no longer has quite the same functions. Warlike music is now only played as an entertainment, and the great epic works with their polemical exaltation of tribal chauvinism and their savage grandeur no longer appeal to the young. This is not to say that laudatory music is dead. It remains with the government for the purpose of election campaigns or with private individuals; it has been 'democratized' in the not very lofty form of quatrains or short poems of circumstance.

In the same way, according to Hugo Zemp's article on the training of musicians in the four West African communities among the Senufo (Ivory Coast),

> . . . today, when the traditional way of life of the chiefs has gone into decline, or completely vanished as a result of changing political and economical conditions, the flute orchestra has lost its raison d'être.

In Morocco, according to A. Essyad in his article on 'Berber music in Morocco',

> The urban way of life tends to be organized differently... These *h'laqi* circles (circles of spectators within which the performance takes place) are decreasing in popularity and even disappearing. Where they still do exist, the nature of the public has changed; it now consists mostly of old men, women and the unemployed.

In the Middle East, according to Amnon Shiloah,

> . . . the number of custodians of the national heritage is di-
> minishing, and the present social and psychological climate
> is not such as to encourage them.

Mireille Ballero laments the disastrous effects of the intrusion of
modern life and technology into folk imagination in India, – an intrusion which is liable to

> . . . kill inspiration rather than provide it with new subjects.
> The transistor is increasingly replacing the spontaneity of
> folklore and making this creative faculty disappear among the
> mass of people.

In Cambodia, as Jacques Brunet sadly notes,

> . . . the traditional artists (whether musicians, sculptors or
> painters) are becoming increasingly rare, since tradition eludes
> them as modernization takes over.

J.C. Eloy, in concluding his article *Musiques d'Orient, notres univers
familier* (Vol. Il, *La musique dans la vie),* quotes Pierre Boulez who, on
returning from Japan, related the story of a manager of a puppet theatre
company who

> . . . no longer could find young people willing to follow the
> long course of study required by this art. They prefer to earn
> a living on television, for instance, and the tradition of puppet
> theatre runs the risk of gradually being lost.

Several musical genres have thus disappeared from non-industrial societies with the encroachment of industrialisation. But the
creative spirit among popular musicians and young people's willing-
ness to learn a difficult art form, one they consider outdated, is also
declining. New music, sometimes called 'renewed music', is springing
up everywhere. This music is often the result of 'acculturation' of
traditional music – a phenomenon that is no less prejudicial to tradition

than the loss of the old musical genres. Let us look at how the process of acculturation evolves, what causes it, and what its results are.

THE PROCESS OF MUSICAL ACCULTURATION

1
The Adoption of Foreign Instruments

– Musical acculturation, at its most elementary stage, evolves from the mere adoption of a foreign instrument used to perform traditional music. The oldest known case may be that of the Chinese importing, in roughly the third century B.C., a four-string, pear shaped lute from Central Asia – the Chinese p'îp'â, also known as the *Hu-gin* (instrument of the 'barbarians'; i.e. the non-Chinese). About the eighth century, the Japanese adopted the Chinese *Zheng*, from which instrument their present-day *Koto* (a thirteen-string zither) is evolved. The Vietnamese have used the *Zheng* of Southern China since the fifteenth century, and from it their *dân tranh* (a sixteen-string zither) evolved.

    Perhaps the most typical case is the adoption of the western violin by several Asian peoples: it has been found in southern India for the past two centuries, in Iran, Morocco, the Arab lands, Turkey, and in Southern Vietnam for about fifty years. The way of holding the bow and tuning the instrument varies from land to land. Perhaps the key to the violin's success in foreign countries is that it has no frets, enabling the musician to perform any kind of scale.

– Foreign instruments are sometimes adopted after undergoing modifications. The Vietnamese use the Spanish guitar, but the spaces between the frets is hollowed out so that tones can be ornamented by varying the amount of pressure used in depressing the strings. The Iranians have replaced the instrument's frets with ligatures.

– Western materials may be used in building traditional instruments. Both the Chinese and the Vietnamese have begun using overspun strings for the bass notes of their sixteen-string zithers. The dimensions of the resonator have been increased to enhance bass tones. This can be found in the manufacture of the Chinese bow-lutes or fiddles *(chong-hu, ti-hu)* and the Vietnamese ones *(tai hô)*.

– Attempts have been made to electronically amplify instruments that are not sufficiently resonant for large concert halls. The Vietnamese monochord *(dan bâu* or *dan tôc hyuên)* is frequently thus amplified. In India, only Balachandar has amplified his *vîma.*

2
Adopting Vocal and Instrumental Techniques

Asian and African singers imitate the vibrato and portamento found in western music. The Chinese play solid chords, rather than arpeggios, on their *p'îp'â* while the Japanese use arpeggios and double strings with the *Koto,* but in doing so, both have neglected that they are putting their instruments at a disadvantage compared to the ones they are imitating: in this case, the Spanish guitar and the harp.

3
Modifications of Performance Practice

Choirs have been organized to perform songs that were originally intended to be softly intoned by a single person. Attempts have been made to form orchestras consisting of traditional Indian instruments and to impose ensemble discipline on the performers whose talents lie in individual improvisation.
In quashing the very essence of the music concerned, all such innovations are nonsense.

4
Changes in Musical Language

Through acculturation, musicians are pressured into harmonizing modal music and using tempered scales in acquiescence to their new audience, which is unaccustomed to the local scales.
It would be beyond the scope of the present article to delve deeply into musicological questions . . ., but Asian and African musicians' many attempts to adopt the idiom and syntax of western music has resulted in them producing music utterly devoid of meaning.

CAUSES OF MUSICAL ACCULTURATION

There are very many causes of musical acculturation.

– First of all, it is commendable that musicians wish to learn new techniques and would like their music to progress beyond that of their masters and predecessors, lending their work a personal stamp.
  Evolution would be slow if they were to rely solely on their own resources, but significant changes follow quickly when they come into contact with neighbouring countries.
– Acculturation is the product of contact between different peoples and civilizations, combined with the added attraction of novelty. The contact between countries of like cultures is very fruitful. We are all aware of the contribution made by Chinese music – particularly that of the Tang dynasty (eighth to eleventh centuries) – to Japanese music, especially the Gagaku court music, of that made by the music of the Tang and Song dynasties (tenth to eleventh centuries) to Korean music, and by the music of the Ming dynasty (fourteenth to fifteenth centuries) to the Vietnamese Lê dynasty (fifteenth to sixteenth centuries). Thai music was deeply indebted to the Khmer tradition and the instruments of the Thai *p'iphat* orchestra are the same as those carved in the bas-reliefs of Angkor. Turkish, Arabian and Persian musicians all consult the same music theorists, and some of the terms found in the Turkish *makam*, the Arabic *maqam* and the Iranian *dastgah* or *avaz* are identical. Several instruments are also found in all three traditions: the *ud* (an unfretted lute with five or six courses of two strings) *canoun* (a psaltery with plucked strings) and *santour* (an instrument with 24 courses of three strings struck by small, flexible hammers called *mezrab*). Contact between countries of diverse cultures has also led to very good results. Several instances that come to mind are the meetings of Japanese traditions and the *champa*, Vietnam and the *champa*, Vietnam and Siam, and of Siam, Cambodia and China.
– Encounters with the West have most significantly led to hybrid musical forms. Both the East and Africa have adopted western tradition. This has been attributed by some to a supposed superiority of western music. In this context, one should keep in mind that the first contacts with the West were in the form of evangelical

missions and these were followed by colonial wars. The colonized peoples suffered from an inferiority complex and tried to imitate the ways of their conquerors, for they were convinced that the superior technology must also be indicative of a superior culture. The final result was mistaking westernization for progress and modernization.

– The development of the mass-media, radio, television and recording apparatus, has accelerated the process of acculturation even more.

Transistor radios have invaded even the most remote regions. Shepherds in the midst of their flocks, farmers in the fields and griots in their tents can listen to music radio broadcasts of music not always of the highest quality – day and night. This urban music influences local composition and improvisation. Television, in the cities, broadcasts the most commercial type of music, the facile 'variety' music that is most profitable to the producers.

The same dangers are an inherent by-product of the recording industry. By dint of being subjected to omnipresent, continual 'musical aggression', today's youth are attracted to and fascinated by this easy-to-write, easy-to-play, easy-to-remember music. They are no longer willing to devote years of their lives to studying the traditional music. After learning a few chords on the Spanish guitar, they can accompany themselves in several months time in singing the songs composed by their compatriots who have been trained in the West. Those who chance to fall into fashion find the opportunity of earning fast and easy money as radio or television stars.

– Along with advances in communications, it has also become easier for musicians to travel. Oriental masters often have the opportunity of performing in the West. Some, impressed by western orchestras, return home with the idea of writing concertos set for their particular instrument and symphony orchestra.

The most immediate result is the production of hybrid music. Etymologically, the terms hybrid and hybridization are not pejorative. Hybridization, biologically speaking, means the crossing of two species – a crossing that may even be advantageous for the sake of variety. In everyday speech, however, a hybrid work is one in which two divergent elements are artificially combined. This term, when applied to language, art or music, implies a certain disdain.

J.C. Eloy, at round table discussions organized by the International Music Council and the ORTF'S Direction of Foreign Affairs and Cooperation, held by UNESCO on April 30, 1971, characterized hybridization as an inevitable phenomenon. The young composer related he could no longer compose in the same fashion after hearing the music of Tibet. At the Lisbon conference of May 1971 on the situation of music and musicians in eastern countries, Salah el Mahdi (Tunisia) pointed out that there is a state of 'permanent hybridization' in effect between the musics of the Mediterranean countries. Alain Daniélou, in his book on music and communication written in collaboration with Jacques Brunet, deplored the disastrous effects of hybridization.

> Melodic forms derived from a modal system are harmonized so that they can be played by modern orchestras or by those artificial ensembles sometimes referred to as 'typical orchestras', apparently in ignorance of the fact that harmony and modes are incompatible. . . All musical forms are affected by this – classical, folk music and light music. A trend towards standardization is spreading in both East and West, gradually effacing the real character of the various musical languages, which lose their style and power of expression without adding anything valid.

In 1968, at the Shiraz symposium on Asian music, and again at the Congress of the International Music Council in New York, the author of these lines distinguished between two sorts of hybridization.

1
Hybridization with an impoverishing effect, sometimes accompanied by the destruction of the national character of one of the two traditions involved; the most common case being when the music of Africa or the East comes into contact with western music.

Oriental and African musicians accompany songs based on exotic scales, using a piano tuned in equal temperament, and now use clarinets, saxophones and even electric guitars in performances of their traditional music. Common chords or arpeggios made up of the component tones of common chords punctuate the phrases of their traditional music.

Alain Daniélou and Jacques Brunet have pointed out the disastrous effects of this sort of hybridization.

> In the new 'Mohori' music of Cambodia. . .a traditional melody is 'enriched' by a 'modern' accompaniment. This applies to all the dance music that can be heard in South-East Asia which is a mixture of jazz, up-to-date rhythms and the pentatonic scale. This evolution proceeds calmly and effortlessly since the radio incessantly broadcasts variety music which then becomes the musical norm.
>
> In addition, there is a sort of madness for gigantism. Traditional orchestras are made to take on such dimensions as to eliminate the musicians' sense of inferiority to the western philharmonic orchestra. From the traditional ensemble, in which each musician improvises on a given theme, new orchestras have been made with each instrument being multiplied by ten so as to arrive at a total that approaches the size of the Berlin Philharmonic, all in the hope of dazzling the foreign tourist and exciting favourable comparisons on the grandeur of both civilizations. Vocal and instrumental techniques are also altered, not to conform to the style of the leading western performers, which would be too difficult, but rather to the more modest styles of Italian, French and American popular singers, whose recordings are often the only ones brought by the noisier westerners on their missions of civilization.

Hybridization is impoverishing because it tries to impose the instruments and style of one tradition on another with which it is incompatible.

2

There have been cases, on the other hand, of hybridization enriching a given culture when the borrowing of foreign elements has led to a new blossoming of the tradition in question. Several examples of this are, for instance, when the music of northern India encountered that of the Islamic tradition, when Japanese court music was enriched by the contribution of the Tang dynasty, Chinese, Korean and Cham music, and when Vietnamese music assimilated both the Chinese and Indian traditions. The effects were beneficial because the borrowed elements were compatible with the original tradition.

Acculturation is a universal phenomenon. What we must try to do is to redirect its potentially destructive forces into constructive ones. The problem is one of compatibility and incompatibility. The combination of compatible elements produces a successful 'graft', but the mixture of incompatible elements leads to 'rejection'. In order to guard against rejection, one must have a very thorough knowledge of one's own national culture and of the culture from which elements are to be borrowed. Unfortunately, the leading champions of traditional music, aloof in their ivory towers and blinded by illusions of their superiority, refuse to permit change and, in many cases, are unfamiliar with any tradition but their own, which they consider to be the only valid one. Young people are interested only in western music, that of their own countries being mere 'folklore'. Given these conditions, neither the old masters nor the young are capable of distinguishing compatible from incompatible elements and are thus inadequate in preventing a process of musical acculturation that is prejudicial to their tradition. In many countries, the new music represents a new need – the need to sing together at mass gatherings. It contributes to the awakening of national consciousness and to preparing the peoples of these countries for the struggle of national liberation, thus fulfilling a historic mission. In most cases however, this music leaves a great deal to be desired from the artistic point of view. Several young musicians, after studying composition at European and American conservatories, have adopted the western musical idiom once and for all. The general public is not yet receptive to their music. They have lost all interest in traditional music, whose public has by now become the minority. Private concerts are held less and less often, while radio and television propagate the new, heavily westernized music.

This author disagrees with the fatalistic argument that traditional music is dying and must soon disappear to make way for another type of music, which though perhaps less authentic, would be more in keeping with the needs of modern society. The music of non-industrial societies is not 'dying', it may be sick, but one must not abandon the ill without first trying to cure the ailment.

If adequate measures were to be taken straight away, the present crisis may turn out to amount to nothing more than 'growing pains'. Needless to say, the rebirth – not the survival – of musical traditions is naturally a problem that primarily calls for a national solution. Cultural and educational organizations, public and private, and the governments of Africa and Asia could improve the teaching of traditional music, raise the living standards of traditional musicians and reorganize musical life. Western countries, however, could aid us in our efforts to rescue our musical heritage by showing interest in our authentic traditional music. Those masters of traditional music who have been invited to perform in western countries enjoy greater prestige among their compatriots. The International Music Council and the International Institute for Comparative Musical Studies and Documentation have not only helped the western public to appreciate Asian music at its true worth, but have also helped to restore the confidence of masters of traditional music in Asia.

If adequate measures are not taken in the near future, this crisis could well develop into an epidemic leading to the loss of what remains of the musical traditions of non-industrial societies – traditions of great value, but how very frail! It would be a loss, not only for the countries involved, but for all mankind.

(Translated from French by Colin J. Norris)

9

EAST-WEST RELATIONS AND THERAPY – MUSIC AND HEMISPHERIC BALANCE
Richard Hees

INTRODUCTION

It is hardly surprising that East-West relationships have been chosen as the central theme for this book: Ton de Leeuw is a composer who is known for his extensive and thorough explorations of various non-Western cultures.

His music is by no means easily accessible. Yet once one has developed a feel for his approach, his efforts to bring together and integrate eastern and western musical elements are impressive.

In a variety of ways his approach distinctly differs from that of many other western musicians who have tended to follow the dictates of fashion with regard to non-western cultures thereby frequently limiting themselves to a simple recapitulation of oriental art's external features. In Ton de Leeuw's music, however, one finds neither a faddish imitation of the East nor a mere assembly of heterogenous materials. As soon as one has opened oneself up to his music one cannot help but be affected by it. Clearly he has succeeded in going beyond the diverse musics by making them a part of himself through his combination of creative power and what he has called 'mutation of mind' (De Leeuw, 1973: 23). This concept of 'mutation of mind' is also valuable within a therapeutic framework, especially at the level where music is – or could be – used in therapy. De Leeuw relates this concept to the idea that music is partly derived from common features and mechanisms of our brain and body. He often refers to the common physiological elements underlying different music cultures. This notion can be readily recognized in his music (cf. *African Studies*, 1954; *Haiku II*, 1968; *Lamento Pacis*, 1969; *Music for Strings*, 1970; *Gending*, 1975; *Invocations*, 1985) but also in his writings where he speaks of "a second layer of musical form, which we might call: the intramusical reality, completing the social reality" [...] "[This] intramusical reality leads us to the realm of universals and underlying formal principles, ever present, deep inside ourselves". (De Leeuw 1981).

What Ton de Leeuw thus intuitively understands and expresses in his writings and even more so in his music, has important implications for theoretical thinking about music therapeutic processes. As an interdisciplinary research field this area, or biomusicology, has long lain fallow while it could provide fruitful advances for both theory and practice of music (in) therapy.

This article uses a biomusicological approach focussing on the interface between the 'intramusical reality' and its effect on the biological organism. To this end clinical examples are used to illustrate the common principles at work in this area. Some basic knowledge about how the human brain works, especially how the two brain hemispheres do or don't interact with each other, is required to grasp these principles. The first section in this article therefore comprises some introductory neuroscientific facts demonstrating the difference in functions between the two hemispheres with an emphasis on their relation to music. Section two shows how functional barriers between the hemispheres can play a role in a variety of mental disturbances. The function music can have in restoring hemispheric balance or overcoming negative consequences due to hemispheric imbalance, is clarified in section three by studying the case of a musical genius.

In section four the question is raised whether the two cognitive modes associated with the two brain hemispheres and operating at an individual level also operate at a cultural level. Within this context special attention will be given to the polarities between western and non-western cultures. Finally section five attempts a synthesis of the insights gained from the preceeding sections using a therapeutic perspective in order to arrive at a better understanding of the concept Ton de Leeuw has called 'mutation of mind'.

1
Music and Aphasia

In the past few decades much progress has been made in the study of the functional differences between the two brain hemispheres.

Before that time, ever since the discovery of the 'aphasia centers' by Broca and Wernicke about a hundred years ago, quite a lot of data was already available. The word 'aphasia' refers to a loss of ability to speak and/or to understand language, and is due to a lesion (= injury) in the part(s) of the brain where language is processed. In right-handed people this is usually in the left hemisphere in rather circum-scribed areas named after Broca and Wernicke. If an injury in one of these areas occurs due to, for instance, a trauma, a stroke or a tumor, one loses the ability to understand words and sentences (called re-ceptive/sensory or Wernicke aphasia) or to express oneself with language (expressive/motor or Broca aphasia).

Of course it is impossible within the confines of this article to give an adequate representative view of the information that has been gathered in the field of brain research. Perhaps it is enough to say that until roughly 20 years ago brain-researchers in the West generally teneted that not only was language processed in the left hemisphere but that all other 'higher' mental functions were as well (Luria 1966). For this reason the hemisphere where the aphasia centers are located was called the 'major' or 'dominant' hemisphere.[2]

More recently, however, the concept of the two hemispheres and their respective functions has been changing. This is partly due to recent findings in brain research (see below), but also to the growing realization that the tendency to think in hierarchical terms is not without bias.

The distinction *'major'* (or 'dominant') and *'minor'* (or 'non-dominant') seems more a societal than a neurological one. The domi-nant or major mode of our culture is verbal and intellectual. If an injury to the right hemisphere did not affect speech or reason, this damage was often considered as minor. Injury to the left hemisphere on the other hand affects verbal functions and this was often seen as major. If one is a scientist, a mathematician or a lawyer, etc., damage to the left hemisphere may prove disastrous. If one is a musician, a craftsman or an artist, however, similar damage to the left hemisphere often does not interfere with one's capacity to create music, crafts or arts. Damage to the right hemisphere on the other hand may well obliterate a career.

Luria's 'Aphasia in a composer' is a case in point. In this study (Luria 1965) he presents the story of an outstanding Russian composer, called Shebalin (1904-1963), who, after a vascular lesion (stroke) injuring the left hemisphere's speech zones, suffered from a severe and pre-dominantly receptive language impairment (sensory aphasia) while preserving his musical abilities. Shebalin was a director of the Moscow Conservatoire, directed a class of composition and had many well-known Russian composers among his pupils. Four years before he died he had a stroke leaving him with severe aphasia and the right side of his body paralyzed (spastic hemiparesis). Working closely with Shebalin, Luria was able to carefully examine the aphasia. He extensively described the impairments in the composer's active speech and in his understanding of speech and how after a few months his active speech partially recovered although defects in perception and in the understanding of speech remained.

Luria states that in spite of the severe impairments of verbal language Prof. Shebalin continued his work as a composer. He worked hard with his pupils, listening to their compositions, analysing and correcting them. He also spent a considerable time on his own creative work. While aphasic, he finished compositions he had started to write before he was taken ill and he created a series of new compositions other musicians considered to be up to standard and not significantly different in quality from compositions of his earlier years. A list of the creative work he published during the years of his illness is given next to a quotation by Shostakovitch stating that Shebalin's *Fifth Symphony*, composed during his illness, 'is a creation of a great master.'

This study does not stand alone. From music history other, though usually less documented or less well documented cases, are known. For example Ravel, who also suffered an aphasia in connection with a paralysis of the right side of his body (which is connected with the left hemisphere). Maurice Ravel unfortunately suffered from a progressive neurological affliction of the left hemisphere starting in 1926, or maybe even earlier (Cytowic 1976). A well-known composition of this period is his famous *Piano concerto for the left hand* (1931), known to be written for Paul Wittgenstein, the Viennese pianist who had lost his right hand in World War I.

Such observations also correspond with the very frequent finding in neurological clinics that aphasia patients, in spite of severe speech difficulties, are often able to sing and – in particular – can even pronounce words when singing they are unable to pronounce in speech. This well-known yet very peculiar phenomenon had already been studied in 1937 by Ustvedt, but his promising attempt to understand this phenomenon for long remained an isolated one. Ustvedt demonstrated that the examination of musical functions in patients with cerebral injuries must be conducted in a manner entirely different from a normal psychological examination. In 1959 Wertheim and Botez made a new attempt and published a 'Plan d'investigations des fonctions musicales' for clinical purposes.

As for the therapeutic potential of this phenomenon: there have been various endeavours to make therapeutic use of music in aphasia rehabilitation. An example is the Melodic Intonation Therapy (Sparks et al. 1976). It is very likely, however, that much better use of the potentials of music in this and other fields will be achieved as soon as a better understanding of the phenomenon of music in relation to language and brain functioning is developed.

Amusia

Theoretically there are many ways to gain insights in how music is processed in the brain (cf. Critchley 1977). One possibility is via the study of amusia, the musical counterpart of aphasia. Amusia is, analogous to aphasia, the loss or impairment of musical ability. Like in aphasia a variety of forms exist, but usually one distinguishes receptive vs. expressive amusia. Receptive amusia refers to a loss or impairment of recognition and 'understanding' of music. The individual tones are heard but not recognized as a tune nor felt as music. Expressive amusia on the other hand is the loss or impairment of the ability to express oneself with music (e.g. sing, whistle, hum a tune or play an instrument).

An example and early description of (expressive) amusia is Jossmann's case of a good singer who lost his capacity to sing as well as whistle after an operation on a right hemisphere artery. The operation itself was successful: the life-threatening arterial defect (aneurism) was perfectly removed, but when the patient awoke from the anaesthesia he manifested an expressive amusia without aphasia in combination with a paralysis of the left side of the body. After a few weeks he recovered from the paralysis but the amusia remained. This meant he could neither sing nor whistle tunes on command. At the same time his recognition of melodies was well preserved (Jossmann 1927).

This example, however rare, suggests that there may be an 'amusia center' in the right hemisphere, just like there is an 'aphasia center' in the left hemisphere. The findings with regard to amusia, however, are much less consistent than those with regard to aphasia.

In other words: while language is for a great part processed in the left hemisphere (in right-handed people) music is processed in the right hemisphere, but not in the same way nor to the same extent as language in the left. It appears from various amusia cases, and also from other data (Critchley 1977) that music is mediated in the left hemisphere as well, at least with respect to certain aspects of music. Which aspects these are is still mostly unknown. Some investigators have found evidence indicating that the left hemisphere is more involved in the processing of music for musicians, i.e. for people with higher musical education (cf. Bever and Chiarello 1974). This suggests that 'higher' aspects of music, i.e. aspects of music that are trained by musical education, are a competence of the left hemisphere whereas 'lower', i.e. more universal aspects of music, are a function of the right hemisphere. This would imply that precisely those aspects of music that are processed in the right hemisphere are an especially promising means of arriving at what De Leeuw calls 'intra-musical reality'.

The particular way the organism resonates to certain of these underlying principles of music offers valuable clues to what could be called the 'lower' or 'depth' aspects of music. Systematic study of the relationships between music and these basic, vital processes is what I call 'biomusicology' (Hees 1980). Amusia is one among various highly valuable objects of investigation for biomusicologists. It provides a promising vehicle for research to help explicate the matrix of (biomusicological) relationships between music and physiological and/or vital and/or depth-psychological processes.

In the same way the study of aphasia has proved fruitful as well. By systematic investigation of aphasia patients, aphasiologists such as Jakobson (1964,1968) discovered depth structures in language appearing to be pre-existent in languages of widely varying cultures (see also: Chomsky 1965; Andreasen and Grove 1980).

Remains the question why a discovery of depth structures in language or music is at all interesting. Jakobson's discovery lends itself to the supposition that there exists an innate predisposition to language at a physiological level. By extrapolation it is possible to hypothesize that there exists a comparable innate predisposition to music. This is in accordance with the fact that the occurrence of music has been described by anthropologists in about all cultures in the world, with only very few exceptions; one is a tribe in Uganda called the Iks, apparently as a consequence of social disruption (Turnbull 1972).

In the context of therapy the power of language to heal by allowing the communication of dreams and free associations, 'the talking cure', has been evident at least since Freud. It may well be that biomusicology concentrating primarily on aspects of music mediated by the right hemisphere will one day be able to establish the innate musical predisposition out of which 'intra-musical reality' is generated.

Perhaps biomusicology will also be able to better explain why and how music can be an effective tool in therapy. In fact, biomusicology may one day even disclose music as a 'Via Regia'[3] to the right hemisphere. I, for one, am convinced this is the case. However, for the reader to even start to consider such a possibility some general understanding of left vs. right hemispheric functioning is indispensable.

Hemispheric specialization for different cognitive modes

The past 20 years has seen considerable progress in the area of hemispheric specialization. This progress is due to the development of various highly advanced techniques.[4] Because of these recent developments a wealth of information showing that we do have two equally important 'halfbrains' mediating two different modes of consciousness has been gained. It has become clear that both the structure and the function of these two 'half-brains' in some part underlie the two modes of consciousness simultaneously co-existing within each of us. Although each hemisphere shares the potential for many functions, and both sides participate in most activities, the two hemispheres normally tend to specialize.

The left hemisphere (connected to the right side of the body) is predominantly involved with analytic, logical thinking, especially in verbal and mathematical functions. Its mode is primarily linear and information appears to be processed sequentially. As this mode of operation forms the foundations of logical thoughts, logic is tied to sequence and order. Here a cognitive mode is mediated for which words and digits are an excellent tool.

As the left hemisphere is specialized for analysis, the right hemisphere (connected to the left side of the body) seems specialized for holistic mentation. Its language ability is quite limited. This hemisphere is primarily responsible for our orientation in space, body image, recognition of faces, artistic endeavour, and it is particularly suitable for music as opposed to words. Generally speaking, it processes information more diffusely than the left hemisphere, and its responsibilities demand a ready integration of many inputs at once. If the left hemisphere can be termed predominantly analytic and sequential in its operation, then the right hemisphere is more holistic and relational, and more synergistic/parallel in its mode of operation. It must be kept in mind that these two delineated cognitive modes are usually integrated and complementary in their functioning.

2

Though many of the above mentioned research methods have been applied to normal subjects, such as students and the like, the impetus to research in this area has come from study with patients. Especially the studies of R. Sperry and his colleagues aroused great interest in the subject of hemispheric specializations. Because the so-called split-brain syndrome sheds light on the interaction between the two hemispheres, it will be discussed here briefly.

The 'Split-brain' Syndrome

'Split-brain' is the name of a condition in which the commissures, i.e. the connecting structures between the two brain hemispheres, have been split surgically in order to relieve a patient from his/her otherwise intractable epileptic attacks.

The effect of this surgical hemispheric disconnection, called commissurotomy, was that a satisfactory and sustained improvement in the seizure incidence usually followed. Moreover no changes due to their split-brain conditions were observed in their day to day life, neither by the patients themselves nor by others. However, Sperry c.s. investigated these split-brain patients and discovered a number of subtle though quite interesting phenomena illustrating that the operation had clearly separated the specialized functions of the hemispheres. If, for instance, a split-brain patient was given a pencil hidden from sight and he could feel the pencil in his right hand, he could verbally describe it, as would be normal. But if the pencil was in the left hand, he could not describe it at all. This has to do with the fact that the left hand informs the right hemisphere which does not possess the capacity for speech. In split-brain persons the verbal (left) hemisphere is no longer connected to the right hemisphere, which largely communicates with the left hand; so the verbal apparatus literally does not know what is in the left hand. If, however, the patient was offered a selection of objects, – a key, book, pencil, etc. – and was asked to choose the previously given object with his left hand, he could choose correctly, although he still could not state verbally just what he was doing.

Sperry gathered a great number of data by means of various specially designed tests. In this way he made manifest a dissociation between the experiences of the two disconnected hemispheres. This dissociation is sometimes even dramatic. He recorded some of his findings with his split-brain patients on film. An illustrative film fragment is the following:

> [. . .] the young woman watches a series of neutral geometrical figures being presented at random to the right and left visual fields and so via the neuronal cross over to the left and right hemispheres. Then a photograph of a nude pin-up is flashed to the right (nonverbal) hemisphere in the course of an otherwise dull series of pictures. The girl blushes and giggles. Sperry asks 'What did you see?' She answers: 'Nothing, just a flash of light', and giggles again, covering her mouth with her hand. 'Why are you laughing then?' asks Sperry, and she laughs again and says: 'Oh, Dr. Sperry, you have some machine!'.

The lady's reactions become understandable when one takes into consideration that the right hemisphere being exposed to the emotion laden information cannot express itself verbally, whereas the left (verbal) hemisphere cannot tell what is going on in the other hemisphere when it is disconnected from the other one due to a commissurotomy. The episode shown on the film is very suggestive indeed. If one did not know of the woman's split-brain condition, one might be tempted to see her reactions as a clear example of perceptual defense and think that she was 'repressing' the perception of the conflictful sexual material – even her final response (a socially acceptable nonsequitur) was convincing (cf. Sperry 1969). Though in this case there is no 'repression' such as in the person with an intact brain who may insist 'I am not angry' while his tone of voice and facial expression simultaneously indicate exactly the opposite; the striking formal similarity between these dissociation phenomena seen in split-brain persons and various similar phenomena seen in clinical practice, have attracted the attention of many researchers and clinicians including psychoanalysts.

An Anatomic Locus for Unconscious Processes?

The psychoanalist Hoppe, for instance, studied split-brain persons extensively before and after their commisurotomy operation (Hoppe 1978). He not only made records of biography, psychodynamics and the usual psychiatric present state examinations, but also made in-depth studies of quantitative and qualitative aspects of their dream and fantasy contents before and after commissurotomy, as well as their ability and tendency to form and make use of symbols.

He found that split-brain persons tended to report a relative absence of dreams and fantasies in the same way also described by Sifneos and others for patients with certain psychosomatic disturbances (Sifneos 1973; Nemiah 1970). There also appeared to be a similarity in the way split-brain persons and these particular psychosomatic (so-called alexithymic) patients make use of symbols. According to Hoppe the quantitative and qualitative impoverishments of dreams, fantasies and symbolization found in both split-brain and the mentioned alexithymic patients derive from an interruption of the preconscious stream between the two hemispheres which in turn causes a separation of word-presentations and thing-presentations. This led him to the hypothesis of a 'functional commissurotomy' in certain cases of severe psychosomatic disturbances (especially those with alexithymic characteristics). With this Hoppe postulates the interesting hypothesis that in patients with certain psychosomatic illnesses there may be a disturbance in the interaction between the two hemispheres (Hoppe 1978).

Loss of Balance Between the Hemispheres

From a somewhat different perspective Galin arrived at a similar conclusion. He assumes that some psychosomatic symptoms and various other psychiatric disturbances as well are due to what he calls a functional disconnection between the two hemispheres (Galin, 1974). He adds to this that in normal, healthy persons mental events in one hemisphere may directly suppress activity in the other one. This is called reciprocal inhibition of cognitive systems and has to do with coping strategies toward situational demands. Only when such functional disconnection starts to lead a life of its own do pathological states arise.

This may happen in cases of (chronic) conflict, for instance when a mother continuously tells her child with words 'I love you, dear', while her face and intonation expresses hatred because of her unconscious ambivalance. Each hemisphere is exposed to the same sensory input, but because of their relative specializations each emphasizes only one of the messages. The left will attend to the verbal cues because it cannot extract information from the facial gestalt efficiently; the right will attend to the non-verbal cues because it cannot easily understand the words.

Usually the left hemisphere is most influential but when the perception of the hateful face by the right hemisphere is strong enough or is not suppressed by the left hemisphere the child may become confused.

The less conscious mental process in the right hemisphere, cut off from the left hemisphere consciousness that is directing overt behavior, may nevertheless continue to lead a life of its own. The ambivalent experience may persist as a memory and thus influence future behavior. This process of ambivalent in-printing has been studied by Bateson c.s. (1956/63) who named the situation where opposite messages are sent, such as by the ambivalent mother to a child, a double-bind. Bateson and his associates found double-bind situations in a great percentage of schizophrenic patients. In this context it may be interesting to note that some patients with schizophrenia have been found to have a thickening of their connective brain structures (commissures) suggestive of an increase in the number of communicating fibers between the two hemispheres (Andreasen, 1982). This has been interpreted as a physiological attempt to restore a disturbed communication between the hemispheres.

There are more examples of disturbances in inter-hemispheric relations. Mandell in the *Comprehensive Textbook of Psychiatry* (Kaplan et al., 1980) states that both the 'obsessional paranoid' mode of dealing with other people – characterized by general negativism, exaggeration of difficulties, preoccupation with difficulties, projection of rage, ruminative self-concern, mistrust and emotional isolation – on the one hand and the 'hysterical-cyclothymic' tendency – a tendency toward bland denial (la belle indifference), high mood, emotionality, impatience with detail and impulsivity – are manifestations deriving from imbalances in inter-hemispheric relation.

Another peculiar clinical phenomenon already pointed out by Ferenczi is that symptoms of the conversion type, such as psychogenic paralyses = paralyses of psychological origin, show a predominance in the left side of the body (Ferenczi, 1926). If this is true this implies that psychological tensions and conflicts tend to be symbolically expressed by the body there where verbal or (externally directed) non-verbal, e.g. artistic expression fails.

Hemisperic Imbalance and Autism

The autistic syndrome or 'early infantile autism' deserves special mention here. This syndrome has increasingly attracted the attention of clinicians and researchers (Kanner, 1943). The term autism is a shorthand for a group of children who manifest a failure to develop normal social relationships. They usually manifest an emotional re-moteness with a lack of eye contact, indifference (or outright repug-nance) to being held, lack of discrimination between parents and other adults, etc. There are usually also severe delays in the acquisition of language as well as deviant forms of language. Often there is a preoccupation with inanimate objects and an obsessive resistance to change. Next to this there may be remarkable areas of normal func-tioning, and sometimes even striking capabilities. What causes this peculiar syndrome is as yet unknown. It has been postulated that inadequate or absent linguistic interaction between mother and child could be a causal factor. However, these deviant interactions have come to be considered to be a consequence rather than the cause of autism.

Blackstock investigated listening preferences of autistic and 'normal' children. He found that autistic children were more attracted to music than other children. By combining his findings with neurophysiological data he was among the first to make plausible that a cerebral imbalance or asymmetry is an important causative factor in the development of early infantile autism (Blackstock, 1978).

Other organic factors have recently been detected as well. Ornitz summarizes investigations in favor of the cerebral asymmetry hypothesis but also presents evidence in favor of influences originating from deeper brain areas, such as brainstem and diencephalic structures (Ornitz, 1985).

In this context it is interesting to note that there are numerous references in the literature to the musical abilities of autistic children (cf. Viscott 1970, O'Connell 1974, Applebaum 1979). Rimland even asserted that musical interests and/or abilities are 'almost universal' in autistic children (Rimland 1964). Yet remarkably few attempts to systematic research have been undertaken with regards to this striking phenomenon. This in spite of the fact that music so clearly appears to have links with the right hemisphere as well as with the deeper brain areas mentioned above. It is known that these deeper brain areas are the very areas where the rhythmic processes of the human organism are generated, such as the brain rhythms that can be registered by the encephalogram, but also to a great extent the heart rhythms, the respiratory and circadian (day and night) rhythms, and many other vital processes that are regulated here, processes which on an auditory level are most clearly expressed in music.

In many parts of the world, isolated case studies have been published in which music was described as a fruitful approach in the therapy of autistic children (cf. Hollander and Juhrs 1974, Benenzon 1979, Willms 1975). Equally impressive is that for 8 of the 11 autistic children in Kanner's follow-up report who later made adequate social adjustments, music played such a major role that this spontaneously occuring activity was spelled out even in the very brief biographies recorded (Kanner 1971).

For all these reasons biomusicological investigation of musical phenomena in autistic children can be expected to provide a rationale for further research in this area, due to its possible clinical, neurological and music therapeutic implications. This, however, is not only the case for autistic children.

3
Music: A Medium for Restoring Balance

Music has also been successfully used in other clinical situations, as for example with the types of mental disturbances mentioned earlier (cf. 2.2 and 2.3). What they have in common is that they are related to an imbalance between the two brain hemispheres. In order to be successful, therapeutic strategies will thus have to include attempts to restore, in as far as possible, a flexible balance between the brain hemispheres.

Music can be useful in achieving this aim. As we have seen music is mostly a function of the right hemisphere. Yet it is also processed in the left hemisphere. Individual cases have demonstrated that for certain mental disturbances music can be an important tool to help re-establish communication by making it possible to express right hemisphere material, mostly repressed emotions, which would otherwise either suppress left hemispheric function or give rise to tensions fostering depressive, psychotic or psychosomatic tendencies. Sometimes music is one of the very few media which contact can be established at all as is the case for some autistic children. More often music can have a function to elicit more general therapeutic effects (Hees 1976).

Of course the context of an official therapy is not always needed for therapeutic effects to occur. Frequently people use music spontaneously as a means of expression and of (re)balancing between the hemispheres. One striking example is that of a composer we all know and many of us greatly admire.

A Famous Case

The left-healing quality of Beethoven's musical creativity has been described by Ehrenwald in his notable article *Beethoven: hero and antihero – Portrait of a right hemispheric genius* (Ehrenwald 1979). Ehrenwald describes here two opposing existential positions in Beethoven's personality, the main, heroic Beethoven as we know him from his music on the one hand, and the anti-heroic side of his personality, that of an ill-tempered, unkempt, dissolute Beethoven 'full of rude energy', as he is described by his contemporaries on the other.

Based on Beethoven's letters, and also his 'Heiligenstadt Testament', Ehrenwald shows his faltering attempts to spell out his emotional predicament in words. But this was by no means his only handicap. Beethoven appears never to have mastered the elementary principles of arithmetic beyond addition and subtraction. And his spelling errors show various features familiar in children with dyslexia. By contrast the original musical scores do not show such disturbances. From the manifold data Ehrenwald hypothesizes that Beethoven had a developmental deficit of the left hemisphere associated with an overdevelopment, if not triumph, of the right hemisphere. However, Beethoven's development was not only determined by these striking flaws in his neurophysiological organization. Ludwig may well have been what is today described as a battered child. This is due to his experiences with an inexorable and unpredictable father who, coming home late at night with his drinking companions, would rouse little Ludwig from sleep and force him to practice until the wee hours of dawn. Being exposed to his father's irrational and unpredictable outbursts of temper in his formative years, in combination with his mother's too early decease seems to have seriously affected his personality development.

Ehrenwald makes it plausible that Beethoven's unequal struggle with his father also carried with it its own rewards. One was his delight in improvisation in the circle of his friends and in the concerthall. It seems to be a direct derivative of his early defiance of his father's insistence on the dreary routine of practicing the scales and of his 'no-no's' to the little boy's attempts at spontaneous self expression. Ehrenwald writes:

> We know today that it was this irrepressible urge that led him to the dizzying heights of creative innovations in virtually all forms of the musical idiom.

Moreover Ehrenwald states that it was Beethoven's ability to express in the musical idiom his rhapsodic mood swings that saved him from mental deterioration and ultimate breakdown throughout his creative period. It channeled his inner turmoil into musical manifestations and helped to drown out the vicissitudes of the other 'anti-heroic' side of his personality. It was a magnificent alternative to diverse somatic and psychosomatic ailments.

Of course this is a case history of a very unusual kind, because we are dealing here with a man of extraordinary musical ability and creative power. Next to this giant the musical processes of less talented people will necessarily occur at an inferior level, yet similar musical and creative processes may be at play in ordinary individuals. While they have no impact on musical world history whatsoever, the impact on their somatic and psychosomatic ailments may be just as great.

Both within and outside of clinical situations numerous music therapeutic cases have been documented since David first played his harp for Saul, or – perhaps more relevant and objectifiable – since music therapists set foot in those clinical settings where the therapeutic impact of music is recognized. In this sense it would have been equally possible to illustrate my point with a research case we studied in the context of the biomusicological seminar at the University of Amsterdam (Van Rest 1985, Kluen 1987). This case would require a considerable amount of space to explain, however, and will be presented elsewhere (Hees 1987).

But whatever difference there may be between Beethoven the musical giant, and an autistic but very musical little girl whose name has to remain unknown, the impressive similarity is that music helped them both to restore a balance somewhere in their soul.

4
Cultural Expression of Hemispheric Polarities

From the recent brain research mentioned earlier we now know that our two half-brains are to be seen as physiological counterparts with respect to their processing of cognitive modes. The concept of a complementarity between two aspects of mental functioning is hardly new, however. Such a concept can be found in many forms of philosophical, religious and psychological endeavour, some of them going back to very ancient times. Cf: Noos and Thymos in Greek civilization (Plato: Logos and Dianoia), Yin and Yang in China, Manas and Buddhi in India (Vedanta), etc.

Not only this duality in human consciouness but also its relatedness to right and left has long been recognized in other cultures besides ours. For instance, the Hopi Indians of the American Southwest distinguish the function of the two hands, one for writing and one for making music. But also other American Indians as well as the Maoris in New Zealand, Australian aboriginals, Hindus, African and Arabian tribes, and many others, manifest a clear right-left polarity (Domhoff 1969). Left is most often associated with bad, profane, feminine, homosexual and with night and death. Our own ancestors had similiar ideas. They were convinced that witches are left-handed; one of the earliest signs of a saint is his refusal to drink from the left breast; girls originate from the semen of the left testicle and boys from the semen of the right one (Domhoff 1969: 588).

Even our language reflects this polarity up to this day. Right is right at any rate, and left-handed can be rather dubious! The child psychologist Janet Brown observed that 3-year-olds use their dominant, mostly right hand for socially accepted actions, whereas they

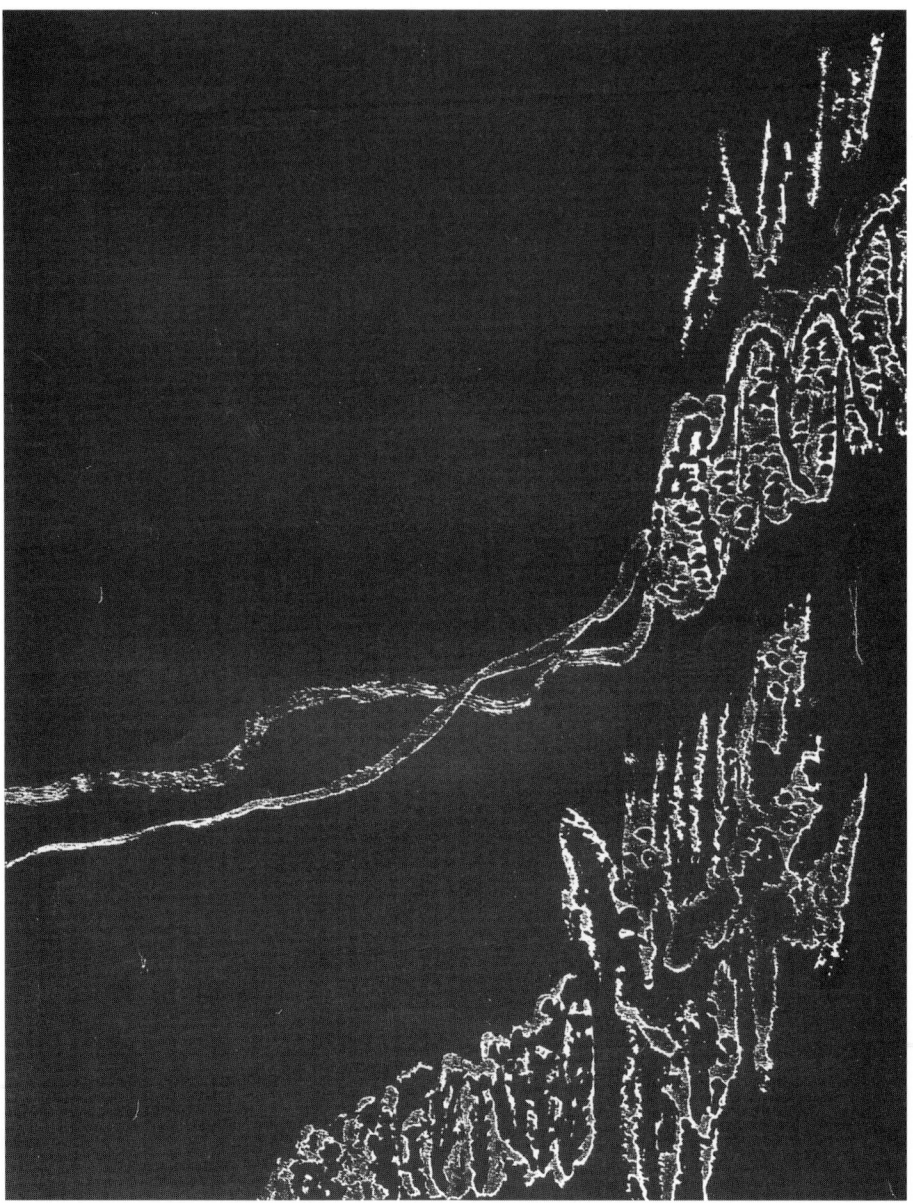

Arlette de Leeuw, "Men go their ways", etching inspired by the similarly titled composition by Ton de Leeuw

use their other hand in contact with their own body or for agressive purposes. In modern man such notions are also still prevalent. Domhoff asked 80 students to rate the concept of right and 80 others to rate the concept of left according to the semantic differential technique. He found statistically significant figures from this sample indicating that Left is characterized as bad, weak, profane, female, unclean, curved, low,mysterious, ugly, night, death or west, while Right means just the opposite – good, strong, sacred, male, clean, straight, erect, high, beautiful, white, correct and east (Domhoff 1969).[5]

The relationship between the evolution of the two brain hemispheres and the cultural history of mankind has been studied by Julian Jaynes. He reported his findings in *The origin of consciousness in the breakdown of the bicameral mind* (Jaynes 1976). In this impressive study he relates various psychological and psychopathological phenomena to cultural history. In particular he traces the origins of consciousness throughout the history of man, when and how it came about, which physiological structures may have been involved, etc. According to Jaynes in this process the specialization of the two hemispheres plays an important role.

Hemispheric Dominance and East-West Dichotomy

It is known that a preponderance of either left or right hemispheric functions may occur in an individual: for one reason or another some persons habitually prefer one mode of consiousness over the other. A lawyer or an exclusively verbal logical scientist for example may manifest a left hemispheric dominance and forget or even deny that they possess another side. On the other hand there are craftsmen, people involved in the 'mystical' disciplines, sculptors and musicians; they will manifest special involvement in the right hemisphere mode of consciousness.

One cannot help but wonder whether such specialization of preference could have developed in cultures as a whole as well. The question then is: could one culture possibly show an affinity toward the left and another toward right hemispheric functions?

With respect to the East-West dichotomy we can state at least in very general terms that in East and West different approaches to knowledge are preponderant. The dominant one in the West tends to be the rational approach, and in the East the mystical approach to knowing. This implies that in the West left hemispheric qualities with linear thinking directed toward mastery through the use of verbal rational modes are especially developed and prized. This is the most apparent in the domain of technical developments and related areas. Nevertheless single-minded pursuit of this mode condemn a society to operate only in these terms. Eventually representation of reality solely in these terms can become a spin-off of its own limitations and remains unresponsive to paradox and to existential paradigms which it cannot define in linear terms.

On the other hand right hemispheric qualities appear to have been especially developed in various eastern cultures particularly those who have retained mystical traditions such as Taoism, Vedanta, traditions inspired by the language of the Upanishads, certain Buddhist traditions etc. These cultures value more introverted, existential and intuitive qualities of mind emphasizing liberation from ordinary human conditions through knowing and understanding a reality which transcends everyday experience.

The great problem for these traditions has always been to translate the mystical experience into ordinary language. Most often this has lead to oral traditions relying on linguistic juxtaposition sounding oracular and incomprehensible to the uninitiated. It is remarkable how often within these traditions music plays an important role as a primary communicative and facilitating modality.

5
Toward a Harmony of (hemi)spheres

Long before modern brain research started to reveal the differentiation in function between the two hemispheres, similar ideas about diverse cognitive styles were intuited by writers in the History of Conciousness. Neumann, for example, an authority in the field of analytical psychology, collated the symbolic and collective material found in individuals during psychotherapy with corresponding products from the history of religion, primitive psychology and other segments of the cultural history of mankind (Neumann 1954). Studying this material he arrived at fascinating conclusions allowing him to reveal the historical emergence of two modes of consciousness, or two 'systems' as he called them. In the later development of western consciousness he shows how this led not only to differentiating but to an actual split between the two systems.

The two systems he described bear a striking similarity to the two cognitive styles now known to be associated with the function of the two brain hemispheres. Neumann saw evidence of this development split in western consciousness depicted in a variety of mythological and related material. He argued that this separation results from any of the following: 1) devaluation or deflation of the unconscious; 2) secondary personalization, that is the personalization, in the course of development, of motifs which are primarily transpersonal and originally appearing as such; 3) exhaustion of emotional components; and/or 4) abstractive processes whereby the unconscious is represented first as an image, then as an idea, and is finally rationalized as a concept.

Neumann shows that the separation of the systems is in a certain sense an evolutionary necessity, because it allows man to dominate his environment. For modern man, however, this inner split carries with it inherent and excessive dangers.

These insights derived from the history of consciousness combined with the scientific data of current brain research, suggest that the dichotomy apparently operating at the organic/biological level is not only reflected at an individual/psychological level but also exists at a cultural/sociological level. Exerting its influence on all of these levels music has the power to stimulate the imagination and enrich emotional life. But it also appears to mobilize spontaneous therapeutic impulses in response to the stresses of everyday life in a way comparable to dreams in the normal, healthy individual. Originating from and impinging on the organism at a (biological) level that is deeper, more primitive and primary than the verbal and conceptual levels of cognition, music may also have an innate restorative influence on individuals who are emotionally out of balance or whose hemispheres are imbalanced in a variety of possible ways.

Seen in this light Ton de Leeuw's concept of a 'mutation of mind' can also be taken to apply to the balancing effects of compensatory tendencies at socio-cultural and individual levels. This is so because intra-musical reality allows the individual psyche to resonate to as well as act upon the collective rhythms of mankind. The mutuality of these processes in music holds true in a broader sense. Neumann, directing attention to this aspect as well, spoke of a rapprochement between human consciousness and the powers of the unconscious hidden in its collective psyche. He saw this rapprochement as man's task for the future.

The eventual healing of man's inner dichotomy is prefigured in the hero. The individual and the story of his transformation are the great human prototypes. Throughout evolution the hero has been the testing ground for collective change just as consciousness is the touch stone of the unconscious.

In Ton de Leeuw's music we apprehend such a hero when we recognize a rapprochement of cultural polarities generated by his creative power and mutation of mind. In (music)therapy we recognize the hero in the patient when he/she is moving – accompanied by the therapist – toward a harmony of (hemi)spheres.

CIRCLES, MIRRORS AND MOTION: AN ANALYSIS OF CYCLICITY IN THE MUSIC OF TON DE LEEUW

Rokus de Groot

LIKE A CRYSTAL BALL

Car nos vignes sont en fleur ends with a melody that is both compelling and calming. This finale of a vocal composition by Ton de Leeuw seems far off until the very last moment. Although fragments of it were already interspersed amidst the heterogeneous patterns of the previous movement, they all vanished, supplanted by percussive sound of the voices. Thus it is very satisfying when these melodic fragments are woven together in musical contours one hopes will never end. We will examine here the close of *Car nos vignes,* the seventh movement, using it like a crystal ball to explore De Leeuw's universe.

The composition is notable for its strikingly elegant examples of those characteristics that are at the root of much of De Leeuw's work. Conspicuous among these are: cyclical patterns; mirror structure; shifting between simultaneously appearing cycles; and continual unfolding.

The aspect of unfolding stands out most clearly among these characteristics. The music begins softly, with a solo tenor, and by the end of the work the entire choir is singing: the result of a steady increase in dynamics and step by step enlargement of parts. In the constantly recurring passages in which unison textures are transformed to heterophonic ones, the degree of complexity also increases. As simple as this may be to point out, one supposes, even on the first hearing, that there is more to this unfolding than the mere addition of parts. This expansion is an elaboration of the unfolding within the melody itself. The music of the seventh movement begins as shown in example 1.

1 *'Car nos vignes sont en fleur', beginning of the seventh movement.*

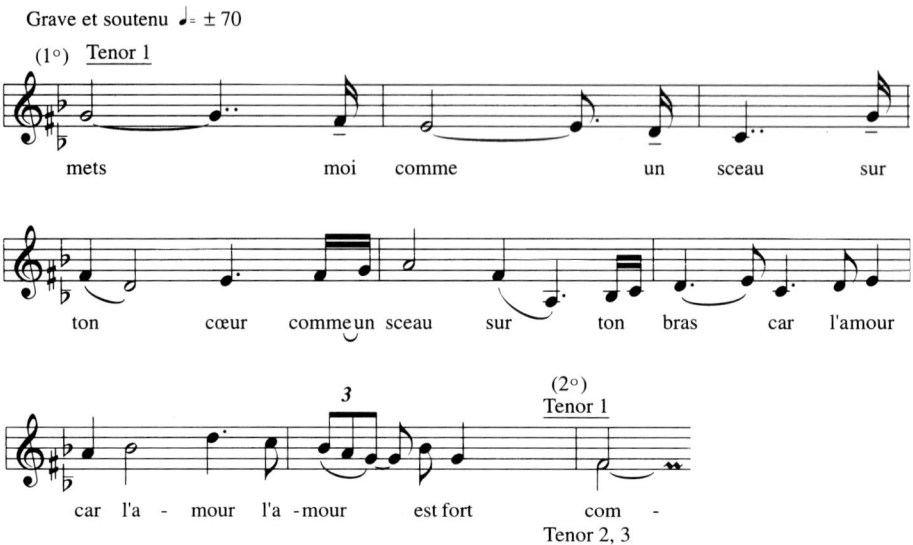

The melody shown in the example is sung again and again, but it is not 'just repeated'. One of the main objectives of this article is to determine the qualities of this melody that continually propel it back to its beginning. Needing a more precise term than 'repetition', we have chosen 'cyclicity', for it implies the (experience of) necessity of repetition.

Naturally, on a first hearing of this closing melody one does not spontaneously grasp its formal subtleties, and the procedures outlined in this article are in all honesty not blatantly obvious. What one hears is a supple, free melody, whose parts lack sharp articulation, the main line of which is from time to time split into individual strands.

THE GAELIC PSALMS OF DAVID

Monophonic textures that time and again blossom in a multiplicity of voices: this is one of the characteristics that in my mind conjures memories of the Gaelic Psalms sung on the Hebrides; the association is reinforced by the calm tempo, the continuity of the music, together with the general repetition of the melody.

These Protestant songs of praise arose as a reaction of the Scottish highlands' folk music culture to melodies that were imported from the Scottish lowlands, England and the continent. The tradition of the lines of the quatrain being recited by the 'precentor' dates from the seventeenth century, when the rhymed version of the psalms and foreign melodies were imposed on this local community – in this way the church community could learn the text – after which the church members would set in one after another. In the highlands this urban homophonic song was thus transformed into the solo song of the folk culture. The collective song, measured in quatrains, became songs of praise with alternating solo recitations, and the multitude of voices joining in, each, in their own way, absorbed in the religious text. This is one of the original choral melodies (see example 2).

2   *Hugh Wilson (1766-1824), the melody 'Martyrdom'.*

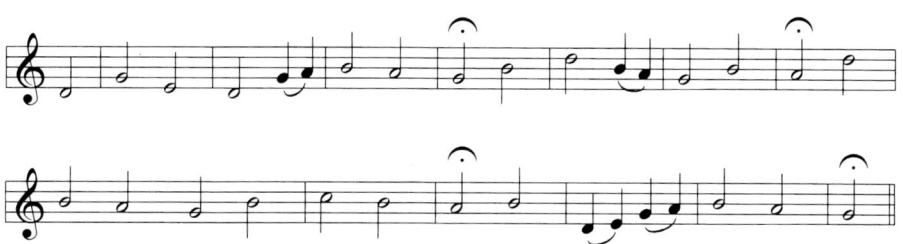

Example 3 gives an impression of how the singers from Lewis would treat this melody during the *family worship*; they and their ancestors had been influenced by folk music models and knowledge of orna-mental patterns of intonation: 'musically this attitude leads to drones, of various kinds, and imitative effects. And to cacophony.'

This is an interesting case for anyone concerned with 'authen-ticity and acculturation'. They are the melodies referred to by the Scottish poet Robert Burns when he wrote:

> Compared with thee, Italian tunes are tame;
> The tickl'd ears no heart-felt raptures raise;
> Nae unison hae they, with our Creator's praise.[3]

This curious music also comes to mind when the seventh movement of *Car nos vignes* has reached the conclusion of the second unwinding of its melodic cycle (see example 4).

3   *Transcription of Psalm 20, verse 5, on the melody 'Martyrdom', sung by Murdina MacDonald (precentor) and her family, at a family service of worship in Ballantrushal, Lewis, Scotland, 1964[2]. The transcription was made from the recording issued on the L.P. 'Gaelic Music from Scotland', Ocora OCR 45, Side B, no.3.*

4 *'Car nos vignes sont en fleur'. A crotchet has been removed from the rhythmic pattern of Tenor 1 at * and the same value has been added at **.*

A CIRCLING DANCE

The term cyclicity is so often heard in reference to the music of Ton de Leeuw that it would be worthwhile here to review its meaning with the help of a simple example. Reproduced below is a melody from the Hindustani *kathak* dance.

5   *Transcription of a Hindustani Lehrà. The Art of Gopi Krishna, The Gramophone Company of India Ltd, ECSD-2373, side 1.*

This constantly repeated melody is a *lehrà*, a melody marking the first beat of a rhythmic pattern for both the listener and the dancer, a necessary aid when we consider the extreme complexity at times of the drum and dance patterns. One could expect that an especial sensitivity has developed in this North Indian tradition for the shaping of the repetition. Of course, anything may be repeated – simple habit will aid acceptance – but the repetition will not sound convincing if one cannot sense its necessity.

The Indian melody is comprised of two groups of unequal length and its cardinal points are not sharply delineated: the final tone is also the opening tone. This contributes to the melody's strong sense of continuity. Example 6 offers a proposal for the division of the melody in its component parts.

6   *Rhythmic analysis of example 5.*

The shortest part of the melody follows the longest: rhythmically it is an abbreviation. This abbreviation could easily be resolved if the melody's asymmetrical characteristics were to be removed, as shown in example 7.

7   *Transformation of melody 5.*

Also note that if the melodic sections are rounded off with longer note values, the emphasis on the first beat tends to disappear (see example 8).

8   *Transformation of melody 5.*

These last, invented, examples also demonstrate that the original melody, with its falling and rising motion, is not perfectly symmetrical, which would lead to an impression of stasis, and has instead a distorted symmetry of motion.

The sense of the necessity of repetition seems to be partially a result of the unequal length of the melodic sections: the audio-psychological experience of 'drive' goes hand in hand with the structural phenomenon of 'abbreviation'. This impression of necessity is reinforced by the fact that the closing tone also serves as opening tone. And it is additionally stimulated by the melodic historical tradition: in Indian tradition the low C of the example could serve as a melodic closing tone while the high C could be the rhythmic closing tone. As these functions do not coincide, the melody is 'doomed' to turn in circles. The music is more than repetitive; it is cyclic.[4]

MIRROR STRUCTURE . . .

When the melody of *Car nos vignes,* shown in the first example, is examined purely as a series of pitches, one is immediately struck by its nearly exact mirror structure (see example 9).

9 *'Car nos vignes sont en fleur', seventh movement. The mirror structure of the pitch cycle.*

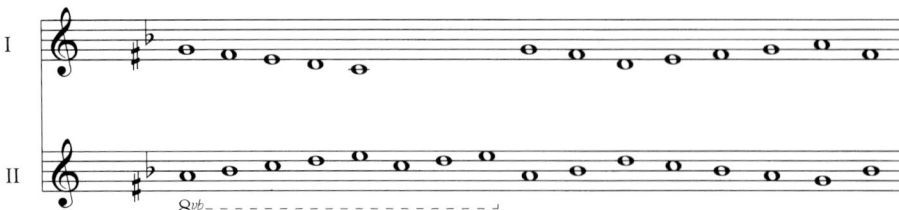

Here both halves (I and ll) are placed above each other in such a way that one can envision a horizontal symmetry-axis: a landscape reflected in water. Mirror symmetries are quite common in nature and are not infrequent in art, especially in the decorative arts.[5] But what does mirror symmetry imply in music?

In the form presented in the example above, the symmetry has no musical meaning. Music is, after all, a temporal art. Translating these musical sounds into a visual metaphor, we could say that from left to right we first view a landscape, and allowing the gaze to wander in the same direction we then see it reflected in a lake. This is an example of the absurdity of visual-auditive comparisons. These types of analogies are even precarious in the case of vertical axes. A vertical symmetrical axis divides an image of Mount Fuji equivocally in rising and falling slopes, but 'mirrored' scales actually do relate to each other in this way; while the distinction right and left is irrelevant in the first case, the difference between before and after is essential in the second. The visual relationship of image and mirrored image stresses the aspect 'replica' (wiph inversion), but auditive relationships underline the aspect 'complement'. Melodic rising and falling form a pair, just like inhaling and exhaling, tension and relaxation, positive and negative.

On a more abstract level, there may still be a similarity in the psychological experience of melodies like that in the last movement of *Car nos vignes* and visual mirror symmetry; the similarity lies in the impression of balance that is created. This experience may be sprengthened in music by constant repetition, for even though we cannot create infinite music, repetition is one means of dispelling the conception of time as a dimension of progression and change, so that one is not aware of any goal beyond the repeated structure. Moreover, the aspect of repetition makes it more difficult to think unequivocally in terms of *before and after* or even to determine *cause and effect*. If one were to sing the example above from the first to last note and no further, one's strongest impression would be that the second half is the complement of the first half, but if one repeatedly begins the melody anew, where then is the beginning and the ending? Is not the first half equally the complement of the second half? And repetition, albeit of a special type, is precisely what happens in this composition by De Leeuw. One need not wonder at the complementariness of musical motion and counter-motion as it is always present in some form or another. If a melody begins with an ascending motion, then this will necessarily be compensated at some point for otherwise the melody would exceed the range of the voice or instrument (special meanings arise if the melody continues this motion to the very limits, as happens in the last movement of Messiaen's *Quatuor pour la fin du temps*). But what has been merely a tendency in much music becomes 'absolutized' (to use Mondrian's expression) in De Leeuw's music to stricter mirror-forms, as has from time to time previously occurred in western art music. In this sense it resembles the music of Webern, Bach and the Franco-Flemish traditions. What a beautiful moment it is when at the end of the mirror fugues in the *Kunst der Fuge*, the symmetrical, ambiguous diminished seventh chord is followed by silence (see examples 10a and b).

10 a/b *Johann Sebastian Bach, 'Kunst der Fuge', two corresponding excerpts from mirror fugues.*

Let us move on from these aspects of mirroring, balance and their stylization and absolutization. Creating symmetry is certainly not the object in every work of art. At times it is even consciously avoided. There are many examples of this in western art. In the Japanese ritual tea ceremony, certain objects are intentionally placed askew and it is an extension of the age-old Japanese tradition of asymmetry that can still be found in the work of Yohijo Yamamoto and other Japanese fashion designers. If symmetry embodies completeness and rest, asymmetry serves dynamism and change. And the sensitivity to dynamism, thought by some art critics to be the essential characteristic of Zen Buddhism, has exerted a strong influence on Japanese art.[6] Significant in this context is the equilibrium of the well-known, old Chinese symbol for the dynamic character of the relation between *yin* and *yang*, *T'ai-chi T'u*; the outline of the symbol, a circle, circumscribes an infinite number of mirrored symmetrical planes, but the representation of the process taking place within the circle is void of these. We could speak of *rotational symmetry* – note that motion is implicit in this term – with the middle of the circle serving as central point. Asymmetrical distortion of symmetry confers motion on stasis. This is what happens in the Hindustani lehrà shown above, and it is also an aspect of De Leeuw's compositions.

... AND MOTION

The melodic sections of musical example 9 are unequal in length; compared to the first half (I), the extra group of ascending tones, C-D-E, effects a deceleration in the passage of the second half (II). At the same time, acceleration takes place in the second half caused by progressively smaller ascending groups of tones following upon each other; first five, then three and finally two tones (A-B flat, C-D-E, C-D-E, A-B flat). In part because of the addition of the group C-D-E, there is a preponderance of ascending motion by seconds in the melody as a whole. The ascending motion in this melody of 29 tones already begins on the 8th tone and continues until the 24th, including the previously mentioned process of musical abbreviation guiding the music from the lowest to the highest point.

Moreover, part of the melody sounds in fact an octave lower, as has been indicated in example 9. In consequence, the resultant division of registers in middle (in I), low and high (in II) lacks an actual return to the original level.

Descending motion and a return to the middle register are needed to eliminate this double disruption of balance. Both are provided in simple fashion by the repetition of the melody itself! Thus, once again, a certain disruption of balance causes the impression of motion in the melody and of reforging the act of repetition to one of cyclicity.

The rhythm participates in these processes in its own way. The rhythmic cycle consists of simple and compound patterns with a variety of long-short (and incidental short-long) proportions. This variety gives expressiveness and unpredictability to the musical progression. There are no exact repetitions of patterns, with the exception of a single case where the repetition does not follow immediately. The constitution of the patterns is shown in example 11 (page 154), according to their delineation in the score.

Above left:
Spring 1965, in the garden of his home in Hilversum with, from left to right, his children, Patricia, Dominique, Ariane and Isabelle.

Bottom left:
At a symposium in Manilla, 1966. Seated from left to right are Iannis Xenakis, Ton de Leeuw and the Philippine composer Jose Maceda.

Above:
At the festival 'The Autumn of Warsaw', September 1966.

11 *'Car nos vignes sont en fleur', seventh movement, analysis of the rhythmic cycle (initial statement).*

The thoughts behind the schematic representation in the rhythmic example are:

1.   The initial phase of the cycle – at least at its first appearance – is characterized by the regularly gradated abbreviation of the patterns by one crotchet.

2.   The process of abbreviation is interrupted by the introduction of compound patterns with a total length of five crotchets (i^1, i^2) After this comes figure j, which uses the second half of pattern i (the dotted crotchet with quaver); this fragment of figure i appears twice in j^1 which then concludes with a single crotchet not followed by any shorter note value. Long without short, that is a new development; there is a hint of elision and an accelerated transition to:

3.   The third phase in which i^1 reappears, this time however not followed by i^2, but by a pattern that is comparable to j^1 without the first two rhythmic values. The long element within this pattern is distinguished by a division in triplets that is unique to the entire cycle and that could be thought of as a signal announcing its conclusion. A short value is missing at the end of j^2, accelerating the entrance of:

4.   The first phase of the cycle (1). . ., and so on.

In summary, the cycle is characterised by a constant process of abbreviation. The aspect of curtailment of the pitch cycle also contributed to its impression of momentum: the number of tones following the intervals of the fifth filled in with movement in seconds is progressively diminished (see example 9): two after the descending G/C (G-F sharp), one after the ascending D/A (F sharp): and then three tones, followed by two after the ascending A/E (C-D-E and A-B flat), and one following the descending D/G (B flat).

The abbreviation of the rhythmic cycle is manifested on a local level in phase (1) by the removal of a rhythmic value, and on a higher level is the product of the omission of a pattern in phase (3) (i^2), in relation to phase (2), and of the fact that another pattern, j, is presented in abbreviated form. Through this, the cycle plunges forward, as it were, to its repetition.

THE MECHANICS OF THE SHIFTING

Together with these aspects of balance and motion, there is yet another propelling factor (and, at the same time, the opposite of this) in the seventh movement of *Car nos vignes*: the simultaneity of occurrences.

In many of De Leeuw's compositions, one or more aspects are differentiated in a very elementary manner: whether in separate voices or with various aspects of one and the same voice, elements are displaced in relationship to each other.[7] One could call such shifting 'period dissonance'. In the case of simultaneously beginning, repeated patterns of unequal length, this dissonance – the 'beat' between periodic units – is eventually resolved in the concurrence of their beginning. Note that the mechanics of this displacement is also here rooted in 'imperfection'. In the closing melody, this is brought about by the

The recording of Spatial music I *with The Netherlands Radio Chamber Orchestra under the direction of Paul Hupperts took an entire week. From left to right are Ton de Leeuw, sound technician Brico and recording director Akkerman, December 1967.*

On the jury of ISCM in Prague 1967, with the Japanese composer Yoritsune Matsudaira.

inequality of the length of the pitch cycle – 29 tones – and the cycle of rhythmic values – containing 30 elements (see examples 9 and 10).

The combination of a pitch and rhythmic pattern of different lengths in a single melody resembles the relationship between *color* and *talea* in the motets of the Ars Nova: there however, the relationship is guided by the proportions of whole numbers, 2: 3 for example, with an idea of overriding unity. De Leeuw's method is of the additive type that is found so often in the work of Messiaen, where, for example, the difference between the duration of units may only consist of a single rhythmic value.

With each successive repetition of the cycles, identical pitch patterns are projected on new rhythmic values and identical rhythmic patterns are shifted to other pitches. But the original relationships are made audible in the following special way. The composition begins with a tenor 1 solo; tenors 2 and 3 accompany him with the second run through of the rhythmic cycle, and in the succeeding statements he is joined respectively by the basses, altos and sopranos. Each new part is of course subject to the shifting between the rhythmic and pitch cycles in effect at that moment. Regarding the other parts, which had already begun, at a certain moment a small intervention cancels the shifting of the cycles, and the version of the melody corresponding to its first appearance is sung. The first time that this happens has already been shown in example 4.

This method is as simple as it is effective: with the tenor 1 part, which opens the piece and is shown in example 4 where the melody is being sung for the second time, the 'extra' rhythmic value in relationship to the pitch cycle, namely the crotchet, is removed before the close of the rhythmic cycle, leading to the reversal of the shifting that had already occurred between the pitches and rhythms. At the close of the rhythmic cycle, the value is again inserted, as is indicated in example 4 with **. The third time that tenor 1 sings the melody, two crotchets are removed from the corresponding place and later again inserted, and so on, so that with each time the new version of the melody is heard with a newly entering voice, the old version sounds with it. This also applies to all the voices entering after tenor 1, but each of these revert temporarily to their own original version of the melody.

This first begins two bars and later three bars prior to the end of the rhythmic cycle; in each case the voices diverge just before the high D. Of especial poignancy are those moments of heterophonic fanning out coinciding with the words and phrases 'flammes', 'le feu dévorant de l'éternel', 'l'amour', '(le feu) dévorant de l'amour'. At the beginning of the rhythmic cycle following this, after the necessary rhythmic values have been inserted, the voices reach again a unison passage. As the number of voices grows with each repetition, the heterophony becomes increasingly complex but the union of voices immediately after is also increasingly powerful. How this accumulative process works can be seen in the representation of the seam between the fourth and fifth statements of the cycles, shown in example 12.

12 *'Car nos vignes sont en fleur', seventh movement, fourth and fifth statements of the pitch/rhythm cycles.*

The inequality of the lengths of the pitch and rhythmic cycles leads to a cyclicity with a scale, larger than any yet mentioned in this article; it is driven by the elimination of inequality, in the concurrence

of the beginning of the cycles: the moment following the 30th appearance of the pitch cycle and the 29th of the rhythmic one. In art it is
not necessary to present a process in its totality in order to demonstrate
it, and this does not happen in *Car nos vignes* either; using elision, the
original melody returns with the sopranos and altos after the fifth
unfolding of the cycles.

The seventh movement is a masterpiece of balance in motion.
Dominating the unison section is a sense of change caused by the
progress of the shifting process; but in the heterophonic passages the
listener is allowed the unusual temporal perspective of the simultaneity of the possibilities.

Back to the source

"Mets-moi comme un sceau sur ton coeur
comme un sceau sur ton bras
car l'amour est fort comme la mort:
la passion est indomptable comme le séjour des morts
ses flammes sont des flammes de feu dévorant de l'éternel,
des torrents d'eau ne sauraient éteindre l'amour
des torrents ne sauraient énteindre le feu dévorant de l'amour."

(text of the seventh movement of Car nos vignes, from Canticles 8:6,7)

The vocal ensemble in the seventh movement of *Car nos vignes*, like
in the first movement, is treated as one whole, but in a thoroughly
different manner. In the first movement, where a state of slumber is
suggested, the unity is symbolic for the not yet present consciousness
of separation from the other: a musical *nebula*, music *in utero*. At the
end of the first movement the separation seeps into consciousness,
and in the movements that follow, when the woman begins her search,
and the man and woman sing to each other, the ensemble is split up,
with the increase in musical articulation, for instance in choruses and
soloists or in heterogeneous groups; this is especially evident in the
sixth movement, an intense expression of the uncertainties of love.
Then, on a higher level than was heard at the beginning, unity returns
in the seventh movement, with a text in which the feeling of separation
is transferred to one of ecstasy at being united with the Loved One.
Their union is made clear in the increasingly powerful unison, but one
having moments of increasingly varied fanning out of the multitude

Above:
East-West congress of the International Music Council in Moscow, October 1971.

Bottom:
During the congress Ton de Leeuw unveiled a statue of the composer Zachary Petrovitch Paliashivili(1871-1933) on the invitation of the Minister of Culture in Tbilisi, Georgia. Georgian dance was performed as part of the festivities and Ton de Leeuw seized the opportunity to study Georgian folk music.

of voices. Strikingly applicable to these many-voiced passages are
Thorkild Knudsen's words on the Gaelic psalms, music of . . .

> [. . .] individual people, who in the singing fellowship reserve
> the freedom to bear witness of their relation to God on a
> personal basis.[8]

This reference to Scotland also has a personal background.
Returning from field research in 1971, I brought several recordings
of Gaelic Psalm singing and one afternoon years later, I played them
for Ton de Leeuw, who at that time was still one of my colleagues
at the University of Amsterdam. He pushed aside a pile of admin-
istrative work to make the time.

After the music had finished, he sat motionless, and I found
him sitting in the same position a half hour later when I returned from
some work in another part of the building. Finally, he stood up, put
his jacket on and headed for the door, uttering these words:

> After that music it would be senseless to continue with office
> work today.

Whether or not this listening experience was the source of
the last movement of *Car nos vignes* is not really a very important
question. The comparison between these musics will not be a simple
matter. The Scottish psalms come from a collective, more or less
spontaneous transformation of imported melodies and styles of singing
ultimately resulting in a multiplicity of variants and a rich heterophony.
The heterophony and melodic variation of *Car nos vignes* are the result
of a more rational structural design.

This rational structural design is, in varying degrees, characteristic of the tradition of western composition. Here, in the music of
Ton de Leeuw, it is applied in a study of unity and diversity, balance
and dynamism, temporal progression and simultaneity. In this orientation on the essentials of life, De Leeuw combines Mondriaan's
intuitive formalization of lines and proportions in nature with
Mandelbrot's mathematical simulation of natural and social processes:
sorcery with cyclically repeating and interfering patterns.

THE SPATIAL ASPECT IN THE MUSIC OF TON DE LEEUW

Jurrien Sligter

In this article I will examine a series of works in which Ton de Leeuw experiments with various arrangements of deploying musicians:

Spatial music I for 32 to 48 players	1966
Spatial music III for chamber orchestra in 4 groups 1967	
Spatial music IV for 12 players 1968	
Haiku II for soprano and orchestra	1968
Lamento Pacis I, II and *III* for choir and orchestra	1969
Spatial music II for percussion in variable groups	1971
Music for organ and twelve players 1971	
Canzone for 10 brass instruments 1974	
Car nos vignes sont en fleur for a cappella choir	1981

Instead of beginning with analyses – which easily deteriorate into a list of musical examples – and summing up with several obligatory remarks regarding the fundamental aesthetics and philosophy of these works, I would like to confront the reader from the onset with my reasons for investigating precisely this aspect of the composer's work. In conversations with Ton de Leeuw I have time and again noticed that his reactions to musical, theoretical or human problems is always such that the topic of discussion is suddenly placed in a much broader perspective. It is as though the world suddenly becomes larger, more spacious. He is one of those personalities whose 'inclusive thought' gives an opening to psychological space. Because the dividing line between a person and their work is imaginary, we could conclude that the way Ton de Leeuw explores physical space in the works mentioned above, must reflect something of the breadth of his human space. Reciprocally, I hope to demonstrate that the use of spatial effects does not always imply an expression of psychological space.

Let me clarify my point: just as there are people who in conversation create broader perspectives, space, open new vistas, so is there music that generates expansiveness and opens new panoramas. Some people are able to support their view persuasively, even brilliantly, but their listeners are reduced to a state of helplessness for there remains no room for subtle distinctions. Equally, some music compels spellbound listening but its very forcefulness leaves one helpless.

Here is a concrete example: in a lecture I once held on the Second Viennese School of composers, I decided to open the evening with a recording of the overture to *Tristan und Isolde* by Richard Wagner. To save time, and because the music is very well known, I intended to listen only to an excerpt. However when I reached for the volume knob I was unable – in sympathy with the listeners - to stop the music: it had taken complete control of me. Why is it that the *Trio* for flute, viola and harp by Debussy, or a motet by Josquin, generates a liberating psychological expanse, while the music of Wagner, Richard Strauss or the early Schoenberg draws us into a whirlwind of feelings, seeming to cast us in a crippling pit?

Although it is exceptionally difficult to objectively outline the nature of such a psychological question, let alone offer an unequivocal answer, this type of ethical problem is often a significant – and sometimes unconscious – factor in the composer's developing of an individual style. The question of the spatial effect of music brings us to the thoroughly individual way that Ton de Leeuw handles physical space. On many occasions Ton de Leeuw has objected to the romantic artist's subjectivism:

> The concept of creating music to convey one's personal emotions came into existence only later, at a time that the artist considered himself the centre of the universe, a time in which only one form of service existed, the service to one's self. This addiction to self led to boundless over-estimation, pathological circumstances. It is no wonder that romanticism, the first epoch to produce great numbers of artists tipped off balance, could because of this generate enormous psychological tension.
>
> Especially since Beethoven, there has been a rapid expansion of all musical means that would multiply the transmission of these tensions. The artist definitively removed himself from any type of social service; he held a monologue.[1]

It is clear that this view of romanticism is fundamental in De Leeuw's admiration of Debussy, Webern, the music of the Middle Ages and Renaissance, and finally of eastern music. According to this view of romantic music, the limitation of living space is a result of the romantic artist creating a thoroughly individual world, of which he is the centre, and one that is furthermore *exclusive*, in other words excluding any other realities. Let us contrast this with the view of the medieval composer or eastern artist: they attempt to give expression to a collective experience founded on religion or on a cosmic experience in which each man is part of a larger Whole, in other words, an *inclusive* experience.

I would like to return to the interpersonal metaphor that I used to introduce the problem of psychological space in music. Some people are capable of presenting their view in an exceptionally compelling manner – sometimes brilliant – a view that arises in forcefully ploughing through a set path, like a jackhammer. The vision may be fascinating, for all its exclusivity, but it leaves no room for nuance or the input of others. In attending a lecture we are aware of the difference between a compelling presentation and the actual content of the message. With music, however, this difference is decidedly less clear. The content of the message and the means of presenting it – gigantic choirs and orchestras – are inextricably connected.

I must, however, mention a subtle distinction: although the romantic artist places himself on a pedestal, inflates his significance, one cannot neglect that behind the superficial facade, the work of a highly gifted personality deals with generally valid, archetypical aspects. For this reason, I have always found Ton de Leeuw's judgement of romantic art somewhat polemical at very least. The *nocturnes* by Chopin are also part of the romantic tradition, and even if we were to confine the argument to Wagner, it is undeniable that he was seeking symbols that were deeply rooted in tradition and the unconscious. Even Schopenhauer's philosophy – that was an inspiration to Wagner – is characterized by Platonic aspects: music is not primarily a manifestation of the Ego but of the Universal will. 'Trans-subjective elements'[3] are also distinctly present in the music of the romantics. This alone can explain the lasting influence of their music that today is even felt in China, Japan and Korea!

Nevertheless, the fact remains that some romantic composers delineated their view with such overly abundant musical means that 'the listener is reduced to helplessness'.[3] This attitude is thoroughly

Serving on a jury in the Amsterdam Concertgebouw, 1971. From left to right are Jef Maes, Marius Flothuis, André Jurres, Manus Willemsen, Ton de Leeuw, Karel van de Velde, Jos Wouters, Wouter Paap and Caraël.

Jury duties at the home of Olivier Messiaen in Paris, 1974. From left to right are Ton de Leeuw, Olivier Messiaen, Iannis Xenakis and Witold Lutoslawski.

Conducting a rehearsal of 'Gending', September/ October 1975.

With students at the Annual International Workshop for young composers, Queekhoven, 1980.

lacking in Debussy's *Trio* for flute, viola and harp, for example, music that to my mind has a freeing effect and excites a physical and psychological experience of openness.

In order to appreciate the originality of Ton de Leeuw's manipulation of space and the way – new in the sixties – he worked with this aspect in surmounting the compositional problem, let us begin by drawing comparisons with several composers of his generation.

STOCKHAUSEN

The first composer to be named in this regard is Karl-Heinz Stockhausen. His article *Musik im Raum,* dating from 1958, was a significant catalyst for many works experimenting with spatial aspects.

Gruppen for three orchestral groups was composed from 1955-56 and *Carré* for four orchestral groups from 1959-60. Stockhausen found an important source of inspiration in the electronic studio, where the four-track tape recorder made it possible to spread the sound over four speakers. *Kontakte* (1960), for four soundtracks, piano and percussion, is, soundwaves whirling through space, a thrilling experience in live performance.

Why did Stockhausen take up the spatial aspect in his composition? Firstly, there is a formal motivation: spatial effects were applied to compensate for the lack of structural differentiation in 'Punktuelle Musik'. They offered the possibility of creating a polyphony of layers that would remain recognizable through their spatial deployment.

Secondly, there is a historical motivation: as Schoenberg liberated timbre as a new musical parameter, so Stockhausen took the next step in freeing the parameter 'Tonort'. It was a further expansion of musical material. Space is nothing less than the fifth parameter in the process of serial composition. It offered the composer even more compelling means of drawing the listener into its world, in order to nearly overwhelm him. Stockhausen's manipulation of the aspect of physical space certainly does not necessarily mean that his work generates the experience of psychological spaciousness.

His expansive zeal is apparent in his proposal for the construction of new halls:

> Es müssen neue, den Anforderungen der Raum-Musik angemessene Hörsale gebaut worden. Meinen Vorstellungen entsprächen ein Kugelformiger Raum, der rundum mit

Lautsprechern versehen ist. In der mitte dieses Kugelraumes hinge ein Schalldurchlässige, durchsichtige Platform für die Hörer.

[New auditoriums ought to be built complying with the requirements of spatial music. My conception would be a spherical room surrounded by loudspeakers. In the middle of this sphere-shaped room would hang a transparent dais for the listeners that allows the sound to get through].[4]

In later works of Stockhausen, spatial deployment had more than just a musico-technical background. In *Sirius* (1975-77) for four soloists and four tapes, the four players are symbolic of the four wind directions, the four seasons, and so forth.

XENAKIS

Iannis Xenakis is a composer who fundamentally explored the theme space throughout his oeuvre. Considering that he began his career as an architect, this is not surprising. According to an interview with the composer in 1968, Xenakis has been occupied with the relationship between the perception of spatial and temporal phenomena since 1955:

> Je me souviens qu'en 1955-56, lorsque j'avais écrit *Métastasis* et presque terminé *Pithoprakta,* les questions de temps et de l'espace me préoccupaient beaucoup. Je cherchais si des études avaient été faites dans des sociétés plus anciennes ou plus archaïques que la nôtre, pour savoir s'ils concevaient le temps et l'espace de la même façon que nous.
>
> [I remember that in 1955-56, when I had written *Métastasis* and nearly finished *Pithoprakta* I was greatly preoccupied by questions of time and space. I tried to discover whether any studies had been carried out in older and more archaic societies than ours to find out if they percieved time and space in the same way as we do.][5]

Xenakis' well-considered criticism of serialism is also apparent in his spatial compositions. The spatial aspect is more than a mere structural facet facilitating differentiation. How it is used in his work is based among other things on his concept of music as ordered 'sonorous masses'. The stochastic method of composing offers him the possibility

of spatially 'directing' the sound. The spatial differentiation is thus
not only on a larger scale with Xenakis than with Stockhausen, it is
also more functional. The listener can follow processes that occur on
a spatial dimension:

> The speeds and accelerations of the movement of sounds will
> be realized, and new and powerful functions will be able to
> be made use of, such as logarithmic or Archimedean spirals,
> in-time and geometrically. Ordered or disordered sonorous
> masses, rolling one against the other like waves, etcetera, will
> be possible.[6]

Significant in the context of this article is that Xenakis, speaking
for example with regard to the work *Nomos Gamma* from 1967-68,
emphasizes a social aspect as motivating his spatial experimentation:

> The quasi-stochastic sprinkling of the orchestral musicians
> among the audience. The orchestra is in the audience and the
> audience is in the orchestra. The public should be free to move
> or to sit on camp-stools, given out at the entrance to the hall.
> Each musician of the orchestra should be seated on an indi-
> vidual, but unresonant daïs with his desk and instrument. A
> large ball-room would serve in default of a new kind of ar-
> chitecture which will have to be devised for all types of present-
> day music. The musical composition will be enriched through-
> out the hall both in spatial dimension and in movement. It puts
> the sound and the music all around the listener and closes up
> to him. It tears down the psychological and auditive curtain
> that separates him from the players when positioned far off
> on a pedestal, itself frequently enough placed inside a box. The
> orchestral musician rediscovers his responsibility as an artist,
> as an individual.[7]

Elsewhere, Xenakis reemphasizes this social aspect, pointing additionally to a physical significance:

> Le public touche les instruments et les sons: il a une proximité
> très grande. Avec cette disposition-là je change les musiciens,
> je les force à sortir de leur coquille, à devenir vraiment des

artistes, c'est à dire des hommes qui ont une trame dessinée par le compositeur, mais dans une action qui leur est propre, où ils sont pleinement responsables. Alors le public aussi devient responsable de cette manière-là; il est à côté du son, et il est obligé de suivre le compositeur.[8]
[The audience touches the instruments and the sound; there is a great sense of proximity. With that in mind I change the musicians, I force them out of their shell to become real artists, in other words men who are given a direction by the composer, but act entirely on their own and are fully responsible for their action. In this way the audience also becomes responsible; they are alongside the sound and have to follow the composer.]

Noteworthy in this passage is that Xenakis projects his compelling, rationalistic vision on the listener, who is nearly physically forced to follow the path chosen by the composer.

'SPATIAL MUSIC I' BY TON DE LEEUW

In *Spatial music I* by Ton de Leeuw the above mentioned factors play a role: the element of space as a structural determinant and the individualization of the instrumentalist. The work is furthermore an example of the exploration of aleatoric possibilities. Still, the term 'aleatoric' is not applicable here. Ton de Leeuw has always been opposed to the chance manipulations of, for instance, John Cage:

> The optimal control of form and concentration of Zen art could not in my mind coincide with John Cage's principles of chance, that, without adequate mental discipline, could lead to a stream of uncontrolled and non-committal products.[9]

In his introduction to *Spatial music I*, the composer writes that 'the whole progresses within a rigorous temporal structure and a clearly defined spatial ordering'. In studying the 'score' one encounters an ingenious planning propelling the macro-structure through space (refer in ex.1 to the indications 'rear', 'right side', 'front' and 'left side'), while spatial motion can further be found in the micro-structure of each excerpt. I will not give a detailed description of the mechanism of this motion, for, in my opinion, the piece is not characterized by that thoroughly individual manipulation of space that the composer was to exploit two years later in his work.

Although it is clear that De Leeuw's main objective was clarity – in the way that the musical structure and spatial effects are inter-dependent – his results are not really new in comparison to the work of Stockhausen and Xenakis. Compared to the dynamic spatial processes in Xenakis' work, this sought for clarity and lucidity in *Spatial music I* seems somewhat schematic and predictable (see example 1).

1 *'Spatial music I', diagram of form.*

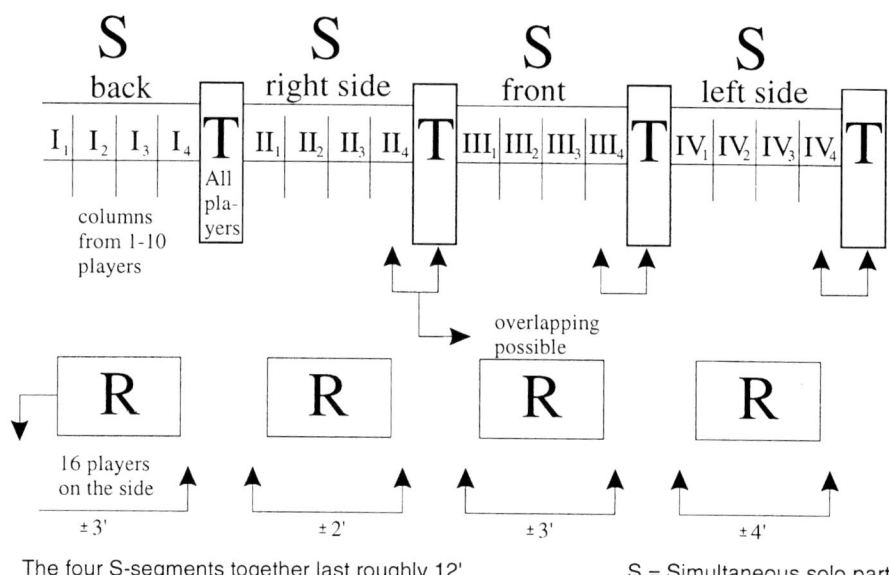

The four S-segments together last roughly 12'   S = Simultaneous solo parts
The four T-blocks - in free succession - also last roughly 12'   T = Tutti
The total is about 24'   R = Players on the side

Like Xenakis, De Leeuw emphasizes the individual responsibility of the instrumentalist:

> It is also asked that the players should have initiative of their own. Since one and the same part must be able to be performed by very different instruments, the indications for playing are to be taken merely as suggestions. Each player should therefore interpret in his way and in accordance with his own capabilities.[10]

'SPATIAL MUSIC III'

Possibly in reaction to the aleatoric elements in *Spatial music I*, a year later De Leeuw composed *Spatial music III* 'for chamber orchestra in four groups'(1967). At first sight it resembles a traditional score in which not a single note is left to chance. For the first time in the series of works dealing with spatial elements, the players are expected to change position during the performance. When, for instance, they move from position I to position II, they play from memory.

   This aspect, that was to return in later works, is not merely a fortuitous discovery, but also plays a significant role in the synthesis between the use of physical space and the creation of psychological space. I will try to clarify this point, based on observations of *Spatial music IV*, which in my opinion is the most successful and individual works of the *Spatial music I-IV* series.

'SPATIAL MUSIC IV'

Noticeable in *Spatial music IV* (1968) is once again the clarity of the total concept. This also manifests itself in the instrumentation: one pianist and two percussionists are placed in a permanent position forming a triangle in the hall (see example 2).

2   *'Spatial Music IV', positioning.*

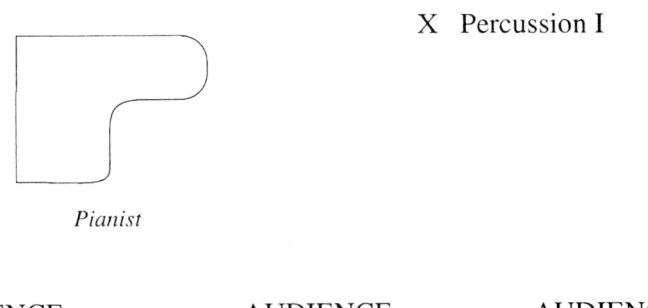

X   Percussion I

Pianist

AUDIENCE   AUDIENCE   AUDIENCE

X   Percussion II

There are also two contrasting instrumental groups which are mobile: a group of five wind instruments and one of four stringed instruments. When the piece begins, only the two percussionists and the pianist are present in the hall. For a minute and a half the first percussionist plays a ritual-like introduction with slow, periodic beats of the tom-tom. Only then do the wind players enter and take up position around the first percussionist. At this point, antiphonal interplay begins between the wind players, the percussionist and the piano soloist. Of importance to the musicians, incidentally, is that when they enter, the hall is already alive with sound, there is already music, which they in turn join in.

In the second phase, the string players enter the hall and group themselves around percussionist II. The ritualistic role of the percussionists is reinforced by the fact that their actions always mark the beginning or end of a structural section. In the middle phase of the piece, this occurs at regular intervals of 20 seconds, a method related to the incisive use of gongs in Javanese gamelan music.[11]

With each structural section of twenty seconds in the middle phase, an instrumentalist moves to a distant position in the hall, so that after nine sections (nine mobile instrumentalists), the players are spread throughout the hall. From their extreme positions, following a short promenade, the wind players regroup in position III around the piano and play the 'chorale'.

From this point on, *centrifugal* and *centripetal* spatial forces were to play a role in De Leeuw's music. At the end of *Spatial music IV* each mobile player follows his own path in leaving the hall in a ritualistic way.

Spatial effects and the structure of this work are clearly directly related. A build-up, as simple as it is effective, is achieved as a consequence of these processions (see example 3). The flexibility of the spatial deployment translates directly into structural differentiation.

3   *'Spatial Music IV', procession through the hall.*

	POSITION I	POSITION II	POSITION III	POSITION I	
entering the hall	around both percussionists	playing throughout the entire hall	only centrally placed around piano	around perc.	almost exiting the hall

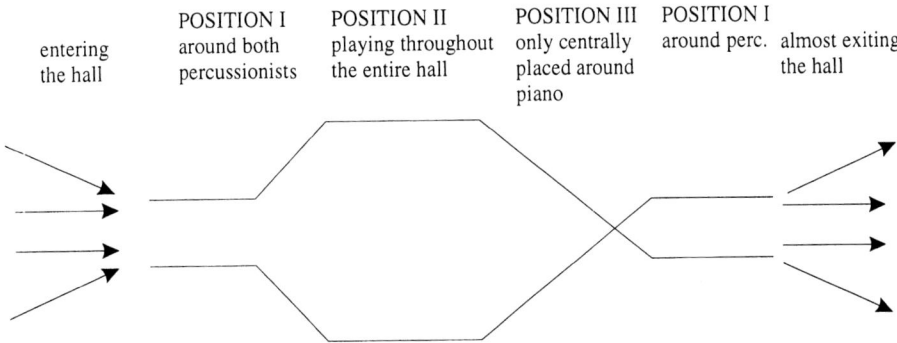

Ton de Leeuw encourages the individualization of the instrumentalist in an original manner through the principle of *free ornamentation*. The player is provided with a 'frame-work' and notes indicating the possible ornamentations. In this way he is granted freedom within certain limits making it possible for him to find an individual interpretation on the level of the micro-structure. The ornamental aspect has, however, even deeper implications to which I will later return. The following passage is from page 18 of the score:

4   *'Spatial music IV', model.*

The composer offers various ways of playing which could yield, for instance, the following:

5   *'Spatial music IV', realization.*

We see here Ton de Leeuw's solution to the problem – one with which Xenakis is also concerned – of individualization of the instrumentalist. The instrumentalist is partially responsible for the working out of the score in De Leeuw's compositions. It is no coincidence that this example is taken from the place where position II is reached in the piece, the position in which the players stand at the greatest distance from each other, thus maintaining the greatest independence.

THE SIGNIFICANCE OF THE SPATIAL ELEMENT IN 'SPATIAL MUSIC IV'

What is now extraordinary in the spatial effect of this piece?

First of all, the spatial deployment has symbolic meaning. The antiphonal interplay between the piano soloist, percussionists and two instrumental groups and the centrifugal and centripetal motion of the individual players moving throughout the available area effectively clarify the relationship between the *individual, soloist, group* and the *whole*. Ton de Leeuw works out an age-old musical tradition here. The path taken by the players in moving through the performance area becomes nearly a symbol for the path of life and reminds one of a Haiku text once used by De Leeuw:

> *Morning-haze:*
> *as in a painting of a dream,*
> *men go their ways*
> (translation: G. Henderson)

Of greater importance than this external, symbolic aspect is the impression made on the listener that the musicians are exploring the space of the hall, probing it to discover its qualities.

While space is itself adapted to the musical demands of Stockhausen and Xenakis, in De Leeuw's compositions musicians and listeners discover the qualities of the space in which they are sitting, an area with an individual nature. The percussionist's ritual introduction in *Spatial music IV* is like the lengthy intonations of the Indian musician who tries to attain harmony with the room in which he performs. In the introduction to *Spatial Music I* we read:

The acoustics of and spatial deployment in the hall are essential factors in playing. It is advisable to review all aspects prior to each performance.[1]

It would be an over simplification to assume that the impression of the performance space being probed is merely a result of the musicians walking around. This impression is also created by the nature of the patterns that are ornamented, in short, the musical material. Each instrumentalist elaborates on a limited and somewhat static musical material. The static element is a consequence of the small range of the melodic material, the use of floating rhythm, and exact or varied repetitions of short formulas. Formulas, motives, sound hesitantly in position II from all corners of the hall, creating a fascinating total-sound. One senses that the players are probing the area to discover its qualities (see example 6).

6   *'Spatial music IV', page 16, winds. The literally or varied repeated patterns are indicated by brackets.*

To create the impression of psychological space, latitude, it is not necessary to work with effects of physical space: listening to Debussy's *Trio* on an old fashioned monophonic record player can also generate the experience of this spatial quality. In other words, it is the musical material, the nature of the music that creates this effect. Inversely, the manipulation of spatial effects – for example in *Kontakte* by Stockhausen – does not automatically create psychological space.

In De Leeuw's music, however, there is a network of relationships between the macro and microstructure, between the spatial effects and the intended effect of the music. The spatial design of the macrostructure serves as a symbol for the course of life. On the level of the microstructure, a correspondence between the choice of spatial deployment and the musical material is evident. De Leeuw's manipulation of spatial effects is not a mere accessory to the music: there is a synthesis between the music, the means in which sound is positioned in the area, and the broadening effect on the listener.

'HAIKU II' FOR SOPRANO AND ORCHESTRA

Haiku II (1968) is one of the most frequently performed of De Leeuw's compositions from this period. It is an impressive work exploring new possibilities of integrating musical form and spatial effect.

The vocal soloist is the only one of the musicians to move about in this piece. In its course, she takes up six different positions, corresponding to the six haiku on which the work is based. While travelling through the hall she meets the six solo wind instruments, each of whom fill many different roles as the work progresses: soloistic, reacting to the vocalist, reacting to each other, and so forth. The wealth of various textures in this piece is so large that I will limit the discussion here to the sixth part, where characteristics typical of De Leeuw's work, like periodicity and variable ostinato, are effectively integrated in the spatial planning.

The structural design of this section lends itself to schematic representation. Six periods, each of ten bars, follow each other, with each being closed by a 'cadenza', of varying duration, played by the four solo wind instruments. Each successive cadenza is clearly longer than the previous one and serves as a recurrent point of repose. The final chord of the cadenza is marked with a fermata, but these are in each case of shorter duration. Because of this, the cadenza (the point of rest) has an internal dynamism. The longest version in period five leads directly to a fortissimo entrance in period six, for the cadenza in period five has no fermata.

September 1980 in Jakarta, Indonesia, at a workshop sponsored by the music department of LKJ, the academy of the arts in Jakarta.

Ton de Leeuw at his home in Hilversum, 1982.

With William W. Austin, author of the standard work 'Music in the Twentieth Century', on the campus of Cornell University, Ithaca, 1982.

The length of each ten bar period is different. There is one chord per bar, each bar being performed by a varied instrumental group. The direction of sound and the timbre are thus relocated ten times within each period (see example 7). The instrumentation, and thus the spatial effect, is also characterized by this periodicity. The second period repeats the succession of instrumental groups heard in the first period; after this periods three, four and five are each shifted one place further in the scheme of the instrumentation. Period six is shifted three phases further in relation to period five (see the arrows in example 8).

7 *'Haiku II' rhythmic structure.*

BAR	1	2	3	4	5	6	7	8	9	10	CADENCE
PERIOD 1	$\frac{4}{4}$	$\frac{4}{8}$	$\frac{3}{4}$	$\frac{3}{8}$	$\frac{3}{4}$	$\frac{3}{8}$	$\frac{3}{4}$	$\frac{3}{8}$	$\frac{6}{4}$	$\frac{6}{8}$	$\frac{4}{4} + 8"$
PERIOD 2	$\frac{3}{4}$	$\frac{3}{8}$	$\frac{2}{4}$	$\frac{2}{8}$	$\frac{1}{4}$	$\frac{1}{8}$	$\frac{3}{4}$	$\frac{3}{8}$	$\frac{3}{4}$	$\frac{3}{8}$	$\frac{4}{4} + \frac{4}{4} + 6"$
PERIOD 3	$\frac{2}{4}$	$\frac{2}{8}$	$\frac{5}{4}$	$\frac{5}{8}$	$\frac{2}{4}$	$\frac{2}{8}$	$\frac{4}{4}$	$\frac{4}{8}$	$\frac{4}{4}$	$\frac{4}{8}$	$\frac{4}{4} + \frac{4}{4} + \frac{4}{4} + 4"$
PERIOD 4	$\frac{2}{4}$	$\frac{2}{8}$	$\frac{4}{4}$	$\frac{4}{8}$	$\frac{3}{4}$	$\frac{3}{8}$	$\frac{2}{4}$	$\frac{2}{8}$	$\frac{6}{4}$	$\frac{6}{8}$	$\frac{4}{4} + \frac{4}{4} + \frac{4}{4} + \frac{4}{4} + 2"$
PERIOD 5	$\frac{2}{4}$	$\frac{2}{8}$	$\frac{1}{4}$	$\frac{1}{8}$	$\frac{1}{4}$	$\frac{1}{8}$	$\frac{2}{4}$	$\frac{2}{8}$	$\frac{2}{4}$	$\frac{2}{8}$	$\frac{4}{4} + \frac{4}{4} + \frac{4}{4} + \frac{4}{4} + \frac{4}{4} + 0"$
PERIOD 6	$\frac{8}{4}$	$\frac{8}{8}$	$\frac{4}{4}$	$\frac{4}{8}$	$\frac{4}{4}$	$\frac{4}{8}$	$\frac{4}{4}$	$\frac{4}{8}$	$\frac{9}{4}$	$\frac{9}{8}$	tam-tam

8 *'Haiku II', scheme of the instrumentation. The arrows indicate the shifts.*

BAR	1	2	3	4	5	6	7	8	9	10	CADENCE
PERIOD 1	brass ↓	Bsn hns.	str.	woodw.	S⁴*	brass	Bsn	str.	woodw.	S⁴	S⁴
PERIOD 2	brass	Bsn hns.	str.	woodw.	S⁴	brass	Bsn	str.	woodw.	S⁴	S⁴
PERIOD 3	hns.	str.	woodw.	S⁴	brass	Bsn hns.	str.	woodw.	brass	S⁴ hns.	S⁴
PERIOD 4	str.	woodw.	S⁴	brass	Bsn	str.	woodw.	brass	Bsn hns.	S⁴ str.	S⁴
PERIOD 5	woodw.	S⁴	brass	Bsn hns.	str.	woodw.	brass	S⁴ Bsn hns.	S⁴ str.	S⁴ woodw.	S⁴
PERIOD 6	Bsn hns.	brass	str.	woodw.	brass	Bsn hns.	str.	woodw.	S⁴ brass	S⁴ Bsn hns.	tam-tam + soloist

* S⁴ = 4 wind soloists

This combination of static (periodicity on several levels) and dynamic elements (variants, contractions and prolongations), characteristic of De Leeuw's work has a direct influence on the spatial effects of the sixth section of *Haiku II*. In the introduction to the score the composer states:

> This is a way of music-making which, in the form of antiphonal and responsorial singing, goes back to the beginning of time. It is perhaps for this reason and because of the way in which the percussion is used that the composer feels he has heard an almost ritual piece of music.

'LAMENTO PACIS I', 'II' AND 'III' FOR CHAMBER CHOIR AND INSTRUMENTS

The variation in the spatial aspect of *Lamento Pacis* (1969) is so extensive that it would be impossible to go into details in this article. The work deserves a separate discussion and repeated performances. I will list the deployment of the singers and instrumentalists, which varies for each movement. The first movement makes reference to the polychoral tradition, in the second movement there is a single instrumentalist, the piccolo player who moves throughout the room, and finally in the third movement the composition ends with the total individualization of all the musicians.

Lamento Pacis I: 2 groups
Coro I + instruments - Coro II
opposite to each other.

Lamento Pacis II: 4 separate groups, distributed over the hall:
group I : 4 basses
group II : 4 altos, flute-piccolo and viola
group III : 1 soprano, flute-piccolo and double bass
group IV :   3 sopranos, 4 tenore, flute-piccolo, two violins, viola, double bass, percussion   *Flute-piccolo is moving from one group to the other.*

Lamento Pacis III: Positioning: gradual transition from one, unique group (section A) towards complete disintegration: *all performers spread out over the hall.*

The diagram makes clear that in the course of the entire work there is an increasing differentiation of spatial deployment. In the third movement, a homage to Ockeghem, a symbolic effect is once again inherent in the transition made by one group towards total disintegration. Like in *Spatial music IV*, where the winds quote Stravinsky when they are grouped with the piano, here we find an Ockeghem (rhythmic) quotation while the choir still functions as a group. Here also, the gradual individualization of all the musicians calls to mind the haiku text: 'Men go their ways'.

Ton de Leeuw did not only experiment with spatial effects in the sixties. A concern with spatial deployment is evident in later works as well: *Canzone* for 10 brass instruments (1974), *Mountains* for bass clarinet and tape (1977), *Car nos vignes sont en fleur* for a cappella choir (1981).

'CANZONE' FOR TEN BRASS INSTRUMENTS

The deployment of the musicians in this work has been indicated by the composer in example 9. The first movement has an introductory character. Using long fermatas, it is divided in four sections, giving the impression of four repeated attempts to begin. The order in which the wind players enter is chosen so that each time a new line is traced in space. The first section begins with F#′ played by the first trumpet. The second section also begins with F#′, but the sound, played by the second trumpet, comes from another direction. The third section is announced by trumpet III and in the fourth section all instruments deployed in the outer ring enter simultaneously. The closing chord is played by all the instruments deployed in the inner ring.

9 *'Canzone', diagram.*

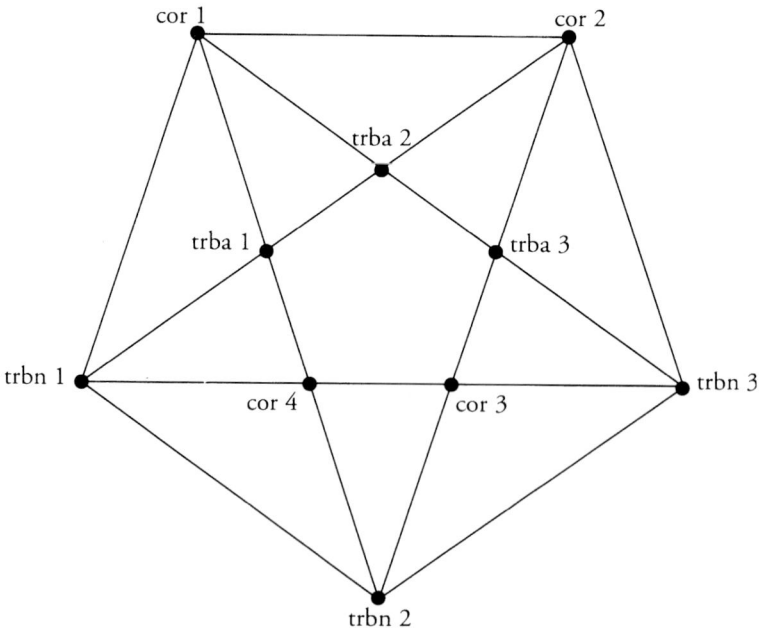

Basing our work on example 9 and indicating the sequence of entrances with arrows, the shifts in space occurring in the four sections can be demonstrated as in example 10.

10   *'Canzone', four diagrams.*

SECTION I

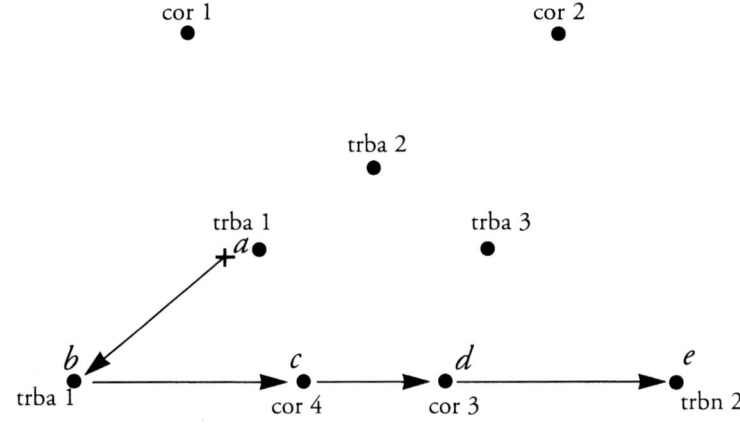

SECTION II

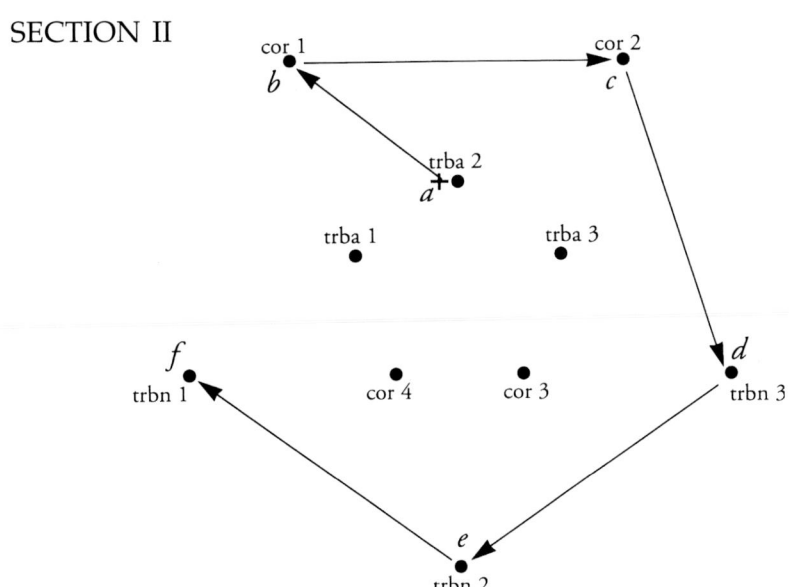

SECTION III

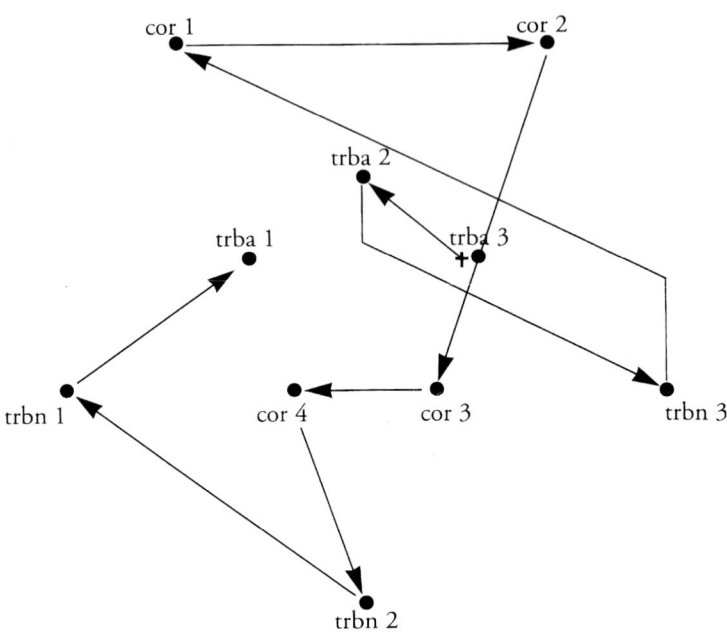

SECTION IV

strike up tutti

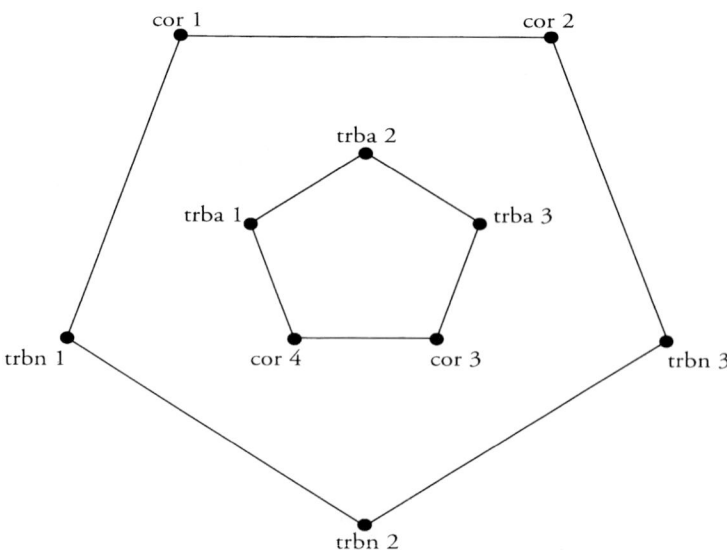

Example 10 clearly demonstrates that the number of entrances increases per section; spatial motion becomes thus more complex with each successive section. Like *Spatial music IV,* the impression is created of probing the space, with small motives of an ornamental nature and a limited range crossing the area. The repeated entrances on F#′ – a central tone from which the music gradually expands its range – is the cause of this impression (see examples 11 a and 11 b).

11a   *'Canzone', section 1, Trumpet 1 entrance.*

11b   *'Canzone', section 2, Trumpet 2 entrance.*

Musical and, at the same time, physical space is being probed! Synthesis is achieved in the fourth section with the instrumentalists in the outer ring taking collective action, after which those of the inner ring close the first movement.

'CAR NOS VIGNES SONT EN FLEUR'

Closing this discussion of experimentation with spatial effects in Ton de Leeuw's work is the example of a recent work for a cappella choir in which he achieves a synthesis between the musical form and spatial effect. Furthermore, the extra-musical implications of the work are indicated by the composer himself.[12] The term 'promenade' would be misplaced here. There is a direct relationship between the positioning of the choir and developments of the musical material, as the following diagram indicates (see example 12).

12   *'Car nos vignes sont en fleur', placement of the choir.*

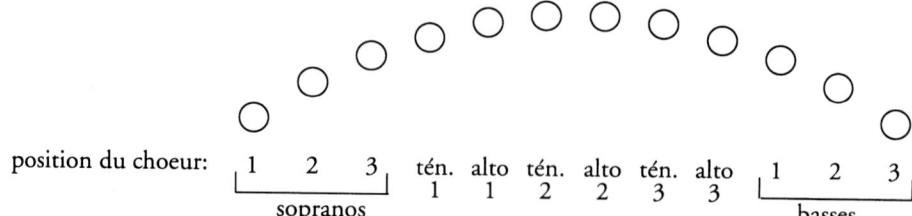

position du choeur: 1   2   3   tén. alto tén. alto tén. alto   1   2   3
                                      1   1   2   2   3   3
                       sopranos   basses

That the spatial effect and musical design correspond closely to each other can be seen most clearly in movement 1, where the tone A, the modal centre of the piece, is sung by tenor 2 and alto 2 during the entire first movement. Centrifugal and centripetal motion from the central A coincides with the spatial motion in the choir. The diagram shows the sequence of the entrances (see example 13).

13   *'Car nos vignes sont en fleur', entrances of the first movement.*

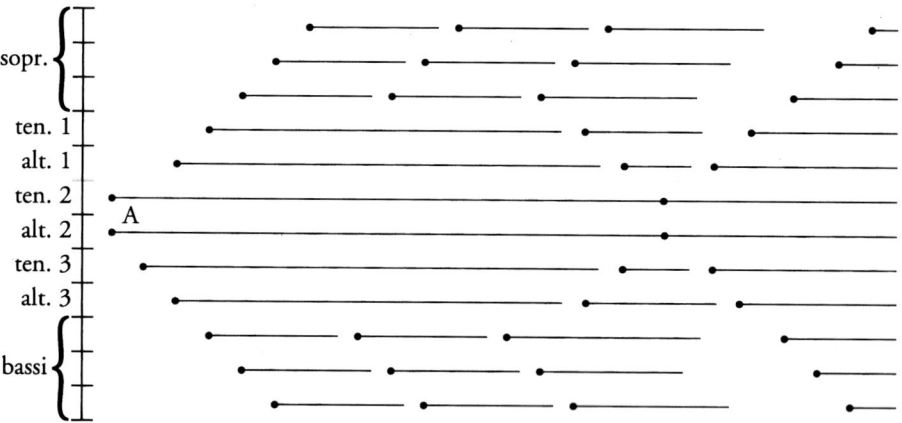

Ton de Leeuw points out the relationship between the beginning of the piece and the process of intonation in the music of India:

> What I would like is that the musical movement would take a long time. The centres of pitch and space must be slowly and firmly established in the singers' minds because it is essential that the singers feel the movement to or away from the centre; when the singer gets out of the centre he must feel it. This must first be established: a musical and a mental condition, like the tuning practices of Indian music, in which,

while tuning his instrument, the musician is also 'tuning' his mind or spirit to the music which he is to play. So I speak of an inner voice, a high degree of correspondence between the music and the musician. The music must have its inner meaning to the musician. The inner voice is a conception of great Oriental music.[13]

14 *'Car nos vignes sont en fleur', entrances of the second movement.*

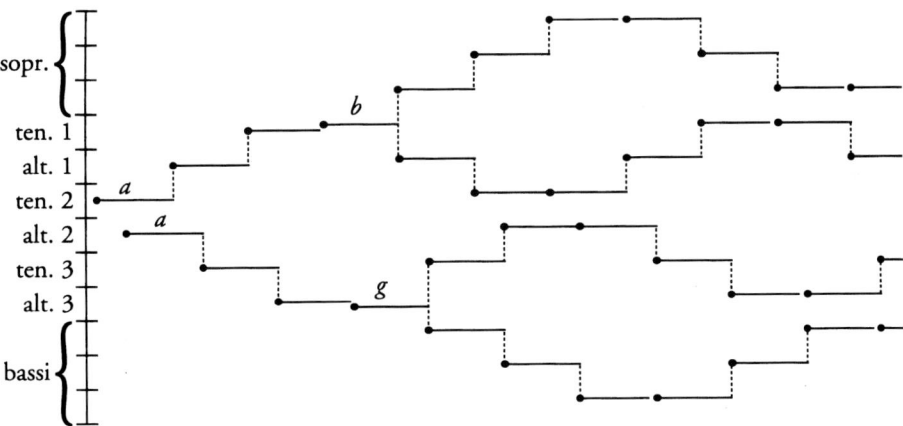

In his article *Back to the source* (1986, rev.1990) De Leeuw writes:

> The bourdon tones A-D-A are symbols of the centripetal background of extended modality and they represent the perfectly balanced inner centre of one who is in deep rest. With slow inhaling and exhaling motions, this centre expands and contracts – in different phases.[14]

The spatial motion of movement II can be demonstrated as in example 14. The diagram shows the sequence of entrances. There is even centripetal and centrifugal movement evident in the tonal material: the tone A progress to B and G, after which the composer gives the following indication: one may choose either ascending or descending intervals, or take the same tone again in order to create centripetal, centrifugal or stable motion in relationship to the centre A.

There are a series of imitations in movement III spread throughout the entire breadth of the choir, which is graphically represented in example 15. The relationship between this increased movement and the text is obvious:

Alors j'ai résolu de me lever, de faire le tour de la ville, dans les rues et sur les places je checherai celui que mon coeur aime. [Then I decided to go for a tour around the city, in the streets and in the places I went looking for the one I love.]

15   *'Car nos vignes sont en fleur', entrances of the third movement.*

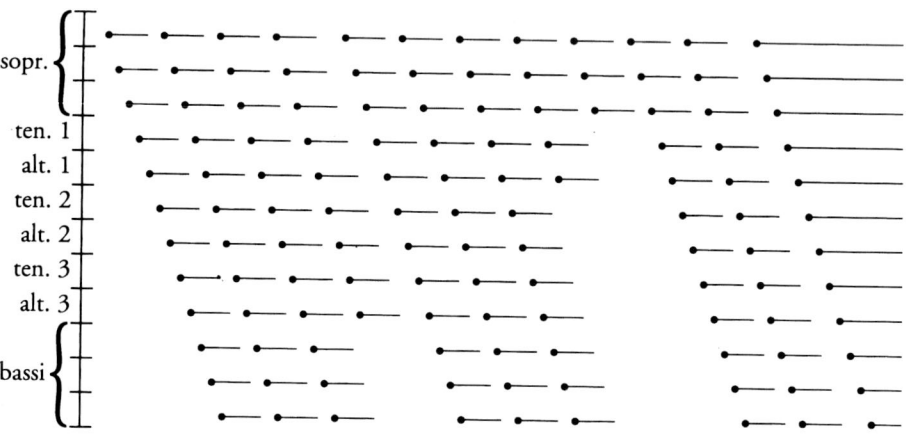

Contrast is created in movement IV between the two central voices, both of which repeat the central E of this movement, and the outer voices who now work as tutti groups. In movements V and VI we find the most heterogeneous spatial treatment of the voices. After the climax in movement VI all of the voices come together again (see example 16).

16   *'Car nos vignes sont en fleur', entrances of the seventh movement.*

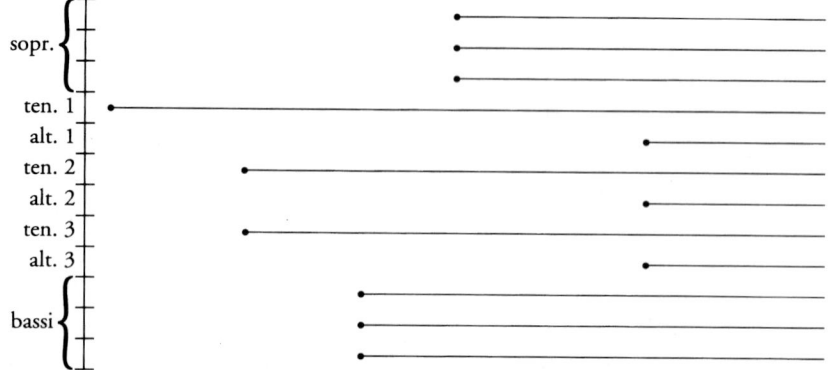

In his comments on the last movement of *Car nos vignes sont en fleur,* Rokus de Groot writes:

> In movement VII of *Car nos vignes sont en fleur,* like in movement I, the vocal ensemble is treated as a single whole, but in an entirely different manner. In the first movement, where a state of slumber is suggested, this unity is the symbol of a not yet conscious realization of the separation from the other: a musical *nebula,* music in *gestation.* At the close of movement I the realization seeps through, and in the following movements, where the woman searches, and the man and woman sing to each other, the ensemble splits, for instance in refrains and solo, or in heterogenous groups, through the increased musical articulation. This is especially evident in movement VI, an intense expression of the uncertainties of love. Then, on a much higher level than in the beginning, unity returns in movement VII, with a text speaking of the end of separation and the rapture of becoming one with the loved one.[15]

The spatial design of the work is not only linked with the tonal material, but also attains a symbolic significance that is closely connected to the text and to De Leeuw's aesthetic and philosophy.

I set out on these commentaries intending to point out the originality of Ton de Leeuw's manner of approaching the problem – of topical interest in the sixties – of spatial deployment. I further proposed that this concern with space is a reflection of the personal breadth of character of the composer.

It should be clear by now that the experience of psychological space is not dependent on the use of spatial effects in music. Even a composition for solo flute (for instance *Reversed Night,* written by De Leeuw in 1971) may be expressive of psychological breadth. Aspects such as floating rhythm, ornamental melody with a limited range but without specific direction, cyclicity and the like, play an important role in creating a non-compulsory musical experience.

Nevertheless, I have shown that the way Ton de Leeuw involves physical space in his work is a clear *continuation* of this musical attempt to create psychological space. Instead of conquering space,

*Ton and Arlette de Leeuw
attending a performance of
gamelan music, including
'Gending', at the
International Ferienkurse
in Darmstadt, 1985.*

*Ton de Leeuw on the terrace of his work
retreat in Vétheuil, France, in the
summer of 1991.*

De Leeuw probes it, allowing the listener to experience it. While in the music of Stockhausen, space, for technical reasons, serves as the platform in which the listener is bombarded with musical events from various corners of the hall, in De Leeuw's music the space in which the music is made takes on a life of its own.

After the winds in *Spatial music IV* have reached their greatest distance from each other, they group again around the piano playing a Stravinskian chorale. In this way they give expression to a super-personal and trans-subjective element in the form of a quotation. It coincides with the moment in which the players, who have been scattered throughout the performance area, join again in a group, thus giving expression to the super-personal element. This dispersion and drawing together, expansion and contraction of physical space, is directly comparable to the centripetal and centrifugal motion of the choir in *Car nos vignes sont en fleur*.

A meaningful correspondence is created between the musical material, spatial experimentation and the philosophy and aesthetics that are fundamental to the work of Ton de Leeuw. The inner breadth of the composer, the psychological space, is reflected in his use of physical space.

A quotation of Krishnamurti, much admired by De Leeuw, seems closely related to *Car nos vignes sont en fleur*, with its text, based on the Canticles, dealing with unification through love:

> If we attain inner *freedom* we will find space. In this space there is energy, not the type that comes into being in the friction of thought, but nevertheless energy. In this space, silence and immeasurable energy is the nameless, the timeless. But it can only be attained through actual, profound love and compassion.

NOTES

INTRODUCTION

1   Excerpt from 'Questions, Ideas and Expectations: Premises and Aims of an East-West *World of Music,* (UNESCO, 1978), XX/2, p.19-33, published in the Dutch edition of this book as 'Vragen, ideeën en verwachtingen'. See also 'Het thema Oost-West', *Composers' Voice 7602,* explanatory text.

2   The term 'ecology of music' is dealt with in 'Back to the source', on p. 73 of this book.

3   See 'Back to the source', p. 73 of this book.

4   Cited from Paul Griffiths, *Modern Music: The avant garde since 1945* (London 1981), p. 268, p. 295-296

5   Karlheinz Stockhausen, 'Interview über Telemusik', *Texte zur Musik 1963-1970,* Band II, ed. D. Schnebel (Cologne 1971), p.76.

6   See De Leeuw, 'Comments', *Proceedings of the International Round Table on relations between Japanese and Western Arts* (Tokyo 1969), p. 322-324.

7   Ton de Leeuw is the originator of international conferences for composers and musicologists that were held between 1974 and 1983 under the name Musicultura in Queekhoven (Breukelen). From 1984 until today these gatherings have been continued as part of the *International Composers' Workshop* (organized by Gaudeamus, Amsterdam).

8   See De Leeuw, 'Introduction', 'The East-West Theme', 'Analysis of *Gending',* 'Five Reflections', *Keynotes 3* (Donemus, Amsterdam 1976), p.66-74.

9   See Carl Dahlhaus, *Die Musik des 19.Jahrhunderts* (Wiesbaden, 1980), Neues Handbuch der Musikwissenschaft Band 6, p. 256-259.

CHAPTER 1

1   These travel diary notes appeared previously in *Mens en Melodie*, 1963, volumes XVIII/5 (p.144-149), 7 (p. 213-216) and 8 (p. 239-243). In 1961 Ton de Leeuw was the recipient of a grant from the Ministry of Education, Art and Science, enabling him to travel for several months throughout India in order to study the music. While there, he lectured on West European music.

2   Dagar brothers, the two greatest performers of dhrupad song, a strict and dignified style of singing from Northern India.

3   Sangeet Natak Akademi, an organization for the arts which branches throughout the entire country.

4   Pahkavaj, a percussion instrument used in accompanying dhrupad song.

5   Barathya Kala Kendra institute: a school in New Delhi for music and dance education.

6   Tampura: a four-stringed instrument that produces continuous, stationary tonic tones. The strings are plucked, no stopping is used and they are never muted.

7   Rasa. There is no precise English translation. It is best described as a type of emotion, with the qualification that this (artistic) emotion is quite different from the subjective experiences of our daily emotional life. Indian theorists distinguish between nine basic types: love, humour (or irony), pathos (or compassion), heroism, wrath, fear, aversion, amazement and serenity. At the time of Bharata, a sage living in the first century after Christ, serenity was   not listed among the rasas, because it was thought that this state precluded any emotion.

8   Raga. Another difficult to define combination of musical, ethical and emotional factors that together form a characteristic individuality. Ragas are often associated with the seasons, or particular hours of day and night.

9   Bharata Natyam and Kuchipudi, two dance styles from Southern India, of which the first is especially highly respected.

10 Carnatic music, music from Southern India.

11 Carthakali, a form of dance drama from Southwest India (Kerala).

12 See footnote 5.

13 Kathak dance, a style from Northern India, influenced by Islam.
14 Manipuri dance, a dance style of Northwestern India.
15 See footnote 13.
16 Parsis, descendants of Persian fire worshippers. A progressive group numbering 100,000, who lay their dead in the 'Towers of Silence', where the bodies are then devoured by vultures.
17 Sitar, the most popular stringed instrument of Northern India.
18 Sarod, also a highly developed stringed instrument.
19 A European state, whose name will remain unmentioned, had its national orchestra perform the following program in India: overture *Euryanthe* by [Carl Maria von] Weber, *Tijl Uilenspiegel* by R[ichard] Strauss, the *Fifth Symphony* by [Ludwig van] Beethoven and several works by Johann Strauss. The following day I read in one of the Hindu reviews: 'The programme concluded with the *Blue Danube* by Waltz...'.
20 See footnote 7.
21 See footnote 11 .
22 See footnote 9.
23 See footnote 10.
24 The European violin is played in southern India, but in a thoroughly different manner; the tuning is also different.
25 Mrdangam, the most important Southern Indian drum.
26 See footnote 6.
27 Tyagaraja, an almost religiously worshipped musician from Southern India, died in 1847.
28 Nagasvaram, a double reeded wind instrument from Southern India.

CHAPTER 2

1   This article appeared previously in *Mens en Melodie*, 1968, volume XXIII, p. 354-359.

CHAPTER 3

1   This article appeared previously in *The World of Music* (UNESCO 1969), XI/4, p, 6-17, and has been re-edited for this publication.

CHAPTER 4

1   This article appeared originally, both in French and English, as 'L'interaction des cultures dans la musique contemporaine' and 'Interaction of Cultures in Contemporary Music' in *Cultures*, (UNESCO et la Baconnière 1973), p. 13-32.
2   See for instance Trân Van Khê, 'Traditional music and Culture Change: A Study in Acculturation', *Cultures* I/I (1973), p. 195-209.
3   These insights are drawn from an interview that I conducted with the composer on Dutch radio in 1971.

CHAPTER 5

1   Opening speech of the Musicultura 1974 congress held under the auspices of UNESCO. It was published in 1978 as 'Questions, Ideas and Expectations: Premises and aims of an East-West Encounter' in *The World of Music*, (UNESCO, 1978) XX/2, p. 19-33.

CHAPTER 6

1   This article was written in the summer of 1986 and was later revised for publication. It has   not been previously published.
2   The correct translation of Sanskrit terms in western terminology – not very lucid in this area – remains a problem. I will later attempt to describe as much as possible.
3   Eliade, Mircea, *Le Yoga*, (Petite bibliothèque Payout, Paris 1954).
4   Thakar, Vimila, *Silence in action*, (Mrs. and Mr. Frankena, Holland 1968).
5   *Trois upanishads* (Isha, Kena, Mundaka), J. Herbert ed. (Edition Albin Michel, Paris 1972). I have chosen this French edition because the upanishads are appended with commentary by no one less than Shri Aurobindo.

LITERATURE CHAPTER 9

Andreasen, N.C., *The broken brain* (Harper & Row, New York 1984).
Andreasen, N.C. and Grove, W., 'The relationship between schizophrenic language, manic language and the aphasis' in *Hemisphere Asymmetries of Function and Psychopathology* Flor-Henry et al. eds. (Elsevier, N.Y. 1980).

Applebaum, E., et al., 'Measuring Musical Abilities of Autistic Children', *J. Autism Developm. Disorders* **9** (3) (1979), p. 279-285.

Bateson, G., et al., 'Toward a Theory of Schizophrenia', *Behavioral Science* **I** (1956), p. 251-264.

Bateson, G., 'A note on the double bind', *Fam. Proc.* **2** (1963), p. 154-161.

Benenzon, R.O., 'Music Therapy in infantile autism', *Brit. J. of Music Therapy* **7** (1976), p. 10-17.

Bever, T.G., and R.J. Chiarello, 'Cerebral dominance in musicians and nonmusicians', *Science* **185** (1974), p. 537-539.

Blackstock, E.G., 'Cerebral Asymmetry and the development of early infantile autism', *J. Aut. Chidh. Schizophren.* **8** (3) (1978), p. 339-353.

Chomsky, N., *Aspects of the theory of syntax* (MIT Press, Cambridge, Mass., 1965).

Clynes, M. (ed.), *Music, Mind and Brain: The Neuro-psychology of Music* (Plenum Press, New York 1982).

Critchley, M., 'Inter hemispheric partnership and interhemispheric rivalry' in *Scientific Foundations of Neurology* (Will. Heinemann Med. Books, London 1972).

Critchley, M, et al., *Music and the Brain: Studies in the Neurology of Music* (Thomas, Springfield Illinois 1977).

Cytowic, R.E., 'Aphasia in Maurice Ravel', *Bull. Los Angeles Neurol. Soc.* **41** (3) (1976), p. 109-114.

Domhoff, G.W., 'But why did they sit in the king's right in the first place?', *Psychoanalytic Review* **26** (1970), p. 586-596.

Ehrenwald, J., 'Beethoven: hero and anti-hero; portrait of a right hemispheric genius', *J. Amer. Acad. Psychoanalysis* **7** (I) (1979), p. 45-55.

Ferenczi, S., 'An attempted explanation of some hysterical stigmata' in *Further Contributions to the Theory and Technique of Psychoanalysis* (Hogarth Press, London 1926).

Galin, D., 'Implications of psychiatry of left and right cerebral specialization: A neurophysiological context for unconscious processes', *Arch. Gen. Psychiatry* **31** (1974), p. 572-583.

Hees, R.O., *Propuesta para una coordinación de las investigaciones musicoterapéuticas y musicomédicos – Introducción a la musicología clínica* (1976). Lecture held at the 2nd World Congress of Music Therapy in Buenos Aires, 1976.

Hees, R.O., 'Muziektherapie en Muziekwetenschap - naar een harmonie van sferen', *T.v. Psychiatrie* **80** (2) (1980), p. 99-123.

Hees, R.O., and Van Rest, E., *Muziektherapie van een 6-jarig autitistiform meisje.* Video demonstration for the Neth. Assoc. for Creat. Ther., in Amersfoort, 1986.

Hollander, F.M. and Juhrs P.D., 'Orff-Schulwerk: an effective treatment tool with autistic children', *J. Music Therapy II*(1974), p. 1-12.

Hoppe, K.D., 'Split brain: psychoanalytic findings and hypotheses', *J. Amer. Acad. Psychoanalysis* **6** (1978), p. 193-213.

Jakobson, R., 'Towards a linguistic typology of aphasic impairments' in *Disorders of Language*, A.V.S. de Reuck & M. O'Connor eds. (Churchill, London 1964).

Jakobson, R., *Child language, aphasia and phonological universals* (Mouton, The Hague 1968).

Jaynes, J., *The origin of consciousness in the breakdown of bicameral mind* (Houghton Mifflin, Boston 1976).

Jossman, P., 'Die Beziehungen der motorischen Amusie zu den apraktischen Störungen', *Mschr. Psychiat. Neurol.* **63**, (1927), p. 239-257.

Jünger, E., *Sprache und Körperbau* (Kostermann, Frankfurt a. M. 1969).

Kanner, L., 'Follow-up study of eleven autistic children' *J. Autism and Childhood Schizophrenia I* (1971), p. 119-145.

Kluen, F., *Analyse van een muziektherapie met een autistisch meisje. Een aanzet tot een biomusicologische benadering* (Doctoral thesis University of Amsterdam, 1987).

Leeuw, T. de, *Les Cultures musicales des peuples: traditions et actualité*, lecture held at the 7e Congrès International de Musique, Moscow (USSR) in 1971.

Leeuw, T. de, 'Influences mutuelles des cultures dans le domaine de la musique', *Revue Cultures* (UNESCO, 1973), p. 13-33.

Leeuw, T. de, *The adaption of Asian Music forms in contemporary Music*, lecture at the Asian Composers' Conference, Hongkong 1981.

Luria, A.R., *Higher cortical functions in man* (Tavistock Publications London 1966) (Originally a Russian text: Moscow University Press, 1962).

Luria, A.R., et al., 'Aphasia in a Composer' *J. Neurol. Sciences* **2** (1965), p. 288-292.

Mandell, J.M., 'Inter hemispheric Relating' in *Comprehensive Textbook of Psychiatry*, H.I. Kaplan et al. eds. (Williams and Wilkins, Baltimore 1980).

Nakamura, K., et al., 'The comparative and developmental study of auditory information processing in autistic adults' *J. Autism and Developmental Disorders* **16** (2) (1970), p. 105-118.

Nemiah, J., et al., 'Affect and fantasy in patients with psychosomatic disorders' in *Modern Trends in Psychosomatic Medicine* Vol. 2, W. Hill ed. (Appleton-Century-Crofts, New York 1970).

Neumann, E., *The Origins and history of Consciousness* (Bollington, Princeton, N.J. 1954).

Noy, P., 'The psychodynamic meaning of music (I-IV)', *J. Music Therapy* **4**/1-4 (1967) (50 pp.).

O'Connell, T.S., 'The musical life of an autistic boy', *J. Autism and Childhood Schizophrenia* **4**(3) (1974), p. 233-239.

Ornitz, E.M., 'Neurophysiology of Infantile Autism', *J. Amer. Acad. Child Psychiatry* **24** (3) (1985), p. 251-262.

Rest, E. van, *Prieya* (Doctoral thesis University of Amsterdam, 1985).

Rimland, B., *Infantile Autism* (Appleton-Century-Crofts, N.Y. 1964).

Sifneos, P., 'The prevalence of alexithymic characteristics in psychosomatic patients' in *Psychotherapy in Psychosomatics* Ruesch *et al.* (Edition Krager, Basel 1973).

Sparks, R., and Holland, A.L., 'Method: Melodic Intonation Therapy for Athasia', *J. Speech Her. Disord.* **4** (1976), p. 287-297.

Sperry, R.W., et al., 'Interhemispheric relationships: the neocortical commisures: syndrome of hemispheric disconnection' in *Handbook of Clinical Neurology, Vol.* **4** (Noord-Hollandse Uitgeverij, Amsterdam 1969).

Turnbull, C.M., *The Mountain People* (Simon and Schuster, New York 1972).

Ustvedt, H.J., 'Ueber die Untersuchung der musikalishen Funktionen bei Patienten mit Gehirnleiden, besonders bei Patienten mit Aphasie', *Acta Medica Scandinavia,* Suppl. **86** (1937), p. 1-737.

Viscott, D., 'A musical idiot savant: A psychodynamic study and some speculations on the creative process', *Psychiatry* **33** (1970), p. 494-515.

Wertheim, N., and Botez, M.I., 'Plan d'Investigation des fonctions Musicales', *Encéphale,* **48** (3) (1959), p. 245-254.

NOTES CHAPTER 9

1   This article is written with many thanks to Prof. Dr. H. van
    Engeland, Drs. R. de Groot, Drs. E. van Rest and Dr. J.C. Hees-
    Stauthamer for their valuable comments on earlier versions of
    the manuscripts.
2   For right-handed people (more than 90% of the population) this
    is the left hemisphere. In the case of left-handedness the same is
    true for the right hemisphere, although here the situation is less
    consistent and more complicated.
3   'Via Regia' is Latin for 'Royal Path'. Freud tended to speak of
    dreams as the 'Via Regia to the subconscious'. With this, he
    emphasized the importance of dreams in learning to understand
    the subconscious. In Freudian psychoanalysis, following this Royal
    Path, that is to say studying the dreams of the patient, is of eminent
    importance to the healing process.
4   Like dichotic listening techniques, computerized encefalographic
    methods, evoked potentials and so forth. The interested reader
    should consult J. Winson, *Brain and Psyche: The Biology of the
    Unconscious* (Doubleday, 1985).
5   As for the geographical direction – west: left; east: right – Domhoff's
    students follow the orientation of the Greeks who looking north
    had their good hand at the right side, from where the rising Aurora
    light came.

CHAPTER 10

1   Knudsen, Thorkild, 'Ornamental Hymn/Psalm Singing in Den-
    mark, the Faroe Islands and the Hebrides', DFS *(Dansk
    Folkemindesamling) Information* (1968) 2, (Copenhagen), p. 5-22. The
    quote is taken from p. 10.
2   Transcription from: Knudsen, Th., op. cit., p. 21-22.
3   From: 'The Cottar's Saturday Night', cited by Morag MacLeod in
    the liner notes of *Scottish Tradition 6, Gealic Psalms from Lewis*,
    Tangent TNGM 120.
4   These conclusions are supported by observations on Hindustani
    rhythm made by Sushil Kumar Saxena. His collection of essays
    on this subject has the fascinating title *The Winged Form* (Sangeet
    Natak Akademi, New Delhi 1979), the poetical summary of the

thought that the internal dynamics of patterns is a necessary element in giving form to a rhythmic cycle *(tāla)*. This cycle is esential to North Indian music. The most important point of orientation is *sama* or *sam:* "central because it both initiates and completes a rhythmic round" (p. 93). "Arriving at the *Sama* should be seen as an impulse of the *bandish* [form] itself. Similarly, the rhythm *itself* should appear to lapse back to the first beat." (p.91). Saxena explains the double position of *sama* – its 'pivotal quality' – by qualifying it as 'destiny' and a 'stimulus to further creation' (p. 135). An important concept of the dynamic shaping of the rhythmic cycle is *āmad,* an Urdu word meaning 'advent' or 'coming'. Musically: *āmad* 'may[. . .]appear to *activate or gather itself* for forward movement' (p. 131); in other words: "*āmad* emphasizes the selfactivation of *tāla*" (p. 143). As musical devices aiding this, Saxena lists the use of *āroha* and *avaroha:* ascending and descending melodic motion (p. 131); moreover the rhythmic pendant of *āroha:* intensifying, bringing rhythmic units closer together so that the successive components of the cycle give the impression of gradated, accelerating motion (p. 141-142, with analysis), with *sama* serving as 'resolution'. With all this attention to dynamic and propulsive aspects, one must keep in mind that it serves in repeatedly reaching the beginning of the cycle and is not explosive activity.

5   See Gardner, M., *Spiegelsymmetrie: Links en rechts in de natuur,* translated by G. Beekman, (Aramith, Amsterdam 1986), especially chapter 5 (original title: *The Ambidextrous Universe: Mirror asymmetry and time-reversed worlds,* (Basic Books, New York 1964).

6   Gardner, M., op. cit., *ibid.*

7   See also De Groot, R., 'Aspects of Ton de Leeuw's musical universe', *Key Notes* 23 (1986, p. 17-31).

8   Knudsen, Th., op. cit., p. 10.

CHAPTER 11

1   De Leeuw, Ton, *Muziek van de twintigste eeuw* (Oosthoek, Utrecht 1964), p. 5.

2   De Leeuw, Ton 'Terug naar de bron' (1986, rev.1990) translated for this book under the title 'Back to the source' on p. 73.

3   Ibidem, p. 97.

4 Stockhausen, Karl-Heinz, 'Musik im Raum', *Texte* band I (1958).
5 'Rencontres avec Iannis Xenakis', *Musique en jeu* (1970).
6 Xenakis, Iannis, *Formalized Music* (1971), p. 236. The original French edition dates from 1963.
7 'Rencontres avec Iannis Xenakis', op.cit.
8 'Rencontres avec Iannis Xenakis', op. cit., p. 4.
9 De Leeuw, Ton, 'Terug naar de bron', op.cit., p. 97.
10 De Leeuw, Ton, Introduction to the score of *Spatial music I*.
11 Kunst, Jaap, *Music in Java* (Den Haag 1973): 'Colotomic structure: The interpunctuation by which the gending (composition) is sub-divided into longer or shorter phrases.'
12 For an detailed discussion of this work the reader is referred to Dominick, Lisa, 'Mode and Movement in Recent works of Ton de Leeuw', *Keynotes,* (Donemus, Amsterdam 1983) nr. 17, p. 15-23, and De Groot, Rokus, 'Aspects of Ton de Leeuw's Musical Universe', *Keynotes,* (Donemus, Amsterdam 1986), nr.23, p. 17-31.
13 De Leeuw, Ton, Introduction to the score.
14 See also p. 89 of this book.
15 See also p. 160 of this book.

LIST OF WORKS

Listed here are (in as far as they are known): the year of composition, setting, duration, the source of the commission (if other than the government and/or the Fund for Creative Music) and publisher (if other than Donemus Amsterdam).

CHAMBER MUSIC

1948	*Scherzo,* for piano (2').
1948	*Trio,* for violin, viola and cello (14') .
1949	*Introduzione e passacaglia,* for organ (8').
1949	*Sonatine,* for piano (7').
1949	*String Quartet.*
1950	*Sonate,* for two pianos (21').
1950	*Four preludes* for piano (9').
1950	*Variations sur une chanson populaire française,* for piano or harpsichord (7').
1951	*Cinq etudes,* for piano (7').
1952	*Four rhythmic etudes,* for piano (8').
1952	*Trio,* for flute, clarinet and piano (13').
1952	*Five sketches* for oboe, clarinet, bassoon, violin, viola and cello (11').
1953	*Danse lente* for piano. Published in the periodical Elsevier.
1954	*Pastorale,* for piano.
1954	*Three African etudes,* for piano (7').
1954	*Lydian suite,* for piano (6').
1955	*Six dances,* for piano (6').
1955	*Andante and vivace,* for flute and piano (6').
1955	*Sonatine,* for violin and piano (7').
1957-58	*String Quartet nr. 1* (9'). Commissioned by the city of Amsterdam.
1959	*Piece for violin,* for violin and piano. Edition Metz.
1964	*String Quartet nr.2* (15').
1964	*Shell,* for flute, viola and guitar (18').
1964	*The four seasons,* for harp (8' 20").

1964   *Men go their ways,* for piano (14').
1966   *Night music,* for flute (9').
1967   *Music for violin* (13').
1968   *The nine rasas,* for piano.
1969   *Music for oboe* (7'). Commissioned by the Stichting
        Cultuurfonds BUMA.
1971   *Reversed night,* for flute (10').
1971   *Spatial music II,* for from 4 to 9 percussionists and electronic
        instruments (60' max.). Commissioned by the NOS.
1972   *Midare,* for marimba (7'). Commissioned by Michiko
        Takahashi.
1972-73 *Sweelinck variations,* for organ (12').
1973-74 *Music for trombone* (10'). Commissioned by the International
        Trombone Association.
1973-74 *Canzone,* for four French horns, three trumpets and three
        trombones (12'). Commissioned by the NCRV.
1974   *Mo-do,* for harpsichord or amplified clavichord (11').
1974   *Rime,* for flute and harp (8').
1976   *Left hand and right hand,* for piano (5'). Commissioned by
        the Rotterdamse Kunststichting. Edition Gerig, Cologne.
1978-79 *Modal music,* for accordion (12').
1984   *Interlude,* for guitar (13').
1987   *Apparences I,* for cello.
1987   *Apparences II,* for clarinet quartet.
1988   *Les adieux,* for solo piano.
1989   *Hommage à Henri,* for clarinet and piano.
1990   *Trio,* for flute, bass clarinet and piano.

VOCAL

1948   *Berceuse presque nègre,* for middle voice and piano (2'). Text
        Paul van Ostayen.
1948   *Diablerie,* for soprano and piano (2'). Text Jan Engelman.
1948   *Goden en zangers (Gods and singers),* for soprano and piano
        (5'). Text Adriaan Roland Holst.
1948   *Die Weise von Liebe und Tod,* for voice and piano (21'). Text
        Rainer Maria Rilke.
1949   *De ueren van de bittere passie Jesu Christi (The hours of the
        bitter passion of Jesus Christ),* for low voice and piano (10').

| 1950-52 | *Vijf liederen op teksten van Lorca (Five songs on texts of Lorca)*, for low voice and piano (9'). |

1950-52 *Vijf liederen op teksten van Lorca (Five songs on texts of Lorca)*, for low voice and piano (9').

1953 *Twee liederen op teksten van Gabriela Mistral (Two songs on texts of Gabriela Mistral)*, for soprano and piano (4').

1953 *Missa brevis*, for a cappella choir (12'). Commissioned by KRO radio. Annie Bank, Hilversum.

1954 *Vier koorliederen (Four Choir songs)*. Medieval text. Annie Bank, Hilversum.

1954 *Prière*, for mixed choir. Text Koran. Annie Bank, Hilversum

1954 *De toverfluit (The magic flute)*, four songs for soprano, flute, cello and piano (11'). Translation Bertus Aafjes. Commissioned by the Galant quartet.

1954 *Acht Europese liederen (Eight European songs)*, for middle voice and piano (12').

1955 *Vier liederen (Four songs)*, for 3 recorders and vocalist (5'). Medieval text.

1959 *Brabant*, symphonic song for mezzo soprano and orchestra (10'). Text Harriet Laurey.

1963 *Haiku I*, songs and interludes for soprano and piano (13'). Commissioned by the city of Amsterdam.

1966 *Psalm 118*, for 3-part choir and two trombones or organ (12'). Commissioned by the Centrum voor de kerkzang.

1968 *Haiku II*, for soprano and orchestra (12^1). Composed in celebration of the fiftieth anniversary of the Rotterdam Philharmonic Orchestra.

1968 *Vocalise*, for solo voice (4'). Commissioned by the Culturele Raad van Zuid-Holland.

1969 *Lamento Pacis I, II and III*, for mixed choir and instruments (27'). Text Erasmus.

1970 *Cloudy forms*, for 4-part men's choir (5'). Text Shi-T'ao.

1970 *The magic of music*, for 2-part choir (4'or 8').

1975 *The birth of music I*, for mixed choir (8'). Text Indian myth. Commissioned by the Cork International Choral Festival.

1981 *And they shall reign for ever*, for mezzo soprano, clarinet, French horn, piano and percussion (18'). Text Apocalypse.

1981 *Car nos vignes sont en fleur*, for 12-part mixed choir (18'). Text Canticles. Commissioned by Radio France for the Atelier Vocal de Radio France.

1983   *Invocations,* for choir, mezzo soprano and instrumental ensemble (35'). Commissioned by NOS radio.

1984   *Chimères,* for two countertenors, tenor, 2 baritones and bass (20'). Text G. de Nerval. Commissioned by Radio France for Ensemble A sei voce.

1985   *Les chants de Kabir,* for 6 voices (30'). Text Kabir.

1986   *Transparence,* for 18-part choir, three trumpets and three trombones (18'). Commissioned by Openbaar Kunstbezit.

1987/88   *Cinq hymnes,* for choir, two pianos and percussion. In celebration of the 25th jubileum of the Kurt Thomas Stichting.

1990   *Natasja,* for solo voice.

ORCHESTRAL WORKS

1946   *Concerto grosso,* for string orchestra (12').

1948   *Treurmuziek in memoriam Willem Pijper (Funeral music in memoriam of Willem Pijper),* for orchestra (20').

1950   *Symphony,* for strings and percussion (16').

1951   *Symphony* for strings (21').

1952   *Plutos-suite,* for orchestra (12').

1954   *Suite,* for youth orchestra (21'). Commissioned by the Stichting Jeugd en Muziek.

1957   *Mouvements rétrogrades,* for symphony orchestra (13').

1961   *Nritta,* dance for orchestra (9').

1961   *Ombres,* for symphony orchestra (14').

1963   *Symphonies of winds* (11'). Peters, New York.

1964   *De bijen (The bees),* for symphony orchestra (17').

1966   *Syntaxis II,* for symphony orchestra (22'). Commissioned by the Utrecht Symphony Orchestra.

1966   *Spatial music I,* for variable setting (32-48 musicians) (24').

1967   *Spatial music III,* for symphony orchestra in four groups and tape.

1968   *Spatial music IV,* Homage to Igor Stravinsky, for twelve players (13'). Commissioned by NCRV radio.

1970   *Music for strings,* for twelve players (11'). Commissioned by the Soloists of Zagreb.

1975   *Gending,* a Western homage to the musicians of the gamelan, for gamelan ensemble (28').

1982   *Alba,* concerto da camera for chamber orchestra (rev.1986) (32'). Commissioned by The Netherlands Chamber Orchestra.

1984-85   *Résonances,* for symphony orchestra (38'). In celebration of the centennial anniversary of the Concertgebouw Orchestra.

CONCERTOS

1948-49   *Concerto for piano* (17')

1953   *Concerto for violin and orchestra* (15').

1961   *Concerto for violin nr.2* (20'). Commissioned by the Nederlands Studenten Orkest.

1970-71   *Music for organ and 12 players* (10').

1987-88   *Concerto pour 2 guitares et 12 instruments à cordes.* Written for the 30th Concours International de guitare de Radio France.

1990   *Danses sacrées pour piano et orchestre de chambre (Concerto for piano).* In celebration of the 30th anniversary of the VARA matinee.

OPERA

1962   *Alceste,* television opera (see below).

1963   *De droom (The dream),* for soprano, alto, baritone mixed choir and orchestra (55'). Commissioned by the Holland Festival.

1990-91   *Antigone,* for mezzo soprano, two choirs and orchestra.

MUSIC FOR TELEVISION

1962   *Alceste,* television opera for choir, soloists and orchestra (48'). Text Euripides. Commissioned by NTS.

1964   *Krishna en Radha,* television ballet for flute, harp and percussion (19').

1969-70   *Litany of our time,* television music for soprano, flute, harp, piano, double bass, two percussionists, 3-part choir, tape and live electronic instruments (36'). Commissioned by VARA television.

MUSIC FOR BALLET

1964   *De bijen (The bees)*, for orchestra (17'). Commissioned by the National Ballet.

1964   *Krishna en Radha*, television ballet for flute, harp and percussion (19').

WORKS WITH ELECTRONIC INSTRUMENTS

1956   *Job*, radiophonic oratorium for orchestra, soloists and electronic instruments (35'). Commissioned by NRU. Prix d'Italia.

1957   *Elektronische studie* (6'47"). Commissioned by AVRO radio.

1960   *Antiphonie*, for wind quintet and four tapes (15').

1965-66   *Syntaxis I*, electronic composition (18'). Commissioned by VARA radio.

1977   *Mountains*, for bass clarinet and tape (18').

1977   *The magic of music II*, for voice and tape (5'45").

1978   *The birth of music II*, radiophonic work for reciter and electronic apparatus (19'30"). Text: myth of the Central American Indians. Commissioned by NOS.

1980   *Chronos*, electronic composition for four tracks (13'08").

1981-82   *Clair obscur*, electronic composition (17'). Commissioned by Groupe de Recherches Musicales.

MUSIC FOR THEATRE

1956   *Medeia*, for oboe and voices. Text: Euripides.

1956   *Le bourgeois gentilhomme*. Text: Molière.

1957   *De Trojaanse vrouwen (The Trojan women)*.

1959   *Wozzeck*, electronic composition. Text: G. Büchner.

1959   *J.B.*, electronic composition.

1960   *Het spel van Adam (Adam's game)*, piece for choir, orchestra and soloists.

MUSIC FOR RADIO PLAYS

1951   *Plutos*, for orchestra and voices.
1955   *De laatste dagen van Pompei (The last days of Pompei)*, for orchestra.
1955   *De stem van de jeugd (The voice of youth)*, for orchestra.
1959   *Het stenen hart (The stone heart)*, for orchestra.

MUSIC FOR RADIO DOCUMENTARIES

1962   *Signalement van het ik (Identification of the self)*, for viola and cello.
1962   *Helpers bij de drempel (Helpers at the threshold)* for viola and cello.

UNPUBLISHED JUVENILIA

1942   *Kyrie Eleison*, two songs for soprano and piano on medieval texts.
1943   *Dodendansen (Death dances)*, for alto and piano.
1943   *Largo and Allegro*, for orchestra.
1945   *Piano sonate I*.
1945-46   *Partita*, for piano.
1946   *Three Inventions*, for piano.
1946   *Kleine suite*, for piano.
1948   *Sonate II*, for piano.
1952   *Ricercare*, for organ.

SHORT BIBLIOGRAPHY

This short bibliography is comprised of two sections:

- Texts written by Ton de Leeuw
- Texts written by other authors about Ton de Leeuw, his work or fields of interest with which his activities brought him in contact.

An extensive bibliography, compiled by Ariane de Leeuw, may be seen at Donemus Amsterdam.

TEXTS WRITTEN BY TON DE LEEUW

1953 'Darmstadt. De Internationale Ferienkurse für neue Musik 1953', *Mens en Melodie* (Het Spectrum, Utrecht 1953), III/8, p. 258-260.

1954 'Samenkomst van Belgische en Nederlandse componisten', *Mens en Melodie* (Het Spectrum, Utrecht 1954), IX/7, p. 205-207.

'Debussy en de exotiche muziek', *Mens en Melodie* (Het Spectrum, Utrecht 1954), I X/12, p. 395-397.

1955 'Brussel. Componistendagen', *Mens en Melodie* (Het Spectrum, Utrecht 1955), X/4, p. 122-123.

'Dodecafonie', in the *Algemene Muziekencyclopedie* (1958), p. 321-323.

1958 *Muziek en techniek* (Hilversum 1958).

Experimentele Muziek. A lecture series held by Ton de Leeuw in the 1957-1958 season for the AVRO Broadcasting company (Hilversum 1958).

'Experimentele Muziek te Brussel', *Mens en Melodie* (Het Spectrum, Utrecht 1958), XIII/II, p. 343-346.

1960 'New Trends in modern Dutch music', *Sonorum Speculum* (Donemus, Amsterdam 1960), nr.4, p. 124-133.

'New trends in modern Dutch Music', *Sonorum Speculum* (Donemus, Amsterdam 1960), nr.5, p. 174-181.

1961 'Mouvements rétrogrades', *Sonorum Speculum* (Donemus, Amsterdam 1961), nr.8, p. 14-15.

1963 'Elektronische Probleme in de Niederlanden', *Melos* (Melosverlag, Mainz 1963), XXX/5, p. 161-163.

'Mensen en muziek in India. Reisdagboekbladen (I)', *Mens en Melodie* (Het Spectrum, Utrecht 1963), XVIII/5, p. 144-149.

'Mensen en muziek in India. Reisdagboekbladen (II)', *Mens en Melodie* (Het Spectrum, Utrecht 1963), XVIII/7, p. 213-216.

'Mensen en muziek in India. Reisdagboekbladen (Ill)', *Mens en Melodie* (Het Spectrum, Utrecht 1963), XVIII/8, p. 239-43.

1964 'Componisten aan het woord (II)', *Mens en Melodie* (Het spec trum, Utrecht 1964) XIX/2, p. 34-39.

Muziek van de Twintigste Eeuw. Een onderzoek naar haar Elementen en Structuur, (Oosthoek, Utrecht 1964; third printing: Bohn, Scheltma, Utrecht 1977).

1965 'Taal en Muziek vandaag', *Mens en Melodie* (Het Spectrum, Utrecht 1965), XX/12, p. 362-368.

1967 Rapport over de wenselijkheid van oprichting van een mobiel ensemble voor hedendaagse muziek, Jaarverslag Raad voor de Kunst 1967.

1968 'Reisherinneringen uit Japan', *Mens en Melodie* (Het Spectrum, Utrecht 1968), XXIII/12, p. 354-359.

1969 'Music in Orient and Occident, a social problem', *The World of Music* (UNESCO 1969) XI/4, p. 6,17.

'Comments', *Proceedings of the international Round Table on re lations between Japanese and Western arts* [Tokyo 1968] (Tokyo 1969), p. 322-324.

'De Sacre du Printemps in aanbouw', *Mens en Melodie* (Het Spectrum, Utrecht 1969), XXIV/10, p. 289-291.

1970 'Muziek in Oost en West, een sociaal probleem', *Mens en Melodie* (Het Spectrum, Utrecht 1970), XXV/2, p. 43-47. [translation of 'Music in Orient and Occident' (1969)] .

'Muzikale confronstate Oost-West', *Mens en Melodie* (Muzikaal Eeuwkwartaal), (Het Spectrum, Utrecht 1970), XXV/12, p. 43-48.

1971 'Les cultures musicales des peuples: Traditions et actualité', *Final report of the Union of composers* (Moscow 1971), p. 35-40.

1973 'L'interaction des cultures dans la musique contemporaine', *Cultures* Unesco et la Vaconniére 1973-74), I/3, p. 13-32.

1974 'Melody', in: *Dictionary of twentieth century music*, (Thames and Hudson, London 1974), p. 467-471.

1976 'Introduction', 'The East-West theme', 'Analysis of Gending', 'Reflections', *Keynotes* 3 (Donemus, Amsterdam 1976), p. 66-74.

1978 'Questions, Ideas and Expectations: Premises and Aims of an East-West Encounter', *The World of Music* (UNESCO, 1978), XX/2, p. 19-33.

'De muziek der Toekomst', *Prana* (1978), III/2, p. 22-26.

1982 'Hilversum 4: het luisteronderzoek telt de koppen', *Muziek & Dans* (Stichting Kunstpublikaties, Amsterdam 1982), May.

'Muziek zonder omwegen' *Preludium* (Vereniging Vrienden van het Concertgebouw Amsterdam 1982), XL/10, p. 5-6.

1983 'Symphonies of Winds', 'Haiku II', 'And they shall reign forever', *Preludium* (Vereniging Vrienden van het Concertgebouw, Amsterdam 1983), XXLII/4, p. 44-45.

'The adaptation of Asian music forms in contemporary music', *Final Report van de Asian Composers Conference* [Hongkong 1981] (Composer's Guild Hongkong 1983), p. 40-47.

1986 'Résonances', *Preludium* (Vereniging Vrienden van het Concertgebouw, Amsterdam 1986), XLIV/5, p. 40-41.

TEXTS WRITTEN ABOUT TON DE LEEUW

1956   Werker, Gerard, 'Prix d'Italia 1956', *Mens en Melodie* (Het Spec trum, Utrecht October 1956, IX/10, p. 302-303.

1959   Paap, Wouter, TON DE LEEUW in 'composers', *Music in Hol land* (Meulenhof, Amsterdam c. 1959), p. 48-49.

1962   Wörner, Karl H., 'Höllandische Musiker Gegenwart', *Schweizerische Musikzeitung* (Hug & Co, Zürich januari/februari 1962), CII/I, p. 5-8.

1963   Paap, Wouter, 'De componist Ton de Leeuw', *Mens en Melodie* (Het Spectrum, Utrecht May 1963), XVIII/5, p.134-140.

1971   Manneke, Daan, 'Ton de Leeuw, Music for Strings', *Sonorum Speculum* (Donemus, Amsterdam 1971), nr. 48, p. 17-26.

        Manneke Daan, 'Ton de Leeuw and his Music for Organ and 12 Players', *Sonorum Speculum* (Donemus, Amsterdam 1971-72), nr. 49, p. 7-12.

        Wouters, Jos, 'Ton de Leeuw (1926)', in: *Nederlandse componistengalerij: Negen portretten van Nederlandse componisten* (part 1) (Donemus, Amsterdam 1971), p. 17-49.

1974   Moore, Sylvia, 'Reflections on Musicultura 1974-1976', *Sonorum Speculum* (Donemus, Amsterdam 1974), nr.57, p. 30-39.

1975   Samama, Leo, 'Westerse confrontatie met de gamelan: 'Gending' van Ton de Leeuw', *Mens en Melodie* (Het Spectrum, Utrecht November 1975), XXX/II, p. 332-334.

        Schneider, Sigrun, *Mikrotöne in der Musik des 20. Jahrhunderts* (Bonn 1975).

1979   Helm, Everett, 'The Music of Ton de Leeuw', *Keynotes* (Donemus, Amsterdam, June 1979), nr.9, p. 3-12.

1980   Wouters, Jos, 'Leeuw, Ton de', in *The New Grove Dictionary of Music and Musicians* (Stanley Sadie ed., Londen 1980), vol. 10, p. 603-604.

1982   Smit, Sytze, 'Een zenderredactie voor Hilversum IV', *Muziek & Dans*, maart 1982, VI/2, p. 7-11.

1983 Dominick, Lisa, 'Mode and Movement in Recent Works of Ton de Leeuw', *Keynotes* (Donemus, Amsterdam 1983) nr.17, p. 15-23.

1986 Markus, Wim, 'Music and Time. Observations on Arnold Schoenberg and Ton De Leeuw', *Keynotes* (Donemus, Amsterdam 1986), nr.23, p. 14-16.

Coenen, Alcedo, 'Muziek zonder grenzen', *Ton de Leeuw 60* (A. Coenen e.a. ed., Amsterdam 1986), p. 2-5.

Groot, Rokus de, 'Aspects of Ton de Leeuw's Musical Universe', *Keynotes* (Donemus, Amsterdam 1986), nr.23, P. 17-31.

Samama, Leo, *Zeventig jaar Nederlandse muziek 1915-1985. Voorspel tot een nieuwe dag* (Querido, Amsterdam 1986), p. 230-241.

1988 Marot, Jacques, 'Ton de Leeuw, compositeur, ethnomusicologue, philosophe', *Septentrion* (Stichting Ons Erfdeel, België 1988), XVII/3, p. 1-4.

DISCOGRAPHY

And they shall reign forever (1985), Jane Manning, mezzo soprano, and an instrumental ensemble conducted by David Porcelijn, Donemus cv 8502 s.

Antigone - Music drama (1991), Netherlands Radio Chamber Orchestra, Martine Mahé, mezzo soprano and conductor Reinbert de Leeuw, NM CLASSICS 92036.

Antiphonie (1960), Donemus cv 7803 s.

Apparence II (1987), The Netherlands Clarinet Quartet CD 89-101.

Car nos vignes sont en fleur (1981), Radio Chamber Choir conducted by Robert Gritton, Donemus cv 8502 s.

Clair obscur (1981-82), Donemus cv Special 1986/6 s.

Cinq Hymnes (1993), Netherlands Chamber Choir conducted by Huub Kerstens and Reinbert de Leeuw, NM CLASSICS 92025.

De droom (1963) Soloists, choir and orchestra conducted by Bruno Maderna, Radio Nederland RN 518-520.

Gending (1975), Gamelan Ensemble Amsterdam conducted by the composer, Donemus cv 7602 s.

Haiku I (1963), Anne Haenen, soprano, and Ton Hartsuiker, piano, CBS LSP 14514 s.

Haiku II (1988), Dorothy Dorow, soprano, and the Rotterdam Philharmonic Orchestra conducted by Edo de Waart, Donemus DAVS 7172/2 s.

Hommage à Henri (1989), Sjef Douwes, clarinet, and Jan Gruithuyzen, piano, NM CLASSICS 92020.

Interlude (1984), Wim Hoogerwerff, guitar, Donemus cv 8701 S, Donemus CVCD 8701 CD, Radio Nederland 85131.

Invocations (1983), Jane Manning, mezzo soprano, Radio Chamber Choir and instrumental ensemble conducted by David Porcelijn, Donemus cv 8502 s.

Lamento Pacis I, II and III (1969), NCRV Vocal Ensemble and instrumental ensemble conducted Marinus Voorburg, Donemus DAVS 7273/4 s.

Les adieux (1988), René Eckhardt, piano, NM CLASSICS 92020.

Linkerhand en rechterhand (1976), Monique Copper, piano, Attaca Babel 8421-6 DS.

Litany of our time (1969-70), Joan Carrol, soprano, instrumental ensemble and electronic music conducted by Jan Vriend, Donemus cv Special 1986/6.

Men go their ways (1964), Theo Bruins, piano, Donemus cv 7904 s. Ivo Janssen, piano NM CLASSICS 92028.

Midare (1972), Michiko Takahashi, marimba, Donemus cv 7602 s: Michael Jullich, Moers Music O 1068 – West Germany; Michiko Takahashi and Ichiro Masuda, Digital Recording System – Pioneer Studio – Tokyo, LOB •4 LSM 2003.

Missa Brevis (1953), Ensemble Arti Vocali conducted by N. Kronenburg, Eurosound ES 46.251-313. 10.

Modal music (1978-79), Miny Dekkers, accordion, Mirasound Musica KS 20.7055. NM CLASSICS 92013.

Mountains (1977), Harry Sparnaay, bass clarinet, Donemus cv 7801 s.

Mouvements rétrogrades (1957), Utrecht Symphony Orchestra conducted by Paul Hupperts, Donemus DAVS 6103 M; Concertgebouw Orchestra conducted by George Szell, Donemus CVCD 9/bfo

A-5 CD; Residentie Orchestra conducted by Ernest Bour, Residentie Orkest 8814.791/786 s.

Music for strings (1970), Radio Philharmonic Orchestra conducted by Jean Fournet, Donemus DAVS 7273/4 s, Radio Nederland RN 6808.047.

Music for violin (1967), Jos Verkoeyen, violin, Donemus cv 7602 s.

Night music (1966), Abbie de Quant, flute, Donemus cv 7602 s.

Nritta (1961), Concertgebouw Orchestra conducted by Bernard Haitink, Radio Nederland RN 517.

Ombres (1961), Concertgebouw Orchestra conducted by Bernard Haitink, Donemus DAVS 6301 M.

Spatial music I (1966), Radio Chamber Orchestra conducted by Paul Hupperts, Donemus DAVS 7001 s.

String Quartet nr. 1 (1958), Gaudeamus Quartet, Columbia 33 CXH8, Omega 145.543 45t. *String Quartet nr.2* (1964), Gaudeamus Quartet, Donemus CV 8302 S, Philips 6500.881 s. *Study* (1957), Donemus CV 7803 s.

Sweelinck-variaties (1972-73), Lien van der Vliet, Donemus Composers' Voice CVCD 16.

Symphony of winds (1963), Radio Philharmonic Orchestra conducted by Ernest Bour, Donemus DAVS 6604 m; Rotterdam Philharmonic Orchestra conducted by Edo de Waart, Teleac TEL 8905 cd.

Trio (1990), The Trio, NM CLASSICS 92020.

Five songs (1952) on texts of Garcia Lorca, Guus Hoekman, bass, and Gérard van Blerk, piano, ES 46.675.

ABOUT THE AUTHORS

Rokus de Groot (1947), composer and musicologist, conducted research and published on the aesthetics and techniques of contemporary composition, and the relationship between eastern and western music. He obtained his Ph.D on a dissertation about the recent works of Ton de Leeuw (University of Amsterdam, 1991). He teaches musicology at the University of Amsterdam. Since 1994 he also holds a personal chair at the University of Utrecht, 'Music in the Netherlands since 1600'; this chair is an initiative of Centre for Netherlands Music (CNM). He has taught at the Universidad Nacional Autonoma de Mexico in Mexico City in 1990 and 1992, and has given guest lectures at a number of universities and conservatories, e.g. in the U.S.A (University of California and Los Angeles, 1992), Russia (Tchaikovsky-Conservatory in Moscow, 1994). He has conducted field research in Scotland and North India. His compositions explore the expressiveness of melodic contours (among other pieces, *Kontur* for soprano saxophone, 1982; *Winds of a far air*, for flute and soprano saxophone, 1991; *Songs of Mira Bai*, for high voice, 1993).

Richard Hees is a psychiatrist affiliated with the RIAGG (Regional Institute for Mental Health). After completing his medical studies, Hees conducted research in the field of music therapy in the United States. As a result of this research financed by the Dutch Foundation for Pure Scientific Research, he organized, together with musicolgist and composer Rokus de Groot, a doctoral study group for biomusicology at the department of musicology at the University of Amsterdam. In his private practice Hees teaches and supervises music therapists. His current research interest is in the biological aspect of music and its therapeutic implications for hemispheric dysfunction. He is especially interested and experienced in music and autism; music and aphasia/amusia; and music and musicogenic epilepsy. Playing the piano is his favorite musical recreation.

Ton de Leeuw was born on November 16, 1926 in Rotterdam. Following his musical education with Louis Toebosch and Henk Badings, he left for Paris in 1949 to study under Olivier Messiaen and Thomas de Hartmann. His life-long interest in non-European music subsequently led him to study ethnomusicology with Jaap Kunst in Amsterdam (1950-54). From 1954 until 1959 he worked as a music director at the former Netherlands Radio Union. After this he was a professor of composition at the Amsterdam (Sweelinck) Conservatory, where several years later he became both director of the institute and head of the electronic studio. Next to this, De Leeuw was a senior lecturer at the University of Amsterdam. He has been active in the Netherlands in the renewal of the orchestral repertoire (for example his much-discussed proposal for the formation of a mobile ensemble) and the musical policies of Dutch radio (the Hilversum IV plan). Between 1958 and 1976 he gave hundreds of radio lectures on contemporary music and non-western music.

In 1961 De Leeuw made his first study trip to Asia to research classical Indian music. He later visited other Asian countries, also with the aim of studying their music on the scene. From the seventies onward, his activities abroad became more extensive. He has often, for instance, conducted workshops for young composers abroad and has also served as a guest professor in many European, Asian, Australian and American universities. De Leeuw is the author of numerous articles published in various national and international periodicals. His book, *Muziek van de twintigste eeuw* (Music of the twentieth century) appeared in 1964 and has since then been reprinted several times. Since 1988 Ton de Leeuw has lived in Paris, dedicating himself primarily to his composition.

William Malm studied composition at Northwestern University and ethnomusicology at the University of California in Los Angeles (UCLA), specializing in Japanese theater music. He taught at the University of Michigan, 1960 - 1993, and directed the Stearns Collection of Musical Instruments.

Jurrien Sligter studied piano with Jan Wijn, composition with Ton de Leeuw and music theory at the Amsterdam Conservatory. Next to this he studied conducting under David Porcelijn and Lucas Vis. He conducted the ASKO orchestra and ASKO ensemble and from 1984 until 1989 he was the conductor of the DELTA ensemble. He is a professor of music theory at the Utrecht Conservatory where he also conducts contemporary music ensembles. In 1984 he organized a Ton de Leeuw festival in Amsterdam and Utrecht, in which the composer's entire oeuvre was surveyed for the first time. In 1988 he founded the ensemble 'Gending', a gamelan orchestra that concentrated on the acculturation between the East and West. In 1989 he founded the BASHO ensemble which is dedicated to performance of twentieth century music in relation to other art forms.

Trân Van Khê was born in South Vietnam and studied physics, chemistry, biology and medicine in Hanoi, and later political science and musicology in Paris. He was 'directeur de recherche' of the Centre National de la Recherche Scientifique de Paris (1971-1987), taught ethnomusicology, was president of the Conseil Scientifique de l'Institut d'Études Comparatives de la Musique et de la Documentation and member of the International Music Council of UNESCO.

ACKNOWLEDGEMENTS

Brommet, F., Paris, 62
Buurman, B., Amsterdam, 92
Cinétex, Hilversum, 20
Ferguson, C., Hilversum, 20
Gideonse, T., Amsterdam, 156
Jansen, W., Amsterdam, xi
Leeuw, A. de, Paris, 135
Partican Pictures, Amsterdam, 23
Stevens, J.C., press photo bureau, Hilversum, 23
Veer, J. van der, 166

As far as has been possible, we have attempted to trace the people and agencies holding the rights for the photographs. Those who have not yet been approached are requested to contact Centrum Nederlandse Muziek, Hilversum, The Netherlands.

The musical examples have been produced by:
Donemus, Amsterdam
Nirota, Koedijk

The graphic examples have been produced by:
Werner Studio, Amsterdam

INDEX

Page numbers in italic refer to music examples or illustrations. Citations in the list of works, bibliography and discography are not registered in this index.